If the Shoe Fits...

How to Develop Multiple Intelligences in the Classroom

By

Carolyn Chapman

Foreword by James Bellanca

SkyLight

PROFESSIONAL DEVELOPMENT

Arlington Heights, Illinois

If the Shoe Fits...
How to Develop Multiple Intelligences in the Classroom

Published by SkyLight Professional Development
2626 S. Clearbrook Dr.
Arlington Heights, IL 60005
Phone 800-348-4474, 847-290-6600
FAX 847-290-6609
info@skylightedu.com
http://www.skylightedu.com

Creative Director: Robin Fogarty
Editors: Erica Pochis, Liesl Banks-Stiegman, Julia E. Noblitt
Type Compositor: Donna Ramirez
Book Designers: Bruce Leckie, Michael A. Melasi
Cover Designer and Illustrator: David Stockman
Production Coordinator: Amy Behrens

Library of Congress Catalog Card Number 93-79952

Printed in the United States of America.

ISBN 0-932935-64-8

1037McN

Item Number 1180

Z Y X W V U T S R Q P O N M L K

06 05 04 03 02 01 00 99   15 14 13 12 11

Dedication

To all the students and teachers in today's schools.
May this be the key that opens the door to lifelong learning.

Table of Contents

Foreword

In his seminal work, *Frames of Mind,* Howard Gardner persuasively theorizes about the existence of a set of multiple intelligences. Gardner has done more in this decade (1983-1993) than any other scholar in the cognitive sciences to advance an expanded view of human intelligence. The idea of a single IQ score undermines the now widely accepted concept of multiple ways of knowing and learning. To believe a single quantitative measure can possibly reveal all the gifts of which the human mind is capable puts unnecessary limitations on our concept of human development.

As with any theoretical breakthrough, it takes creative studies and experimental ventures by those on the front line to uncover the real power inherent in an emergent theory. Carolyn Chapman, a former teacher, veteran educator, and internationally known consultant who works directly with school personnel at every level of the educational arena, offers just that: a practical approach to the theory of multiple intelligences that can be embraced by novices and seasoned staff alike.

Cleverly characterized by different shoes, an indelible image is created for each of the seven intelligences, not only for the teachers but for the students as well. For example, who can mistake the array of football cleats that signify the teamwork embedded in Gardner's interpersonal intelligence? Or who can ever forget the practical, tough hiker's boot for "climbing the rugged path of competitive technology" in the realm of the logical/mathematical intelligence?

With this rich metaphor of the shoes, the author sets the stage for two of Gardner's more striking principles: just as the shoes are varied in style, combined differently, and are interchangeable depending on personal preference or appropriateness, so too are our multiple intelligences; and just as shoes are influenced by the culture in which they exist, so too are our multiple intelligences.

Filled with ready-to-use activities for the high school lab, the middle school cluster, or the primary play area, *If the Shoe Fits...* is a teacher-friendly guide to "encounter," to "employ," to "educate," and finally to "embrace" multiple intelligences in the classroom.

Without a doubt, this newest addition to the growing literature on multiple intelligences is a sparkling edition of well-grounded, theoretical background, significant considerations for the reflective practitioner, and fresh, exciting, and appropriate lessons for immediate classroom use.

If the shoe fits... wear it; wear it well; wear it long; ...but don't wear it out.

James Bellanca
Executive Director
IRI/SkyLight Publishing, Inc.
August 1993

Acknowledgments

I must confess, I never dreamed my ideas would one day become a book. Many times while working with educators throughout the last twenty-three years, people would urge, "Carolyn, you really should write a book." My answer was always, "My talent is in reaching students through my workshops, seminars, and sharing sessions. I would rather walk, dance, sing, and talk about my ideas than write about them." However, with encouragement and assistance, I developed my own verbal/linguistic intelligence further—the end result being, *If the Shoe Fits...: How to Develop Multiple Intelligences in the Classroom*.

Every child I have taught and each teacher with whom I have worked is a part of this book. I have acquired the strategies, tools, and activities found in this book from them. Without the valuable experiences we shared together, *If the Shoe Fits* would not have been possible.

I would like to express my gratitude to Jim Bellanca, the executive director of IRI/Skylight Publishing, Inc. It is an honor to work as a member of his team of expert consultants—Robin Fogarty, Kay Burke, Beth Swartz, and Bruce Williams. Jim's support, knowledge, and input are the forces that brought this book to fruition. The guidance and assistance he gave me during this project were invaluable.

I am grateful to Roslyn Brown, director of the Effective Teaching Program at New York State United Teachers, and her colleagues Howard Rotterdam and Arlene Harris of New York City's Special Education Support Program (SESP) for reviewing the book and providing their valuable insights and suggestions.

Thank you to my husband and my best friend, Jim Chapman. His continuous support, true understanding, and high expectations gave me the drive and push I needed to accomplish this goal. We have had hours of sharing, laughing, and working together trying to "make these shoes fit."

In addition, I wish to thank the IRI/Skylight Publishing staff led by Robin Fogarty. This highly creative team has maintained its wit and professionalism through agonizing delays and hectic deadlines. I greatly appreciate the work of Julie Noblitt, Erica Pochis, Liesl Banks-Stiegman, David Stockman, Donna Ramirez, Amy Behrens, Bruce Leckie, and Mike Melasi.

Introduction

In 1983, Howard Gardner published his book *Frames of Mind* in which he outlined his theory of multiple intelligences. According to Gardner, everyone possesses at least seven intelligences and each person's blend of competencies produces a unique cognitive profile. In 1995, Gardner identified an eighth intelligence. Gardner's theory provides a framework for a metamorphosis of education at all levels of learning. I believe that the theory of multiple intelligences is a critical key to opening the doors of learning. My strong belief in Gardner's research is the basis of this book.

My personal philosophy has always been that every child can learn. It is our responsibility as educators to find each student's particular way of learning. Putting the theory of multiple intelligences into practice can help this philosophy become a reality. We must learn how to develop all of our intelligences and embrace the philosophy that all students are "learner-abled." We should remember that it is not "how smart we are, but how we are smart" that is important (from the American Broadcasting Company home video, *Common Miracles: The New American Revolution in Learning*, 1993).

Educators *can* make a difference in the learning of each student. Unfortunately, in today's classroom, so many students are not learning. Often these students are labeled as at risk, low achievers, or unmotivated. These students tend to perform at a level less than their capabilities because of low expectations on the part of educators, low self-esteem, and society's acceptance of their lower achievement levels. Many students in gifted and talented classes are unmotivated learners as well. This is due to the focus in our schools on two intelligences—verbal/linguistic and logical/mathematical. We are not teaching to all of the intelligences, areas in which these students have special abilities.

About the Book

This book is designed to begin to remedy these situations and to bring about a change that incorporates the theory of multiple intelligences. It is organized around the basic questions that many classroom practitioners ask.

Chapter 1 explains Gardner's theory in layman's terms. It gives readers a picture of how Gardner derived his theory, how intelligences are developed, and the definitions of the eight intelligences. Readers will also gain an understanding of the elements necessary to create a brain-compatible classroom, how to meet the needs of special students, methods of mediation, and other viable ideas for implementation.

Chapters 2 through 9 are dedicated to each of the eight intelligences. Each chapter demonstrates a variety of ways to understand and implement Gardner's theory. Sections include:

☐ *What Is the Intelligence?* — Defines each intelligence in a paragraph or two using simple terms. This section describes the characteristics of the intelligence.

☐ *What Is the Developmental Path for This Intelligence?* — Describes in chart form the skills from this intelligence that appear on basic, complex, and higher-order levels.

☐ *How Is This Intelligence Developed in Other Cultures?* — Offers readers a global understanding of the intelligences because all cultures value and stress the eight intelligences differently.

☐ *How Can This Intelligence Be Used for Problem Solving?* — Illustrates how people tend to use this intelligence to solve problems using a variety of short vignettes.

☐ *Who Is the Student With This Intelligence?* — Tells how a student with a strength in a particular intelligence will act and provides signs to look for that help educators identify these students.

☐ *The Comfort Zone: What Helps This Student Learn?* — Offers examples of situations that enhance learning for students with a certain intelligence.

☐ *The Discomfort Zone: What Hinders This Student?* — Provides explanations of conditions that may hamper learning for students with a particular intelligence.

☐ *How Do You Catch This Student's Attention in the Classroom?* — Gives strategies to capitalize on a student's talents and develop his or her intelligence further.

☐ *How Do You Meet the Challenge of the Special Student?* — Outlines methods to help special students learn in ways compatible with their strengths.

☐ *What Activities Promote Learning With This Intelligence?* — Lists several teaching techniques to use in the classroom that enhance each intelligence.

☐ *How Do You Create an Environment for This Intelligence?* — Explains exactly how to foster an environment that stimulates and is compatible with the eight intelligences.

☐ *Lesson Examples That Target This Intelligence* — Gives specific, easy-to-implement lesson examples designed to focus on a specific intelligence.

☐ *Make Your Own Lessons* — Offers a template for creating lessons of your own to target the eight intelligences.

☐ *Teacher Reflection Page* — Encourages readers to reflect on their own personal use of the intelligences, how they are promoting them in the classroom, and how to improve their teaching toward the intelligences.

☐ *Journal Page* — Gives readers a place to record their progress in understanding and teaching the multiple intelligences.

Bringing the book full circle, the last two chapters feature more holistic views of the multiple intelligences. Chapter 10 synthesizes the eight intelligences approach to learning by delineating a number of methods to integrate curriculum and instruction. Among the integrated models are ways to nest, share, web, and thread the multiple intelligences into the various learning experiences.

In addition to this synergistic approach to developing human potential through the multiple intelligences, the final chapter, chapter 11, addresses the grading dilemma with practical ideas for assessing the multiple gifts of the learner. Included in this section are suggestions about collecting and selecting artifacts for portfolio assessment, ways to align outcomes, set criteria, and engage in "the grading game." The chapter ends with sample reporting instruments.

How to Use the Book

Some readers immerse themselves in the eight intelligences by using the book sequentially. They begin with the outcomes section and move systematically through the chapters on the eight intelligences, capping off the experience with ideas on assessment. Others prefer to dip in and out of the book choosing chapters of particular interest. For example, some plunge into the chapter on the musical/rhythmic intelligence because they feel *most* comfortable with this one, while others gingerly glance through the section on the bodily/kinesthetic because they feel *least* comfortable with that one.

Regardless of how the book is used, the reader can be assured that myriad ideas—both conceptual and concrete—bombard their thoughts as they try on the various shoes for size and fit. The book is the practitioner's manual for knowing, learning, and teaching about the multiple intelligences.

C H A P T E R

1

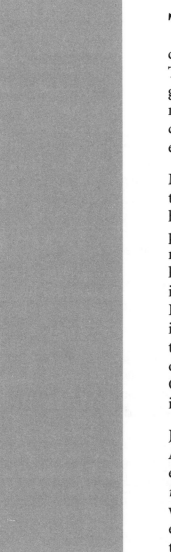

If the Shoe Fits...

There are many misconceptions about intelligence. One misconception, disproven by modern research, is that all intelligence is fixed. That misconception argues that individuals die with the same intelligence with which they are born. Another one, also disproven by modern research, is that there is only one intelligence. Other misconceptions that spring from these two are likewise challenged by modern research.

Many scholars of intelligence have contributed to the debunking of these misconceptions as they have explored the inner frontiers of the human brain. Reuven Feuerstein, Jacob Rand, and their associates pioneered the work on cognitive modifiability through cognitive mediation. Roger Sperry investigated the different ways the right and left sides of the brain process information. Paul McLean provided the insights into the triune brain. Robert Sternberg, Stephan Ceci, and David Feldman have studied the development of different types of intelligence. The development of each intelligence depends on how the individual is nurtured. Howard Gardner and his colleagues developed the theory of multiple intelligences. In this theory, Gardner holds that every individual possesses several different and independent capacities for solving problems and creating products.

Just what is this thing called "intelligence" by these "brain" people? According to Gardner, ". . . a human intellectual competence must entail a set of skills for problem solving—enabling the individual to *resolve genuine problems or difficulties* that he or she encounters and, when appropriate, to create an effective product—and must also entail the potential for *finding or creating problems*—thereby laying the groundwork for the acquisition of new knowledge . . . the ideal of what is valued will differ markedly, sometimes even radically, across human cultures, within the creation of new products or posing of new questions being of relatively little importance in some settings" (Gardner, 1983, p. 60–61).

In the traditional view of intelligence, the notion is that the individual's single capacity is fixed. Following the definition of fixed intelligence established by Binet, single, fixed intelligence consisted of the ability to use language and do mathematics. Whole educational systems were built on Binet's understanding. His tests marked the student for life. The IQ test results showing how well or poorly a young person could analyze language or mathematics made an indelible and immutable mark. From this single score, a permanent tattoo, the student's path was set.

After Feuerstein and his colleagues had disproven Binet's notion of the fixed intelligence, Gardner and his peers developed the theory of many intelligences. The first important key to understanding Gardner's theory is that intelligences are of consequence in a particular cultural setting. After years of studying the cognitive development of normal, gifted, and brain-damaged young people at the Boston University School of Medicine, the Veteran's Administration Medical Center of Boston, and Harvard's Project Zero, and after the study of problem solving in cultures around the world, Gardner postulated his theory of multiple intelligences. He groups the eight intelligences into three categories.

The *language-related* intelligences, verbal/linguistic and musical/rhythmic, he describes as "object free." These two intelligences reflect the structure of individual languages. For instance, some linguists consider the Japanese language to have a very analytic form. This form enables them to perform analytic tasks more easily. On the other hand, the French language is image filled. Thinking in pictures helps develop the verbal capabilities.

The second category he calls personal forms (interpersonal and intrapersonal intelligences). In this category he includes the *personal-related* intelligences that reflect the powerful restraints inherent in the personal vision of self, expectations of others, accepted norms of thinking or acting, and cultural pressures. What an individual wants to become competes with a multitude of discordant voices that may make major changes in that goal.

The third category he calls *object related*. In this category he includes bodily/kinesthetic, visual/spatial, logical/mathematical, and naturalist intelligences. The object-related intelligences are subject to the structure and function of the objects that the individual must work with for solving a problem or making a product. How the learner uses canvas and brushes is going to be different from how he uses clay and a scalpel.

It is essential to remember that the definition of intelligence highlights problem solving and product making as the most important elements. This suggests that intelligence is more than what we can observe in a person's action and speech. What seems most important is the decision-making processes that occur before the actions. For instance, when a basketball player comes down the floor and makes great moves to the basket that leave everyone else watching in amazement, what mental operations triggered those moves? When a concert violinist stuns her audience with her choice of technique, why did she decide on that precise sequence? Ultimately, it is these nuances of choice that define the intelligence.

The Eight Intelligences

There were many candidates for "intelligences" that met his definition. However, after applying numerous criteria, only seven intelligences remained. He has since added an eighth intelligence.

VERBAL/LINGUISTIC INTELLIGENCE

 The verbal/linguistic intelligence is concerned with the uses of language. People with this intelligence possess a particularly strong sensitivity to the meanings of words and a skilled aptitude for their manipulation. According to Gardner, these people have "the capacity to follow rules of grammar, and, on carefully selected occasions, to violate them" (1983, p. 77). On yet another level—the sensory level—those with a heightened verbal/linguistic intelligence are able to communicate effectively by listening, speaking, reading, writing, and linking. They also have a strong awareness of the varying functions of language, or more specifically, its power to stimulate emotions. Poets, authors, reporters, speakers, attorneys, talk-show hosts, and politicians typically exhibit verbal/linguistic intelligence.

MUSICAL/RHYTHMIC INTELLIGENCE

 As Gardner describes, "There are several roles that musically inclined individuals can assume, ranging from the avant-garde composer who attempts to create a new idiom, to the fledgling listener who is trying to make sense of nursery rhymes (or other 'primer level' music)" (1983, p. 104–105). Each of us holds musical capabilities to some degree, the difference is that some people have more skill than others. No matter what range of talent, we all possess a core of abilities necessary for enjoying a musical experience. These consist of the musical elements of pitch, rhythm, and timbre (the characteristic elements of a tone). People with a more highly developed musical/rhythmic intelligence are singers, composers, instrumentalists, conductors, and those who enjoy, understand, or appreciate music.

LOGICAL/MATHEMATICAL INTELLIGENCE

 The logical/mathematical intelligence incorporates both mathematical and scientific abilities. Mathematicians are typically characterized by a love of working with abstraction and a desire for exploration. They enjoy working with problems that require a great deal of reasoning. A scientist, however, is "motivated by a desire to explain physical reality" (Gardner, 1983, p. 145). For scientists, mathematics serves as a tool "for building models and theories that can describe and eventually explain the operation of the world." Mathematicians, engineers, physicists, astronomers, computer programmers, and researchers demonstrate a high degree of logical/mathematical intelligence.

VISUAL/SPATIAL INTELLIGENCE

Visual/spatial intelligence involves the unique ability to comprehend the visual world accurately. Those with visual/spatial intelligence are able to represent spatial information graphically and have a keen gift for bringing forth and transforming mental images. Artists and designers have strong visual/spatial capabilities. They have a certain responsiveness to the visual/spatial world as well as a talent to recreate it to produce a work of art. Also among this group are sailors, engineers, surgeons, sculptors, cartographers, and architects.

BODILY/KINESTHETIC INTELLIGENCE

The bodily/kinesthetic intelligence is based on the gift of control of one's bodily motions and the talent to manipulate objects with deftness. It is possible for these elements to exist separately, however, most people possess both. In addition, people such as inventors and actors tend to have a great deal of bodily/kinesthetic intelligence because the role of their bodies is so critical to their occupations. Others with substantial bodily/kinesthetic intelligence include dancers, acrobats, and athletes.

NATURALIST INTELLIGENCE

Man's adaptation and survival in his environment is the key component to the naturalist intelligence. It is the study of science. Individuals with a strength in this intelligence can recognize and distinguish between and among a variety of species of plants and animals, as well as make other distinctions and categorizations in "nature" (Gardner 1995). Those strong in this intelligence are hikers, botanists, scientists, oceanographers, veterinarians, gardeners, and park rangers.

INTRAPERSONAL INTELLIGENCE

The heart of intrapersonal intelligence lies in the ability to understand one's own feelings. These people instinctively comprehend their own range of emotions, can label them, and can draw on them as a means of directing their own behavior. In Gardner's words, "the intrapersonal intelligence amounts to little more than the capacity to distinguish a feeling of pleasure from one of pain, and on the basis of such discrimination, to become more involved in or to withdraw from a situation" (1983, p. 239). Examples of those with higher-than-average intrapersonal capabilities include the introspective novelist, wise elder, psychologist, or therapist—all of whom possess a deeper understanding of their feelings.

INTERPERSONAL INTELLIGENCE

Unlike intrapersonal intelligence, which is directed inward, interpersonal intelligence is one that focuses outward to individuals in the environment. The most basic skill among those with a high degree of interpersonal intelligence is the talent for understanding others. Those exhibiting this intelligence have the gift for noticing and making distinctions among other individuals, and more specifically among their "moods, temperaments, motivations, and intentions" (Gardner, 1983, p. 239). For example, at a very simple level, this intelligence includes the ability of a child to notice and be sensitive to the moods of adults around him. A more complex interpersonal skill is that of adults being able to read the intentions of others, even when hidden. People exhibiting this intelligence include religious and political leaders, parents, teachers, therapists, and counselors.

The Criteria

Gardner identified eight criteria for the existence of the intelligences.

Criterion 1 – Potential Isolation by Brain Damage

Gardner postulates that an intelligence is autonomous when it can be obliterated or preserved, in isolation, upon trauma to the brain. For example, speech can be impaired or totally absent following a head injury.

Criterion 2 – The Existence of Prodigies, Mentally Handicapped Individuals with Savant Behaviors, and Other Exceptional Individuals

Although each individual presents a jagged profile of the eight intelligences as unique as one's fingerprint, there are rare cases of what Gardner calls, "highly uneven profiles of abilities and deficits." In these examples, again, the particular intelligences can be scrutinized in isolation. The super-occurrence or total absence of a faculty in itself suggests the very existence of that intelligence.

Criterion 3 – An Identifiable Core Operation or a Set of Operations

It appears, according to Gardner's work, that an intelligence is sparked by certain kinds of stimuli inherent to the particular intelligence. For instance, the verbal/linguistic intelligence can be set into motion by the reading of a familiar line that in turn triggers the words remaining within that context. "'Twas the night before Christmas," primes the pump and one spews out, "and all through the house, not a creature was stirring, not even a mouse." The core operation of the verbal/linguistic intelligence has been activated.

Criterion 4 – A Distinctive Developmental History, Along with a Definable Set of Expert "End-State" Performances

As illustrated throughout this text with the developmental path diagrams, each intelligence presents a traceable path toward proficiency—basic, complex, and higher order. Gardner also states that although all individuals pass through the various stages, only those with unusual talents may develop the highest levels of expertise. For example, although we all experience the early awkwardness and eventual smoothness of figure skating, only the highly trained talent can execute the complex jumps and spins of the double and triple axel.

Criterion 5 – An Evolutionary History and Evolutionary Plausibility

The idea that our existing intelligences link back to species of long ago is also part of Gardner's thinking on this concept of criteria for an intelligence. He suggests an intelligence becomes more credible if it has some evolutionary roots that can be traced to today's phenomenon. A simple illustration is the early cave drawings and archeological artifacts and pottery that precede modern art in the area of the visual/spatial intelligence.

Criterion 6 – Support from Experimental Psychological Tasks

Demonstration of a particular intelligence seems to be a reasonable criterion, Gardner suggests, and often that demonstration is illuminated through the experiments of cognitive psychologists. For example, the ability to detect a logical pattern or visualize and solve a jigsaw puzzle are typical investigations of the logical/mathematical and visual/spatial intelligences.

Criterion 7 – Support from Psychometric Findings

Along similar lines of psychological experimentation are the standardized tests that provide complementary evidence of the existence of an intelligence. Although Gardner cautions one to use these measures gingerly, he nevertheless includes this traditional criteria as yet another test of validity and reliability. If one performs well on an abstract reasoning problem, evidence of a logical/mathematical intelligence is more than implied—it becomes explicit.

Criterion 8 – Susceptibility to Encoding in a Symbol System

Gardner's common-sense approach to what an intelligence is, is exemplified in this criterion as he explains that what makes a particular intelligence useful to humans in problem solving and production is the ease with which it can be "exploited." For example, the fact that language and mathematics, graphic illustrations, dance, choreography, and musical notation can be encoded into universally understood symbols allows easy access and use of the intelligences.

Gardner is the first to advocate that his list of eight ways of problem solving and making products is not all encompassing. The current list identifies those which up until now have met the eight criteria. Continued study by Gardner, his colleagues, and others who accept the definition and the criteria may identify one or one hundred more intelligences.

Underlying Principles

In understanding the theory of multiple intelligences, it is important to understand some principles of intelligence to which Gardner's work is connected.

EACH INTELLIGENCE IS MODIFIABLE

A variety of factors can cause the intelligence to expand. Recent theorists suggest that there are predictable factors that will impede development or even cause the intelligence to regress. A close-to-home example is found in the field of early childhood education. Middle-class students come from homes where the mother's higher education creates a family culture conducive to early linguistic development; children from economically deprived and less well-educated homes come from a family culture where verbal readiness for school may not be valued or possible. The child who grows up in an upper-middle-class suburb of Charlotte, North Carolina, with two college-educated parents has a greater chance to enter school ready to read than the child who grows up in the back mountains of Appalachia where parents have little or no knowledge of preschool language development.

ALTHOUGH EACH CHILD MAY BE BORN WITH A DIFFERENT CAPACITY, THE INTELLIGENCE CAN BE "GROWN" AND THEREFORE TAUGHT

Wilma Rudolph may have been born with a giant bodily/kinesthetic intelligence. Or she may have had that intelligence more carefully honed than most students. Michael Jordan may have more bodily/kinesthetic intelligence than anyone who ever played basketball, or some combination of factors, most of which appeared to have developed after his adolescence, that caused him to develop his capacity to an unmatched degree. And what of Mikhail Baryshnikov, William Shakespeare, and Madame Curie? The critical point in any of these instances, as with all individuals, is not that they had a specific capacity when they were born, or that the culture nurtured them to a certain degree; the point is that they developed their special intelligences well beyond what they were born with.

EACH PERSON IS BORN WITH ALL THE INTELLIGENCES

Because of the different cultural influences each person experiences, some intelligences develop strongly, others slightly, and some not at all. Gardner identifies eight intelligences that meet his criteria. Gardner believes that every normal individual possesses a unique blend of the eight intelligences.

Four Stages of Development

We can recognize at least four distinct stages in the development of an intelligence. Factors in an individual's cultural environment can speed or slow that process.

- *The First Encounter.* From the earliest moments after birth, the young child encounters the cultural influences that will facilitate the development of his or her dominant intelligences. These encounters activate the senses and start what brain researchers might call the "dendrite connection." The more stimulation, the stronger the connection. As the child manipulates ideas, the more the intelligence is developed. In a household where the mother sings to the child, the child's musical intelligence is honed. In the household without sound, the child is less likely to develop the musical/rhythmic abilities. A logical extension of the "encounter" theory is that an individual even at a late age can develop an intelligence. Although this "late bloomer" may not have a lifetime of experiences, she may well enrich her life with this new intelligence. For instance, think of the number of modern women who return to school after raising a family and who may encounter for the first time the beauty of mathematics or the richness of language.

- *The Employment.* In this stage, the individual receives many opportunities to exercise and strengthen an intelligence. Young Navajos learn about traditional pottery making and clay sculpting as they watch elders work. As soon as their hands are strong enough, they are taught how to wet and mold the clay. In rural Illinois young farm children receive chores. From caring for the smallest animals, they graduate to operating machinery and assisting with planting and harvesting and entering prize heifers in the state fair.

- *The Formal Education.* From learning by doing, with the guidance of parents and elders, the next step is basic training in solving problems and making products. In Switzerland, the young student may take an apprenticeship with a watchmaker; in New York City, the aspiring dancer may join the Martha Graham Dance Company; in Rochester, the composer may attend classes at Eastman; in San Francisco, the would-be scientist may settle into her high school physics class. In each instance, the student works with master teachers. These teachers structure lessons that enable the student to refine her creativity and problem-solving skills. If this formal preparation helps the student to understand the key concepts and to apply the problem-solving skills, then the student is ready to embrace the intelligence. If the formal education mires the students in the memorization of facts without the deep understanding that facilitates application, the student will need additional formal education.

- *The Embrace.* With the basics for problem solving and making products in an intelligence in place, the individual can embrace it fully. The apprentice becomes a watchmaker; the dancer is assigned a part in an upcoming production at Lincoln Center; a small orchestra selects the new composition for its next tour; the physics student gets accepted at Cal Tech. The students accept immersion into the life of the intelligence—thinking, feeling, and sensing its nuances as they apply what they are learning to more and more complex problems. The watchmaker fiddles with the design of a new watch for use in outer space; the dancer practices a lead part; the composer writes a pivotal piece; the physics student selects a doctoral program.

As Fogarty, Perkins, and Barell (1992) have noted, the highest refinement of any intelligence comes when the ability to problem solve moves from within a topic or discipline to "somewhere" in real life. To clarify "somewhere," Fogarty et al. distinguish "near transfer" from "far transfer." With near transfer, the learner solves additional problems in the same discipline. For instance, the teacher teaches students how to establish cause-effect relationships in a chemistry experiment about waste management. The student who makes near transfer replicates or duplicates that experiment with different garbage, but sees no other use for what he is doing. However, a different student understands the experiment enough to extrapolate the basic problem-solving approach and applies it to solving a community waste problem in

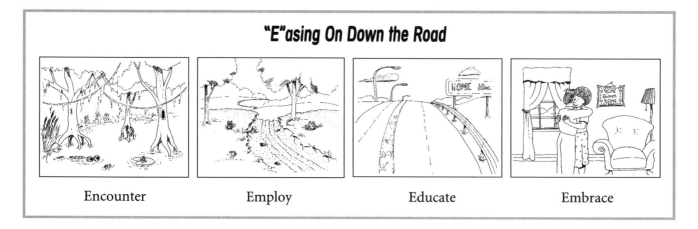

"E"asing On Down the Road

| Encounter | Employ | Educate | Embrace |

IRI/SkyLight Training and Publishing, Inc.

his town. This mindful abstraction to a real-life problem situation is characterized as "far" transfer.

In each of the four stages, the individual experiences different feelings. In the first stage, Encounter, it is natural to experience great discomfort. Some might compare this stage to walking in a swamp. The feet sink into mire, mosquitoes bite, snakes slither past, the heat rises, and moss scratches the face. Travel is slow and difficult. The path disappears. The traveler gets lost, bogged down, and frightened. Frustration is high as the traveler wonders, "Why am I doing this? I feel so stupid."

In the second stage, Employ, the discomfort declines. It is as if the traveler has climbed out of the bog and found a rough path. Some stretches are smooth and clearly marked. Obviously well traveled, the path's direction is clear and easier to follow. Occasionally, a fallen tree or a mud slide forces a detour. Travel is faster and the frustration is less severe.

In the third stage, Educate, the traveler finds a paved highway. There are many road signs. One sign indicates how far it is to the next town. A highway patrolman drives by and offers advice. The traveler finds a rest stop. In the shelter there are maps displayed. The traveler can chart the distance and estimate the time of arrival. Occasionally the traveler has to stop for a rest, but quickly recovers and moves on.

In the final stage, Embrace, the traveler arrives home. She opens the back gate. Under the rock, she finds the house key. As she opens the door, she hears a welcome greeting from her spouse. She smiles and he gives her a hug. Home sweet home.

TEACHERS CAN MODIFY THE INTELLIGENCE OF STUDENTS

The Feuerstein principle of cognitive modifiability suggests there are two basic ways to increase the problem-solving capabilities: first by creating the right conditions for helping the development and second by removing the conditions that hinder development.

It is especially important that students encountering an intelligence in the early stage experience a classroom that facilitates the development of the various intelligences. Such a classroom is rich with posters, bulletin boards, learning centers, activities, and lessons that promote the development. This does not mean that every room encourages every intelligence all the time. Some teachers use different intelligences to create a monthly theme. Others target one intelligence for the year in each subject. In the upper grades, the discipline (e.g., English, trigonometry) already targets the focus intelligence. In these cases, teachers select one or two supporting intelligences for consistent use in the semester or year.

Elements of the Brain-Compatible Classroom

The classroom environment that best facilitates the full development of the intelligences is sometimes called "brain compatible." For the brain to function fully, it is beneficial for the classroom to provide five elements: trust and belonging, meaningful content, enriched environment, intelligent choices, and adequate time.

TRUST AND BELONGING

The brain-compatible classroom is an inclusive classroom. Here each child feels that she belongs, can contribute, is considered important by the teacher and her peers, and is challenged by high, consistent expectations. When the teacher ignores the child and does not call on her to answer questions, when peers make fun of her or put her down, when the content goals are merely covering the material, completing workbooks, and finishing the textbook, the child cannot feel cared about.

In the brain-compatible classroom, the teacher trusts that every child, no matter how rich or poor, tall or short, black or white, will learn and develop. The rates of growth may vary. (How many times has a worried parent taken a child to the pediatrician because the child did not start reading as soon as her older siblings?) The interests may vary. (How many children in the same family like to do what their siblings do?) Throughout the school years, it is important to keep the faith in a child's natural tendency to learn, to encourage the child with patience, and to remember that rate of learning and interest will always vary. When the classroom is inclusive, the changes will come.

MEANINGFUL CONTENT

For most teachers, curriculum is set by the district. At best, curriculum committees will align the different intelligences with established outcomes or reconfigure outcomes to match development of the intelligences. In the classroom, the teacher can align the multiple intelligences approaches with district outcomes. It is most beneficial when the students understand the lesson outcome along with the clear goals and the purposes of what they are learning. If the goal of a lesson is to learn how to mix oil colors for texture (visual/spatial), the teacher can be explicit in helping students see how that task is connected to painting a more eye-appealing picture (the product). It is even more helpful when the teacher links the product outcome to the lifelong benefits of a strong visual/spatial intelligence.

Product-based outcomes help students make immediate connections to a purpose for learning a skill. When the learning starts with the making of the product itself, they discover a need for the skills. This approach works well with tasks that require math computation and problem-solving skills. The teacher assigns the students to design a treehouse. The architectural rendering will be the product. The teacher includes accurate computation and aligned measurements of all heights, lengths, and widths. The students must check their computation to meet these standards. When they are inaccurate, they will have to pursue instruction and coaching to learn computation and measurement.

Problem-based outcomes challenge students to distinguish means from ends. The goal is the solution of a problem. For instance, a short-story lesson about "The Most Dangerous Game" might have a problem framework that begins with this challenge statement: "You are trapped on an island owned by a man who wants to make you game for his hunt. Your problem is how to do something no other human game animal has ever done: escape alive." After reading the first half of the story, the students will have a clear understanding of the problem. At this point, the students will brainstorm possible solutions, examine consequences, and make a plan for escape. After reading to the end, they can compare their proposed solutions to the main character's and evaluate their own problem-solving approaches.

Product-based outcomes are often linked with process outcomes in the multiple intelligences curriculum. This linkage enables students to apply their understandings and assess their skill development at two levels: (1) reading and writing skills, and (2) problem-solving skills. In the short-story lesson, the students can extend the discussion of the problem by inventing additional similar scenarios for ending the story, write the new story endings, and assess the endings according to criteria which the teacher provides. Students can also evaluate specific reading, writing, and problem-solving skills used in the project. Knowing the criteria for assessment before they start the story enables the students to concentrate more attentively on solving the problem and/or completing the project.

Some schools implementing the multiple intelligences approach are using process-based outcomes. These outcomes use intelligent dispositions or attitudes as the desired outcomes. Logic, metacognitive reflection, inventiveness, and persistence in problem solving are examples of such desired dispositions. Over time, the teacher observes students through the lens of the disposition outcomes she has selected. For instance, in the short-story task, she might use an observation checklist as the students work on the invented story ending. As she notices students using strategies to make new relationships, she will make notes on her checklist. On a later assignment where inventiveness is again required, she will make more notes and look for improvements.

ENRICHED ENVIRONMENT

The classroom that is conducive to learning is a place the learner feels comfortable and not threatened. The room is filled with samplings of students' work and depicts the unit of study. When gazing in the classroom doorway and looking around one sees several obvious clues of a brain-compatible environment. Some of these clues are:
- examples of the focused unit of study
- students' work displayed
- places for independent work such as learning centers and quiet, cozy spots for exploration, study, and reflection
- places for collaborative learning
- hands-on environment with manipulatives
- central place for total class gatherings for discussion and lecturettes. Learners must be made to feel that they are important members of the group and contributors to that enriched learning environment.

INTELLIGENT CHOICES

The brain-compatible classroom structures many choices into the students' day. Building on the trust theme, the teacher outlines parameters and opportunities for choice. The parameters provide the students with high expectations for their individual work at the learning centers and for their collaborative work in cooperative groups. Where needed, the teacher also provides students with the tools and techniques to work in a cooperative group or at the centers.

Constructive choices come in all shapes and sizes in the multiple intelligences classroom. In classrooms where outcomes are delineated, students may choose which tasks to do to accomplish the goal, how to do a task, how to reflect on a task, and how to apply what they learned. The choices provide opportunities to grow in the different intelligences.

Sample task choices include: which book to read, which research materials to use, which graphic organizer to use for gathering information, what character to analyze, which sample problems to use for practice, what materials to use, what problem to investigate, and what product to make.

Choices depend on the teacher's comfort zone with a variety of different instructional approaches. The comfort zone is created by the teacher's know-how, her trust in the students' ability to work with the approaches, and the students' sense of accountability. For the most part, a teacher will have the best opportunity to extend the multiple choices for students by varying how she structures the curriculum. For instance, she might start by teaching vocabulary (verbal/linguistic) through a cooperative jigsaw (interpersonal), a song or rhyme (musical), or movement (bodily/kinesthetic). After she sees that the students can use a variety of approaches for the same task, she can extend to the students the choice of which approach each wants to use. In high school, the algebra teacher can design lessons that reflect the new math standards (logical/mathematical) by structuring problem practice in cooperative groups (interpersonal), using a sequence graphic organizer (visual/spatial) to review the steps of problem solving, and encouraging student self-assessment in a math journal (intrapersonal). After she observes their ability to use these tools, she can scaffold the assignment and have each group select how it will use each tool.

ADEQUATE TIME

The age of technology has its advantages. Through technology we can access new information with the press of a button. From remote spots around the world, ideas can pour into our workplaces. However, this quick access is a double-edged sword, especially in schools. Technology is drowning us in a flood of information. Teachers with limited instructional time and locked curriculum are struggling to stay afloat. Paddling harder does not help.

What can a teacher do to help students work smarter, not harder, in the flood of information? One answer, suggested by Arthur Costa, is "selective abandonment." This approach suggests the removal of outdated, irrelevant, and unnecessary information from the curriculum. To accomplish this task, he suggests the identification of three to five "thoughtful dispositions." The only information selected to remain in the curriculum would be that which is relevant to students' development of these dispositions (Costa, 1991). Another approach, developed by Robin Fogarty (1991) is the integration of the curriculum. Her models place the emphasis on helping students make connections. Gardner and his colleagues advocate using the multiple intelligences as a coordinating element that takes the emphasis off factual information and places it on the making of products and the solving of problems. In this view, the most important information is that which is needed for the problem-solving tasks.

Any restructuring of instruction will take time. Students need time to develop their comfort zones with approaches to learning that are novel for them. If the students have a high comfort level with front-end teaching, textbook coverage, and workbooks, they may not easily take to the challenge of problem solving and product making. Unless the teacher gives up lecture time, turns textbooks into just another resource, and abandons "fill-em-up" workbooks, there will be no time for projects or thoughtful problem-solving activities. Projects and the activities should be the most important elements in the multiple intelligences classroom.

Meeting the Needs of Special Students

When parents and teachers discuss the special needs child, they recognize the special and unique challenge of helping each child reach full potential. Unfortunately, many special needs youngsters are defined by the outdated and narrow, unidimensional definition of intelligence. Although there are many students whose logical/mathematical and verbal/linguistic intelligences are limited, by no means should we assume that these narrow definitions describe the intelligence potential of all special needs students. Nor should these narrow definitions, even when appropriate for students with the most serious developmental challenges in mathematical and linguistic reasoning, limit how these students can develop their other intelligences.

Consider the following examples:

☐ Roger was a bright, highly skilled athlete who also played two musical instruments and wrote compositions for the school's jazz band. A few years ago, Roger was in an accident and was crushed beneath the weight of his car. Roger is now confined to a wheelchair without the use of any of his limbs. His mind and spirit function fully. Labeled physically disabled/physically challenged, should he be locked out from the general education classroom, stopped from writing and playing his music, prevented from talking and laughing with his friends? His IEP mandates a restrictive placement within a special education, self-contained classroom setting.

☐ Annette reads at the fourth grade level. She is in the eighth grade. Her label is learning disabled (LD). She perplexes her teachers. They hear a vocabulary consistent with the abilities of much older students. They know she can solve complex word problems in her head. They see her interact and socialize as easily with adults as with her peers. Yet, she fights reading. She lacks basic word attack skills. Her reading tests show 4.2.

☐ Raul was raised in five foster homes. Due to his uncontrolled fits of anger and self-destruction, Raul was moved from home to home, school to school. Now, helped with psychiatric treatment, he has settled peacefully into his sixth home. His school records, however, have followed him. In his current school, he cannot leave his self-contained class for the severely behaviorally disordered (BD) students. In the lunch room, students who hardly know him, know the label given to Raul. They taunt him. How long must Raul live with such branding?

☐ Jessica is the athlete every coach in the school wants on a team. She excels in every sport. The other middle schoolers see her as a leader. Her never-ending energy and enthusiasm are contagious. She never quits. But, she is not eligible. With her list of telling labels (ADD, ED, LD, etc.) she spends two-thirds of her day in self-contained classrooms at the district center. Her tutors praise her hard work, even as they struggle to keep her attention on the math and reading activities. Because she is mainstreamed for two classes only (P.E. and art), the school board has ruled that she is not eligible for the school teams. They say, "Full academic mainstreaming is necessary for involvement in extracurricular activities."

Your school district may not treat its special needs students in this way. Yet, every day in schools across the nation, similar decisions are being made about these special students. These decisions are often the result of an outmoded view of intelligence and the all-or-nothing concept of intelligence levels.

In the framework of multiple intelligences it is not necessary to label students by perceived deficiencies. Instead, the focus should be on identifying and challenging potential. There is no need to limit potential to reading, writing, and arithmetic. There is the possibility to see potential in at least eight dimensions. Where a child might have an extremely low functioning ability in one of the intelligence areas, there is nothing to say that he or she cannot have high functioning capabilities in another. And even where there is limited functioning ability, that child can improve with the right type of education. In this regard, the special needs child is no different from any of us. All share the ability to encounter, employ, educate, and embrace.

The coming years will bring special challenges to those working with the special needs students.

THE CHALLENGE OF INCLUSION

For more than three decades, national policy has encouraged school districts to separate all special needs children from the regular classroom. Few teachers have received the preservice or inservice training necessary to assist special needs children in the classroom. The mildly learning disabled child is seen as more "treatable" in a labeled classroom than in a "regular classroom" with more highly functioning peers. He joins the endless trek of other labels, including the totally unwelcomed BD student, in and out of classrooms.

As dollar costs for special education exclusion have risen, so too have the concerns over the educational negatives. With the movement of the regular education initiative and the laudable social agenda to include the specially challenged in all aspects of our society by destroying the barriers that have locked them out, inclusion is reaching the attention of educators. The challenge comes not in the goal, but in the means to achieve the goal. Given that the government and the local school district provide classroom teachers with the training, the mandated aides and assistants, and the materials, inclusion will have great benefits.

Especially important will be the training programs. Fundamental will be training programs that help classroom teachers and their peers from special education work together. Such programs

IRI/SkyLight Training and Publishing, Inc.

will not only need to break down artificial distinctions between special education and regular education, they also will need to introduce new understandings about intelligence, its modifiability, and its divergence. From this base will come the practices that will make inclusion easier on teachers and students alike. If, however, the same narrow definitions of intelligence are carried forward, the challenge of inclusion can only end in failure and frustration.

THE CHALLENGE OF CHANGE

Change comes slowly. As society awaits the success of inclusion, many teachers will find themselves still struggling with the day-to-day reality of the old policies and practices. This means that the teacher will have the challenge of doing the best she can in the confines of outmoded and bureaucratic practices.

The theory and practices of multiple intelligences can empower the special education teacher to work with students in new and different ways. First, there is the understanding that this theory opens up new vistas for teaching these students the prescribed curricula. Reading can come through musical rap; math can spring from physical movement. Rather than boring worksheets redone in the resource room, the special student can learn to make predictions, explain why events in a story occurred, and forecast scientific results. By tailoring new teaching methods outlined in this book to individual students, the special educator can use resource room time to help these students construct knowledge for classroom assignments, rather than waste time on forcing memorization and the filling in of blank lines. As the students learn in different ways, they will demonstrate successes not anticipated in the old models of learning.

Mediation

The most beneficial and time-consuming responsibility occurs when the teacher mediates the development of the intelligences. Mediation occurs when the teacher helps the student reflect on what and how she is learning and to apply the insights so that she learns from her experience. This is very much like a baseball coach helping a player improve a bat swing. First, the coach explains, demonstrates, and guides practice with corrective feedback and positive reinforcement. Second, at critical points, the coach asks the player to explain what was expected, to analyze what she did well, to hypothesize what she might do to improve, and to ask questions of the coach. As the player thinks out loud about "swinging the bat," the coach makes verbal and/or pictorial corrections.

Mediation is the process of helping a student think aloud about a task. The goal is to dialogue with the student and help the student dialogue with herself to make the fine corrections in how she thinks about the task. When working with intelligence development in the teaching stage, the guided reflection is the most important step.

Mediation requires time. There is no shoveling of new material. There are quiet looks back throughout each day. The student is guided to look back at the content she has learned. She is given help to review her problem-solving processes and to evaluate her products. The teacher, whether mediating the whole class, small groups, or individuals, guides the students to analyze, evaluate, and apply insights into their development of the intelligences. To find the adequate time for this mediation obviously requires thoughtful selective abandonment.

Multiple Intelligences Schools

Although the culture of American schools gives primary attention to the logical/mathematical and verbal/linguistic intelligences, there are many examples of schools going so far as to redesign curriculum instruction and to take time to create brain-compatible, multiple intelligences classrooms.

HOWLAND SCHOOL OF THE ARTS

With enthusiastic community support, this inner-city Chicago elementary school has used the theory of multiple intelligences as its core. Aided by a grant from the Field Foundation, membership in the Network of Mindful Schools, and co-sponsored by the International Renewal Institute, Inc. and Phi Delta Kappa, teachers, administrators, parents, and students have reshaped this school's approach to formal learning. Using the visual and performing arts as its focus, learning experiences are integrated into holistic units of study with performances and productions as the goals.

ARTS PROPEL

This school's program is a collaboration among Harvard's Project Zero, the Educational Testing Service, and the Pittsburgh public schools. Using what they call "process portfolios," teachers sample a wide range of process skills in the development of different intelligences. The process skills include inventiveness, expressiveness, use of criticism, awareness of the properties of materials, and the ability to work collaboratively.

VANCOUVER PUBLIC SCHOOLS, WASHINGTON

This is a district-wide program that uses the theory of multiple intelligences as the coordinating principle of its curriculum. To reinforce the emphasis on the development of the multiple intelligences, the district progress report card is organized into seven major subheadings that correspond to Gardner's initial seven intelligences. Under each heading, indicators are listed. (See top of next page for an excerpt of the progress report.)

PROJECT SPECTRUM AT HARVARD UNIVERSITY

This is a model that encourages young students to explore their intelligences. In the Spectrum classroom, students can visit learning centers where they choose from a variety of hands-on activities and experiment with a variety of materials in each intelligence. For instance, storyboards, puppets, crayons, and pencils are provided in the verbal/linguistic center. As the students work, the teacher notes the patterns of choices made. A student profile assesses the student's strengths and makes recommendations for extending the various intelligences.

INTERPERSONAL				
SOCIAL STUDIES	1	2	3	4
Concepts				
Shows respect for rights of others				
Recognizes patterns and connections with cultures				
Participation				

Comments:_____

SPATIAL				
VISUAL ARTS	1	2	3	4
Recognizes patterns				
Composition				
Craftsmanship				
Expresses ideas through art				
Completes projects				
Participation				

Comments:_____

INTERPERSONAL				
CITIZENSHIP	1	2	3	4
Cooperates with school staff				
Cooperates with classmates				
Meets responsibilities				
Sets goals				
Completes assignments				
Overall school participation				

Comments:_____

SPATIAL				
GEOGRAPHY	1	2	3	4
Demonstrates map reading skills				
Identifies geographic features				
Relates geographical features to real places				
Participation				

Comments:_____

INTERPERSONAL				
LEADERSHIP	1	2	3	4
Uses influence for greater good				
Provides service				

Comments:_____

This is an excerpt from a progress report for the Vancouver Public School District, Washington. The report was created by Ric Packard.

THE INDIANAPOLIS KEY SCHOOL

Having read *Frames of Mind*, a group of teachers in this inner-city Indianapolis elementary school redesigned the total school program to fit with Gardner's theory. Since its start, the school has been one of the best performers on the Indiana Test of Educational Progress among the Indianapolis schools. Equal time is spent on pursuit of multi-age projects in the arts with study of the basic skills. At the Key School, every student, every week, engages in activities related to the different intelligences that are being developed through this school's curriculum. For example, students might be engaged in a unit of work titled, "The Renaissance: Then and Now." On one day a student might begin by working with puzzles and various games in a room set aside for such activities. Here, this student's ever-increasing skill with spatial relationships, eye/hand coordination, and inquiry into how things work are noted and aided by the teacher who is following a carefully planned, teacher-designed curriculum. All children at Key School will have such an experience during the week.

LINCOLN SCHOOL DISTRICT, STOCKTON, CALIFORNIA

This district is using the theory of multiple intelligences to transform itself into a Smithsonian Institute according to Gardner's thinking about museums for children. The fourteen schools were reorganized into multiple learning sites reflecting the multiple intelligences. Learning is extended into the community with apprenticeships.

LAKEVIEW PUBLIC SCHOOLS, BATTLE CREEK, MICHIGAN

The teachers designed a summer program using activities for the bodily/kinesthetic, interpersonal, logical/mathematical, and visual/spatial intelligences. They started with a desire to use larger blocks of time to facilitate problem-solving work. This led to framing a summer program that focused on multiple intelligences in and outside of the classroom.

MCWAYNE SCHOOL, BATAVIA, ILLINOIS

This school is in the midst of development as a "multiple intelligences school." Armed with Gardner's theory, a small but talented staff of dedicated teachers and Alan McCloud, the principal, are immersed in learning and applying the ideas related to multiple intelligences into a viable model of schooling.

Ideas for the Classroom

These are only a few of the increasing number of schools and districts that are using the theory of multiple intelligences. Throughout the country there are additional examples each year. Some teachers, however, may not have the luxury of participating in such a comprehensive change. Yet they may choose to enrich their teaching within the single classroom by using Gardner's theory. What can they do?

PROMOTE A VARIETY OF INTELLIGENCES

Enrich lessons and units with instructional strategies that promote a variety of intelligences, not just the logical/mathematical and verbal/linguistic intelligences. In this way a teacher can teach the same material but in a different and more motivational way. As Csikszentmihalyi has written, motivation is the most important by-product of the varied curriculum. When students are encouraged to expand their strengths, they are more likely to enjoy their work and to pursue increased competence with confidence (Csikszentmihalyi, 1990).

RESTRUCTURE LESSONS AND UNITS TO TARGET DIFFERENT INTELLIGENCES

Basic skills lessons that lead into projects work well in most disciplines. The projects enable the students to use the basic skills so that they develop understanding and learn to use the skill. To do this, the teacher will have to abandon many facts and concentrate more time on the most important curricular concepts.

INTEGRATE THE CURRICULUM AROUND THE MULTIPLE INTELLIGENCES

Integrated curriculum is not a question of adding something else to the overcrowded curriculum. It is a way to reorganize the material in new ways. Fertile and thought-provoking themes thread through the required material and help students note what is most important to learn. For more ideas about integrating the curriculum with multiple intelligences, see chapter 10.

RESPOND TO INDIVIDUAL NEEDS

In this age of inclusion, multi-age grouping, and the detracked classroom, a teacher may feel overwhelmed with the diversity in her classroom. By using the theory of multiple intelligences, she can differentiate instruction for special needs. Cooperative learning (interpersonal) will help her group and regroup students for specific lessons.

For instance, she might use heterogeneous groups to practice a math concept. After the guided practice, she can regroup students based on degree of mastery. For the "wow" students, she can form a group that applies the concept to a problem-solving project that incorporates the concept. For the "O.K." students, she can form several groups to do more practice. For the "not yet" groups, she can reteach using a different set of manipulatives (visual/spatial). In other instances, the teacher can individualize by the intelligences she wants students to develop. For instance, in language arts, the teacher might group the students by an intelligence that is not strong. After discussing a novel, she can assign each group to do a character analysis in a product that expresses their ideas in ways other than an essay. One group might draw a sketch, another write a song.

MAKE HOLISTIC, LEARNER-CENTERED OUTCOMES

The multiple intelligences approach allows a teacher to individualize learner outcomes within district- or state-mandated outcomes. After diagnosing each student's strong intelligences, the teacher can initiate an individualized learning plan that details which supporting intelligences the student will develop. As the teacher plans lessons, she can use these plans as a reminder for how she wants to group students and what types of strategies she will select. She will not, however, limit these outcomes to the now out-of-date "split brain strategy." This approach came from a narrow interpretation of Sperry's right brain/left brain split. His studies gave us a new understanding of how each of the brain's hemispheres affect learning. Gardner's work has since extended what Speary found. Gardner's work supports the notion that the brain processes with both hemispheres simultaneously in many complex ways.

If the Shoe Fits . . .

The summary of what a teacher does with the multiple intelligences is pictured in the shoe metaphor. In the closet are many pairs of shoes. Each has a different use. Each helps its owner in a different way. When the shoe fits properly, the owner's feet are comfortable. When the shoe slips and slides on and off the heel, it slows the pace. When one pair fits more snugly than another, the owner tends to favor the comfortable pair. And of course it's more beneficial to have lots of shoes that fit just right, for multiple shoes, like multiple intelligences, serve multiple purposes.

The shoe metaphor leads to many implications for classroom and school changes. Many go beyond curricular and instructional modifications. The theory can lead to:

1. A new way to understand the complete child including strengths and weaknesses
2. Elimination of the need to label students or isolate large groups of students for special instruction
3. Elimination of the need to ability group and track students
4. The creation of problem-centered schools with activities outside the school walls
5. The establishment of multi-age classrooms that group students by developmental age and interest
6. The assessment of learning in a range of authentic learning experiences
7. The opportunity for every student to excel in at least one intelligence
8. Students who excel by understanding and applying what they have learned
9. Teachers who mediate learning
10. The elimination of letter grades

Today's classroom requires that the teacher adapt his or her teaching to meet the diverse challenges of today's students. When we begin to think of students as diversely intelligent rather than measuring each child against one fixed standard with an outdated instrument, the logical/mathematical IQ test, we will begin to see a true change in the performances of students.

IRI/SkyLight Training and Publishing, Inc.

Journal Page

Reflections on My Pathway to the Intelligences

_____
_____
_____
_____
_____
_____
_____
_____
_____
_____
_____
_____
_____
_____
_____
_____
_____
_____
_____
_____
_____
_____
_____
_____
_____
_____
_____
_____
_____
_____

Verbal/Linguistic Intelligence

The tap shoe is the communicating shoe to represent the verbal/linguistic learner. The shoe makes the tapping sounds that tell us the message of the dancer. This symbolizes interpretation. When the dancer moves to the beat and taps out every sound, we interpret the full message.

What Is It?

The verbal/linguistic intelligence is the ability to use with clarity the core operations of language. The communicating of humans by reading, writing, listening, speaking, and linking are the significant components of this intelligence.

If the Shoe Fits... It Looks Like

Jeff, our communicating student, thinks well in words and expresses himself beautifully. He has a well-developed language ability, enjoys reading, writing, listening, and speaking, and is able to link new knowledge to prior experiences. Jeff fits well in today's classroom.

Wearing the Shoe in Life – Career Choices

- Author
- Speaker
- Attorney
- Talk-Show Host
- Politician
- Actor, Actress
- Teacher
- Religious Leader
- Salesperson

"E"asing On Down the Road of the Verbal/Linguistic Journey

Create a print environment.

Find out interests.

Set up centers for reading, writing, listening, and speaking.

Educate

Provide time for improving communication skills.

Teach necessary skills.

Have a variety of printed materials available.

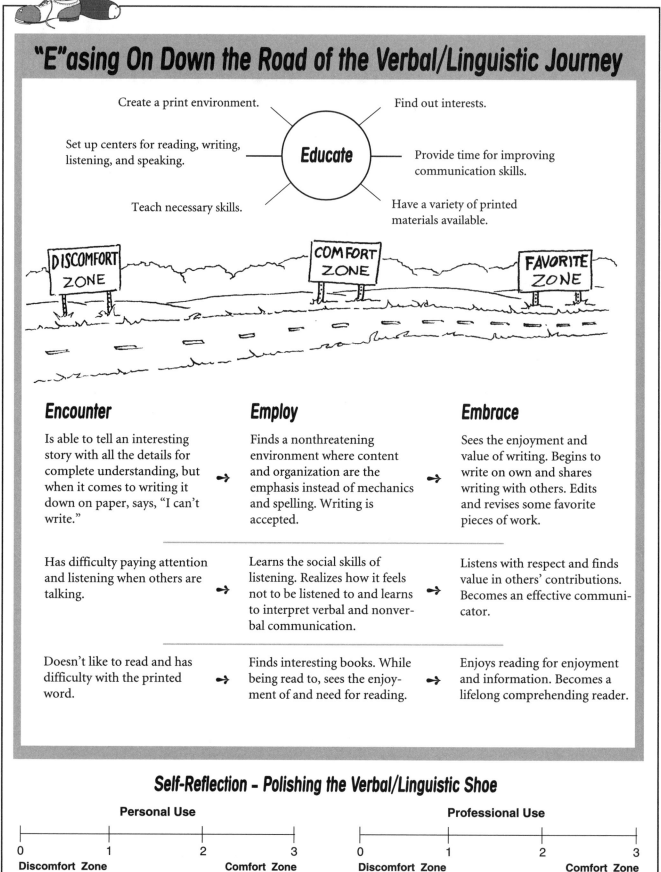

DISCOMFORT ZONE

COMFORT ZONE

FAVORITE ZONE

Encounter

Is able to tell an interesting story with all the details for complete understanding, but when it comes to writing it down on paper, says, "I can't write."

Has difficulty paying attention and listening when others are talking.

Doesn't like to read and has difficulty with the printed word.

Employ

Finds a nonthreatening environment where content and organization are the emphasis instead of mechanics and spelling. Writing is accepted.

Learns the social skills of listening. Realizes how it feels not to be listened to and learns to interpret verbal and nonverbal communication.

Finds interesting books. While being read to, sees the enjoyment of and need for reading.

Embrace

Sees the enjoyment and value of writing. Begins to write on own and shares writing with others. Edits and revises some favorite pieces of work.

Listens with respect and finds value in others' contributions. Becomes an effective communicator.

Enjoys reading for enjoyment and information. Becomes a lifelong comprehending reader.

Self-Reflection - Polishing the Verbal/Linguistic Shoe

Personal Use

```
0          1          2          3
Discomfort Zone        Comfort Zone
```

Professional Use

```
0          1          2          3
Discomfort Zone        Comfort Zone
```

"It is reasonable to assume that the liberally educated man should know something of the structure of his language, its position in the world and its relation to other tongues, the wealth of its vocabulary together with the sources from which that vocabulary has been and is being enriched, and in general the great political, social, and cultural influences which have combined to make his language what it is" (Baugh, 1978, p. 1). Such thoughts might well coincide with Gardner's description of highly developed verbal/linguistic intelligence.

In American schools, the attention given to language outpaces that given to any other intelligence. Nothing seems to grab more headlines than perennial battles over the teaching of reading and writing. Whole language? Phonics? Phonetics? Process writing? Language experience? Strategic reading? Reading and writing across the content areas? and on and on. On top of these arguments comes the battle over testing. Standardized tests? Writing samples? Testing bias? Aptitude or achievement? Out of all this comes more time spent with reading instruction and more concern over test results. When all is said and done, everyone has a pet theory, but few are happy with the readers that schools are producing.

The tap shoe fits the verbal/linguistic intelligence. This shoe was selected for many reasons. First, this shoe makes the tapping sounds and the noise tells the message. As people communicate, whether socially or formally, they are sending a message. Humans communicate by reading, writing, listening, speaking, and linking. This shoe represents interpretation. When the dancer dances to the beat and taps out every sound, we relate to prior experiences, look at what is going on right then, and think about the future. We as learners base our communication on the past, present, and future. Also, the body language of the other dancers completes the full message. Our verbal and nonverbal signals complete our full message as we communicate with others.

Given all the pressures to raise reading scores, what can the teacher do to develop the verbal/ linguistic intelligences of her students? First, she needs to avoid the "magic recipe syndrome." This comes from the advocates of the "one right way " to teach reading and writing to every child. "Just follow these five steps and add water." Second, she needs to recognize that reading and writing are developmental processes. There is no arriving; there is only constant travel along the path of betterment. This means that day in and day out she models correct language usage, consults and coaches students with their writing, demonstrates better ways to communicate, supports and encourages budding authors, and spends much time reading aloud to her students. Third, she can discover opportunities for language instruction in every subject. No discipline is more easily integrated across the curriculum. For those teachers who teach in other disciplines separated from language arts or English, responsibility for the development of reading, writing, speaking, and listening is sometimes shunted aside. However, this avoidance works only to the disadvantage of students' linguistic development. Fourth, she remembers that language development is the key to learning. By providing a variety of writing and reading experiences, a language-rich environment, and many opportunities for each student to read, speak, hear, and write language; by keeping ready a variety of methods to assist special challenge readers; and by empowering each child to become a strategic reader, the teacher will better ensure the development of the verbal/linguistic intelligence in all her students.

What Is Verbal/Linguistic Intelligence?

Verbal/linguistic intelligence helps the student produce and refine language use in its many forms and formats. The ability to form and recognize words and word patterns by sight, by sound, and for some by touch, is the start. After learning to read and write in the basic patterns, the more advanced learner goes on to distinguish the many formats of language including stories, essays, and poems, and the techniques of language such as metaphor, hyperbole, symbol, and grammar. These are enriched with meaning by abstract reasoning, conceptual patterns, feeling, tone, structure, and an ever-expanding vocabulary. Ultimately, the peaks of language development are reached by those who combine sound and sense in unique patterns to express universal thoughts and to speak to the hearts of the many.

What Is the Developmental Path for This Intelligence?

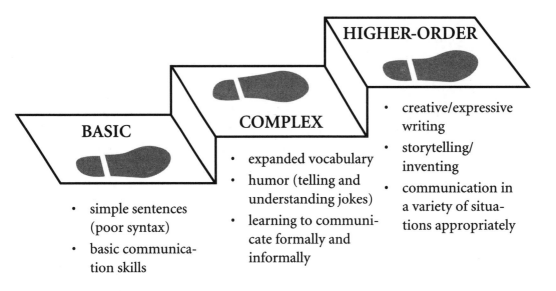

BASIC
- simple sentences (poor syntax)
- basic communication skills

COMPLEX
- expanded vocabulary
- humor (telling and understanding jokes)
- learning to communicate formally and informally

HIGHER-ORDER
- creative/expressive writing
- storytelling/ inventing
- communication in a variety of situations appropriately

How Is This Intelligence Developed in Other Cultures?

Many cultures around the world have retained an oral language tradition. The storyteller is an esteemed figure among many Native American tribes. While Gutenberg's press was printing the first mass production books, the inhabitants of North America were painting word pictures for their children. Myths, fables, and heroic stories were passed from one generation to the next by word of mouth.

Gutenberg did not end the oral tradition in Europe, but he facilitated the dominance of a written tradition. He sped up the production of the printed word begun by the monks with their elaborate manuscripts. He enhanced the opportunity for the growing middle class to learn to read and write.

In Europe, it is contended that Great Britain leads in the provision of literary greats. From the publication of Chaucer's *Canterbury Tales*, the plays and poems of Shakespeare, the productions of Donne, Swift, and Coleridge, and the works of T.S. Eliot, it is hard to find a nation that took greater advantage of the printed word. Some would argue that Russia, Germany, Spain, and France produced written works of similar or greater merit, but few will contend that these countries produced so many high-quality literary stars.

How Can This Intelligence Be Used for Problem Solving?

Problem solving with language is evident every day.

- ☐ When Robin saw the red light twirling behind her, she looked at her speedometer. "Oh, Officer," she said when he appeared beside her stopped car. "I know I was going fast. But this is an emergency. There are three hundred teachers waiting at a workshop for me. Traffic was so slow on the expressway that I had to rush these last few miles. . . ."

- ☐ John looked puzzled for a moment. Then he looked at the group and spoke. "I believe the problem is the software for three reasons. First, the hardware is operating fine. Second, we put our best people on the project and they were inhibited as much as anyone else. Third, there is no other choice. Given that scenario, let me tell you what our alternatives are. Then we'll evaluate the alternatives and decide what we want to do."

- ☐ Bruce wrote his solution on the computer. He was pleased with the result. His solution was clear and precise, and it argued the case for cutting costs succinctly. The other managers would be surprised that a bean counter could actually write a persuasive memo.

- ☐ Mary was excited. This was her first court case. She felt confident that she could argue this case against Clarence Darrow and win. There was no doubt in her mind that the brief she had written should get an award.

Who Is the Student With This Intelligence?

Jeff, our verbal/linguistically intelligent student, thinks well in words and expresses himself beautifully. He fits well in the traditional classroom because of his strengths in reading, writing, and speaking.

The student with a well-developed language ability is one who is an effective communicator who enjoys reading, writing, and public speaking. He expresses himself well on paper and in oral delivery. Because he thinks in words, he links ideas effectively and translates these ideas to paper with ease. As a reader, he is very strategic. Without cuing, he checks his prior knowledge, uses textual clues to guide himself through reading passages, and as a result he puts himself in the middle of stories and comprehends easily.

When it comes to expressive language, he finds negotiation, compromise, descriptive detail, logical argument, and fluent/flexible thinking easy to communicate. Given encouragement for his highly tuned reading and writing skills, he finds school "a breeze."

There are many children, some who are very bright in other domains, who struggle with written language in ways that perplex the most experienced teacher. Verbally the child may sound very capable, but she resists reading with all her might. This child does not need "time out" from reading and writing tasks. She needs a peer coach, an older child, or a grandparent volunteer to work one-on-one with encouragement, muscle exercises prescribed by an optometrist, and reading remediation strategies suggested by a reading specialist.

The Comfort Zone: What Helps This Student Learn?

Dylan Thomas, the Welsh poet, sings the praises of being surrounded with words when he was "young and green among the apple boughs." The verbal/linguistic child likes words, words, words. Before school starts, he likes words. Given the shortest moment, he will read and write. When encouraged, he will read more of whatever is in print: comic books, poems, magazines, and novels. The more opportunities the teacher gives to write, this student will write. This can include anything from a one-line ad, the balloon dialogue for a comic strip, or a portrait of an artist. The comfort zone is expanded for this child when there are many opportunities to read and write in a print-rich classroom with a teacher who encourages literary adventures.

When it comes to ensuring that all readers develop their verbal/linguistic capabilities, it is beneficial to recognize the new research that tells classroom teachers about the characteristics of successful readers. Beau Jones and her colleagues at the North Central Regional Education Laboratory, a federally funded research institute in Oak Brook, Illinois, have identified seven characteristics. Successful readers:

1. Take responsibility for constructing meaning by using their prior knowledge.
2. Develop a repertoire of reading strategies to use with varied text structures and genres.

3. Think strategically—plan, monitor their comprehension, and revise their strategies.

4. Perceive themselves as productive, proficient learners who are in control of their thinking and learning.

5. Have strategies for what to do when they do not know what to do.

6. Persevere in the face of contradictory or inadequate information.

7. Know that their own success is a direct result of their effort, ability, and determination.

Jones further declares that the evidence shows that all students can acquire these characteristics when they are the target of reading instruction. She advocates instructional models that (a) are collaborative, (b) center on the thinking skills of reading (e.g., metacognition, prediction, clarification), and (c) use the multiple intelligences.

The Discomfort Zone: What Hinders This Student?

Because this student has more highly developed language sensibilities than most, criticism, humiliation, negative comments, sarcasm, favoritism, and belittling more readily result in "a turn off." When classroom walls, bulletin boards, and bookshelves are word bare this student gets little stimulation. If the language curriculum focuses always on the mundane (grammar) and the practical (vocabulary worksheets) without stirring the imagination or encouraging students to become strategic readers, this student will shut down.

How Do You Catch This Student's Attention in the Classroom?

Verbal/linguistic learners, sensitive to the nuances of language, need special encouragement to take communication risks. Authoring a poem, short story, novel, or essay that shares the special meanings this student sees and feels is a risky business. To avoid the risks, the child tends to write safe, not stretching use of the language to her capabilities.

Encouragement is critical, especially for the budding writers. When the student says, "I'm not sure," "I can't do. . .," or "This just isn't what I want to say," ask, "What aren't you sure about?" "Why do you think that?" "Why do you feel that way?" and "What do you want to say?"

Listen patiently, paraphrase, "Is this what you are saying. . . ?" Ask clarifying questions, "Can you help me with an example?" Affirm her strengths, "I really like the way you. . .,"and help her explore options, "What would happen if you tried. . .?" Your enthusiasm, invitations to try again, high expectations for the quality of her work, and understanding of her literary capabilities will build her self-esteem and help her over the risky barriers she perceives.

What Activities Promote Learning With This Intelligence?

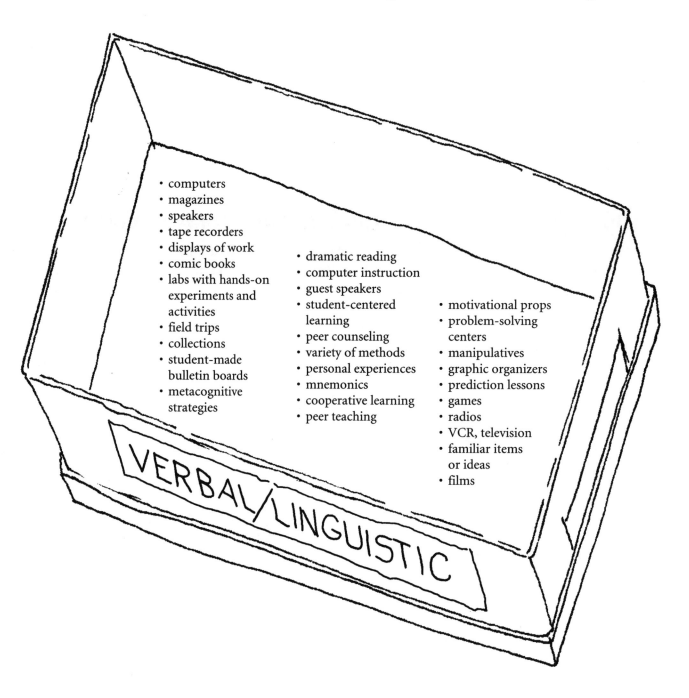

- computers
- magazines
- speakers
- tape recorders
- displays of work
- comic books
- labs with hands-on experiments and activities
- field trips
- collections
- student-made bulletin boards
- metacognitive strategies

- dramatic reading
- computer instruction
- guest speakers
- student-centered learning
- peer counseling
- variety of methods
- personal experiences
- mnemonics
- cooperative learning
- peer teaching

- motivational props
- problem-solving centers
- manipulatives
- graphic organizers
- prediction lessons
- games
- radios
- VCR, television
- familiar items or ideas
- films

VERBAL/LINGUISTIC

To build this student's confidence, invite her to visit the primary classrooms and read aloud with a "little brother" or "little sister." She can read a book the primary child or teacher selects, a big book she creates with the child, or one of her own creative works.

In your classroom, hold a reading time. Be sure this student gets a regular chance to read to her peers at this time. You may structure this in pairs, cooperative groups, or before the entire class. Remember to lay down guidelines so that put-downs are banned.

Finally, if this student is reluctant to read or write, don't let her distract you with avoidance misbehaviors. Keep her at the task. If you don't have many chances to give her one-to-one attention, pair her with a one-on-one coach who will model, encourage, and give caring reinforcement. Work with a middle school teacher or high school program to identify older students who can do this one-on-one work.

How Do You Meet the Challenge of the Special Student?

The way this intelligence is developed in the traditional classroom makes life miserable for many special needs children. This is especially true for those labeled "learning disabled."Although textbook companies earn billions of dollars each year by selling consumable workbooks filled with matching, fill-in-the-blank, draw-a-line, and circle-the-answer questions that ask students to guess over and over which fact goes where, these special needs students get bored more quickly than other students. With workbook mania five hours a day, few students learn much of anything; the LD child learns nothing more slowly. Which best practices can help develop the child who finds it difficult to learn in this intelligence? Refer to the Dynamic Dozen Plus 1 in this chapter for the key elements and practices to reach these learners.

How Do You Create an Environment for This Intelligence?

The literate environment begins with the classroom walls and ceiling. On bulletin boards, above the blackboard, and on any blank wall inside the room or out in the hallway, display students' creative use of language. Whether in kindergarten or high school, every student should see his or her work in a gallery. When students know their work will receive prominent attention for all to see, they will spend more care in the creation. Mix the signed, displayed work with their visual products. Essays, short stories, poems, concept maps, Venn diagrams, cartoon strips about characters in a story, ad campaigns for favorite books, and student-made books—all make a rich display.

When a display of work is done, select the very best for your classroom library. This is a low-cost way of building a classroom library. In addition, it will provide future students with models for their work. Add favorite books nominated by students, magazines, newspapers, catalogs, and pamphlets to your library collection. House it in a corner of the room with a rug or soft pillow for easy reading.

Posted directions for classroom procedures and guidelines facilitate easy reading practice. When teaching a new process in science, introducing behavior guidelines for cooperative learning, starting math problem solving, or teaching a new thinking skill, make a procedure chart. Use choral reading with the whole class to review these charts on a regular basis. On the next page is an example of a procedure chart for learning the skill of prediction by remembering the word BET.

Predicting

Base on facts.

Express probabilities and possibilities.

Tender your bet; take a guess.

In addition to the visual print displays, the literate environment is enhanced with a variety of reading and writing experiences. The mnemonic READER outlines some key strategies.

Enhancing the Reading Experience

Read to the students every day.

Encourage self-selection of reading materials.

Allow for read-alone and read-to-a-partner time.

Demonstrate good reading strategies.

Explain to students how to use prior knowledge and text clues.

Recognize and celebrate effort given to reading each day.

To enhance the writing experience, the mnemonic WRITER suggests a variety of basic strategies.

Enhancing the Writing Experience

Write with your students every day.

Review the writing process on a regular basis.

Invite students to read their writing to a partner or the whole class.

Teach students new techniques for thinking through their writing.

Encourage risk taking in new ideas and new formats.

Remember, the more a person writes, the better writer he or she becomes.

In addition to these basics which encourage student reading and writing, there are many helpful strategies that work in any classroom with students of all ages. Here is a selected list, a dynamic dozen plus one.

IRI/SkyLight Training and Publishing, Inc.

The Dynamic Dozen Plus 1

1 – STORY TIME

In story time, students read all types of literature. Every day they can hear favorite stories, poems, text selections, news releases, and other articles. Reading to students models good reading and develops their love of books! It is natural for a child to want favorite books read over and over again, so set aside a time to read favorites and a time to read a new book of your choice. Read to students every opportunity you get! These special sharing times are fun as the students are discovering more about the world, increasing their vocabulary, and witnessing the joys of learning how to read. Story time does not have to be long. A short, quick selection that holds students' attention is preferred over a long, rambling piece.

Suggestions for Story Time

What to Read

1. Read selections that you enjoy and feel are worthwhile.
2. Choose favorite selections that fit the themes of your classroom study and levels of interest of your students.
3. Enjoy selections chosen by you and some selected by the children.
4. Select personal experience stories.
5. Include some fables, myths, or folk tales.
6. Read a favorite story with lots of action and intriguing characters to create interest in the listeners.

Reading Aloud

1. Get everyone in a comfortable spot.
2. Choose a selection that you and the children like.
3. Read as long as you have the listeners' attention.
4. Have fun with the stories. Laugh at the funny parts.
5. Put yourself in the setting and the character through your voice and a prop.
6. Stop at key points and have students predict what might happen next.

Storytelling

1. Choose a story to tell that you love!
2. Read the story to yourself many times aloud.
3. Close the book and jot down the parts you remember.
4. Reread the story from the book.
5. Revise your notes.
6. Tell the story from your notes.
7. Close your eyes and visualize where each scene in the story takes place.
8. Tell the story over and over from your notes.
9. Put in voice tones for moods and inflections for characters.
10. Practice in front of a mirror.
11. Before you tell it to an audience, tell it to a close friend or family member.
12. Find an audience (your students)!

2 – INDEPENDENT READING TIME

Set aside a time for all students to read something of their choice. During this time, you can read too. The more children read the better readers they become. A variety of reading materials should be available for student selection. Provide books that they have heard in story time, a classmate has recommended, or is of great interest. Saturate the students with things to read. When students read books of personal interest, they practice comprehension strategies and respond to reading materials as individuals. Your classroom collection can include favorite books on different subjects and at varied reading levels, newspapers, magazines, pamphlets, dictionaries, and encyclopedias.

3 – GUIDED PRACTICE: GUIDED READING

Guided practice is done with the total class or small reading groups. The selection is read and discussed. Skills are taught in mini-lessons during this time. Language and reading are integrated in all content areas. The integration of academic areas connects the core of the curriculum. As students read, they are given opportunities to think, discuss, and then form their own opinions, with a solid background to explore for further knowledge. In many classes, teachers are forming literary study groups with students working with the same piece of reading.

4 – LANGUAGE EXPERIENCE

A Language Experience activity involves writing down what a student says. This dictation is usually written on a chart, the bulletin board, or sentence strips so that students are able to read the language over and over again. It is amazing how much of this published material the children can read, enjoy, and comprehend. This is because these works are made up of their own spoken language on paper.

Language Experience activities are done with small groups or the total class. Students gather around a chart or stand near the chalkboard for this activity. The teacher or another student writes on the chalkboard or the chart. The students dictate their language and it is written down. This may be lists of brainstormed words or phrases, random ideas or sentences, or a story based on a central theme. Many ideas that used to be written on chalkboards, shared, and then erased are now kept for reference, for review, and to add to as learning continues on the subject. The charts are displayed at eye level to make a rich print environment in the classroom.

A Lesson Format for Language Experience

1. All students gather around the teacher at a central location to see the chart.
2. The teacher has a big chart tablet and markers of various colors.
3. The teacher sets the prewriting stage with an introduction of the subject. This must be done well to generate thought around the central subject or topic.
4. The teacher calls on individual volunteers to give the sentences. Sometimes the child's name is written by his or her sentence.

IRI/SkyLight Training and Publishing, Inc.

5. The teacher writes the sentences on the chart by adhering to the following guidelines:
   a. Always use correct English and spelling.
   b. Model the correct formation of the letters.
   c. Say the word at the beginning and then say every letter in each word as it is formed on the paper and have students repeat it.
   d. When you get to the end of the word, say that word and have the students repeat.
   e. When you get to the end of the word, read the sentence thus far.
   f. When a sentence is complete, read the entire sentence and have the class repeat it.
6. At the completion of the chart, read the whole story and celebrate.
7. Display the chart at eye level for rereading.

When Is a Good Time to Use These Lessons?

Language Experiences work best:
1. At the end of a story or unit to sum up all that the students have learned.
2. To sequence events in a story.
3. To describe a character, event, or holiday.
4. As a spin-off from a discovery center where students have been observing something (e.g., an experiment, object, or animal).
5. To follow up a field trip, visitor, or creative class experience.
6. To celebrate "the special student of the day."
7. To establish class rules.

Suggestions for Following the Writing of the Chart

1. Point out a skill you would like to reteach by marking where it occurs on the chart.
2. For the first few days after the chart is written, display it near the writing center. Then move it to another location at eye level.
3. During learning center time, allow students to read the print around the room to a partner.
4. Reread the chart or parts of it during center time.
5. If the chart is an activity for sequencing, cut it apart and place it in the game center for students to put it in order.
6. Allow students to illustrate the chart story.
7. Encourage them to write spin-off stories about the same subject.

Word Brainstorming as a Language Experience

1. It is fun to list words or phrases on a big cut-out shape that fits the topic or theme.
2. Create interest with an exciting prewriting activity that motivates students and gets their thinking power going.
3. Call on individual students to provide words or phrases.
4. As students suggest a word, say the word, say each letter, ask students to say the word, and then repeat the word.
5. Reread the list thus far.
6. Display the words at eye level and reread the lists during transition times.
7. Remind students of the list during creative writing time.

Language Experience Works Well as a Motivation for a Single Student

1. Motivate the child to tell a story to another student, to the teacher, or into a tape recorder. This experience will be successful if the child is able to relate the story to his or her personal experiences, if it is based on a reading that was recently enjoyed, or if it pertains to a subject that this student wants to talk about.
2. During the telling of the story, the story is written down.
3. The student needs to illustrate the story.
4. This information is then used as the basis of instructions.
5. The story may be published in the student's folder, displayed around the room, or bound into a book.

5 – SHARED READING TIME

Students love to read together. Invite students to move to a comfortable spot with a partner or a small group of students and read to each other and discuss the literature. This might also be the time for students to share their own writing or to tell about a favorite book.

As a variation, the teacher reads the material and the students read along from their copy or from the teacher's book. The students should be actively involved during this reading. Choral read alongs, reader's theater, plays, role playing, or movement activities encourage active participation in read along.

The purpose of the shared book experience is to create a natural environment for literacy learning and to stimulate a home read-aloud situation.

Best Selections for Shared Reading

1. Are timely with interest, level, and focus.
2. Use predictable language or happenings.
3. Have warmth, mystery, or humor.
4. Have flow with a strong story line.
5. Have characters or situations with which children can identify.
6. Place strong emphasis on a particular skill that can be taught through the book sharing process.
7. Use natural spoken language.

Reading Stages

Initial Reading Stage
1. Present story introduction.
2. Read the selection aloud to the students.
3. Discuss the story. Use prediction and summarizing strategies.
4. Repeat the book or the section with students joining in where appropriate with motion, sound, or words.
5. Follow up with related activities.

Independent Reading Stage
1. Invite students to choose a partner.
2. Instruct them to share a book and sit side by side.
3. Ask them to take turns reading and listening.
4. Give instructions for difficult words.
   a. Read to the end of the sentence.
   b. Look at the pictures.
   c. Try to sound out the word.
5. Tell them to praise their partner with warm comments.

Extension Activities

1. Drama
   a. Role play the story.
   b. Develop plays and then perform them in cooperative groups.
   c. Role play with the total group.
   d. Use puppets.
2. Listening
   a. Tape record stories of the class readings for the listening center.
   b. Read stories over and over again.
3. Rereading
   a. Put the words on sentence strips or on charts around the room and have partner reading.
   b. Make class books of favorite stories with the children's illustrations.
4. Skill Instruction
   a. Teach or reteach skills that fit with the particular selection.
   b. List book examples on a chart.

All-Grade Sample: A Lesson Plan

Title: *Alexander and the Terrible, Horrible, No Good, Very Bad Day* by Judith Viorst

This book is loved by all from second grade through adults. To get the full effect of the character's feelings, it helps to practice before reading out loud to the class. Wear a little boy's hat to create interest. Enjoy reading this wonderful adventure!

Skills
The skills that might be emphasized in mini-lessons before or after reading this story are: point of view, sequencing, and brainstorming "bad day" feelings, likes, and dislikes. In the middle school and high school, English classes use this story as a model to illustrate how (1) an author depicts feelings and captures the reader's emotions, (2) an author creates a point of view, and (3) sequence is created. Use this story as a model before going to more difficult literature or before assigning a story creation.

Extension Activities
1. Write terrible-day stories and illustrate them.
2. List on a Language Experience chart or sentence strips all the bad things that happen to Alexander, put in order, and display.
3. Make a class book.
   a. Use cooperative learning groups.
   b. Request one page from each student.
4. Have students draw Alexander and themselves on a happy or terrible adventure.

Primary School Sample: A Lesson Plan

Title: *The Little Mouse, the Red Ripe Strawberry, and the Big Hungry Bear* by Don and Audrey Wood

Day 1
1. Show the book cover and discuss what the story might be about.
2. Talk about the title, author, and illustrator.
3. Talk about the title page.
4. Create an interest and an excitement in the story.
5. Show the pictures through the book.
   a. Cut out a huge mouse shape for writing the describing words that the students hear.
   b. Brainstorm words about the mouse's feelings.

Day 2
1. Read the story and let all hear the flow of the beautiful dialogue and look at the illustrations. This will be a successful story time!
2. Reread the story with one of the following suggestions:
   a. Stop after each question in the script and let the students answer.
   b. Refer to the list of brainstormed words from Day 1 and see which feeling best explains the mouse on each page now that the story has been heard.
   c. Role play the story as students read along with you for the second reading. Decide on different movements and noises to make at certain points in the book.
   d. Discuss the mouse's problem and solutions.

Day 3
1. Select a skill to reinforce that fits with the story, such as adjectives, sequencing, problem solving, or opposites.
2. Reinforce a unit of study such as mice, fruit, fears, sharing, or feelings.

Extension Activities
1. Tape record the story for the listening center.
2. Write other mouse and bear adventures.
3. Draw illustrations and write text, making the Big Class Book.
4. Practice math concepts of fractions and division by making a fruit salad for all to eat together.
5. Create different endings for the story.

6 – A NONTHREATENING AND PRINT-RICH ENVIRONMENT

Students have to know that their attempts at authorship will be accepted and encouraged. Literate classrooms promote risk taking in reading and writing.

Make the classroom a literate environment with students' creative work displayed, language experience charts hung, and relevant language posted everywhere. The classroom should be student centered with stories, artwork, and other creations displayed. Post directions for procedures so students can read along when you give directions. Special bulletin boards and projects should display the students' work. This makes the students feel like they are an important part of the classroom.

Display reading materials of all kinds so that each class member knows there is something in the classroom that he or she will like to read. Always add books or articles that you read orally. Students should be saturated with books and other reading materials.

7 – WRITING TIME

Writing opportunities are provided for the students and the teacher to write creatively. Each room needs a writing center to encourage writing. Writing lessons are planned following the writing process. Daily journal writing is a must in the language-rich classroom! The more students write, the better writers they become! Students have to feel they are in an environment where their writing is accepted.

8 – INDEPENDENT, COOPERATIVE, AND COMPETITIVE LEARNING

Students work in cooperative learning groups to develop communication skills and think through problems to develop knowledge. After the teacher establishes the cooperative group ground rules and gives the assignment, the teacher then becomes the facilitator and the mediator during the group work time. The group comes to an agreement and completes the task through a cooperative process. Some examples of cooperative activities to assign in language classrooms are book making, discussions about literature, the editing and revising of writing projects, and the writing of stories, poems, raps, songs or cheers, comic strips, ads, video scripts, and plays.

Cooperative Writing Activity: Creating a Book

After assigning the topic and the group roles (refer to chapter 9, Interpersonal Intelligence), each group brainstorms and comes to an agreement about the items that go on the chart or poster or in the book. The artifact is made, displayed, and the celebration can begin.

Primary School Sample Lesson

1. Each student creates an animal, monster, vehicle, or something personal during art or at the art center.
2. The cooperative groups are formed.
3. The groups create a big book about the objects created. There will be forced connections. This fun activity focuses on story development through group cooperation.
4. The books are bound and shared with the other class members.
5. The books are then placed in the reading center for all to enjoy.

Middle School Sample Lesson

1. Each student writes a description of an imaginary character.
2. The cooperative groups are formed. The members identify the relationships among the characters that they each bring to the group.
3. They add a setting, conflict, and ending.
4. The teacher types the stories so they may be read aloud to the class.
5. The teacher binds the class collection and adds it to the class library.

High School Sample Lesson

1. Make an "invent a story" matrix based on literature the class has read. See the model below.

Main Character A	Main Character B	Conflict	Setting	Ending
young soldier	old miser	man vs. self	the countryside	tragic
little kid	ex-con	good vs. evil	the inner city	boy marries girl
woman doctor	politician	man vs. nature	the ocean	happy
rich teenage boy	writer	man vs. man	a small town	cliff hanger
artist	nurse	husband vs. wife	a forest	bad guy wins

2. Each group selects one entry from each column via a random technique.
3. Each group writes a short story using the selected entries.
4. Each group reads its story to the entire class.
5. Each group binds the story into a collection for your class library.

9 – LANGUAGE LEARNING CENTERS

The classroom has designated labeled spaces for centers. An appropriate center activity is one that is not overwhelming but challenging enough to be interesting and require thought on the part of the student. There are two types of learning centers. One is the Exploratory center, where children have opportunities to initiate their own learning experiences with the materials available in the center. The other type is the Structured center where the teacher provides the materials and the task or tasks.

Daily schedules can include a freedom of choice for center time. During this time the teacher is engaged in active floor talk, moving from center to center. Center time should last at least an hour. This gives the students time to complete work and/or go to more than one center. Students should choose where they want to work. The teacher's role during center time brings more quality to the effectiveness of centers. The teacher is constantly moving among the students, discussing what they are doing. This is a time of the day when all elements of effective communication are in practice. Busy noise and on-task behavior are observed and evaluated. When the teacher is moving from center to center, she is asking effective questions, probing, praising, and encouraging students to think critically and problem solve. A teacher must be an effective "people-watcher." An hour of effective center time can be a beneficial part of the day. An effective management system and interesting centers will make this time a favorite part of each day.

Exploratory Centers

These centers allow students time to play, explore, and discover the manipulative, its purpose or purposes, and its relevance to their individual world. This time is essential for individual growth and awareness.

Structured Centers

Structured centers allow students to work independently or with peers on specific tasks assigned by the teacher. There might be one task or several choices. Either way the student is practicing, discovering, or creating.

10 – INTEGRATING CURRICULA APPROACH

It is very difficult to develop one intelligence without impacting the other intelligences. In the literate classroom environment, this is especially true. What the teacher does with each lesson in the language-rich classroom is target the verbal/linguistic intelligence and recognize that she can support the lessons with selections from the other intelligences.

Verbal/Linguistic

Students talk among themselves and come to a consensus on the story's topic, theme, subject, and focus.

Logical/Mathematical

Students sequence the events as the story unfolds.

Visual/Spatial

Everyone makes an animal out of construction paper and names that animal. Students glue the animals in a book and use markers to make a setting, background, cover, and title page.

Bodily/Kinesthetic

Students brainstorm a list of all the actions that this animal can do.

Naturalist

Students study an animal of their choice. They research the animal's habitat and basic needs for survival.

Interpersonal

Students bring their animals to their cooperative group of four or five. These animals become the characters of a group story.

In the upper grades, the integration is just as easy. For instance, if the high school teacher wants to encourage her English students to integrate visual/spatial and logical/mathematical intelligences, she can structure the matrix activity to include a drawing of the setting selected for the story or have the students sequence the story on a storyboard. If she wants to integrate other subject areas, she can make the matrix include characters or events drawn from history or science discovery.

By integrating the curriculum in the language classroom, the teacher encourages the students to make the connections and see the unusual relationships that force language development. These connections and relationships become the foundation for forming new concepts and expressing new ideas in new ways. From the youngest students to the oldest, the discovery of the rich power of new thinking through language is an empowering tool.

11 – ASSESSMENT AND EVALUATION

The best evaluation of any program is through teacher observation! Assessment is an ongoing process being done by the student and the teacher. The use of portfolios, writing folders, checklists, audiotapes of the student reading, and a teacher's log book are very valuable ways to assess in the language-rich classroom. As the assessment data is gathered, the teacher is able to evaluate the students.

12 – CELEBRATION AND FUN

There is always time for celebration in the effective classroom. Opportunities to share are invaluable. Through book talks, the completion of a unit, wall displays, and bulletin boards of students' writing, artwork, and projects, the students are tuned into learning. The room is personalized with students' work developing a rich print environment. It is student centered. When the motivating elements are going on in the classroom, there is a feeling of fun. This is because the lesson and the learning are things the students are interested in and can relate to from personal experiences. The learning is natural. Teachers and students enjoy the classroom where students communicate effectively through all the elements and enjoy using their language.

List of Energizing Celebration Cheers

Radical	WOW!	YES!	Standing O
Standing O! Yes!	Table Rap	Awesome	Thumbs-up
Happy Clam Clap	High Five	Wah-hoo!	Excellent Guitar

(from What to Do with the Kid Who...: Developing Cooperation, Self-Discipline, and Responsibility in the Classroom, by Kay Burke, p. 72)

PLUS 1 – METACOGNITION

In recent years, reading teachers have heard the term metacognition used over and over. In brief, a metacognitive strategy is one that helps students think about their thinking before, during, and after reading. Other related strategies, such as checking prior knowledge, using textual clues, making predictions, observing text structure clues, and visual organizers, help students plan how they will approach a reading task, observe their thinking as they proceed through the text, reflect on their strategic approach, and decide how they will read differently.

In the classroom, metacognition moves on a spectrum from what the teacher directs to what the students choose.

Teacher-Led Metacognition

Metacognitive Questions
When the teacher is reading to the students, she can introduce metacognitive questions before, during, and after the story. Factual questions and other one-word response questions do *not* help metacognition. Here are some helpful metacognitive questions:

1. What do you think will happen in this story?
2. What do you already know about this author?
3. As we read, think about some strategies you can use to help your understanding of the characters, theme, and plot.
4. Let's stop. How have you been using your strategies?
5. Let's stop. Predict what will happen next. Why do you think so?
6. What did you do to work hard in understanding this story?
7. Describe the skills you used to understand the story, character, and plot.
8. How else do you think the story might have ended? Why?

Graphic Organizers
These visual aids help students listen with attention. During a reading, the teacher can direct the students to fill in the sequence of events on a sequence chart, make an attribute web of a character, or use a concept map to chart themes. At appropriate breaks in the story, the teacher stops and allows time for additions to the charts.

Metacognitive Assessment Questions
After a reading, the teacher can elicit and list on the board multiple responses to such questions as:

1. What did you do well so that you understood the story?
2. What might you do differently to improve your understanding?
3. How can I help you improve your understanding of future readings we do?

Have students explain and clarify the strategies they list. Help students who did not add to the list see how they can use the strategy in a self-directed way.

Student Use of Metacognitive Strategies

1. Scaffolding is the technique of transferring the use of a strategy from a teacher-directed task to a learner-directed task. Following extensive teacher modeling, the teacher, step by step, moves control of the strategy use to the students. Ultimately, the teacher wants to have students make their own decisions about the strategy use. Note the sequence below.

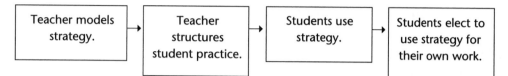

Teacher models strategy. → Teacher structures student practice. → Students use strategy. → Students elect to use strategy for their own work.

   a. Post charts with the questions that you have been asking students. After you have modeled the question-asking several times, stop and do a think-pair-share.
   Assign a question from the chart or allow pairs to select one to use during the think-pair stages. After a few minutes of pair talk, ask for volunteers to share with the class. Repeat the procedure several times during the story.
   b. Move next to posting the questions in your centers. Structure an assignment to use the questions.
   c. Have students pair and select a book to read to each other (or pair a strong reader and a weak reader with the strong reader assigned to read). Have the pairs select from the list the pair-share questions they will discuss.
   d. Invite students to do a process book report. When the students select a book for independent reading, they will also select three to five metacognitive questions to respond to in their journals as they read.

2. In addition to scaffolding the metacognitive questions, the teacher can scaffold the use of a graphic organizer as a strategic reading tool. See the example below.

Teacher guides creation of concept map. → Teacher and students make chart of concept map elements. → Groups read story and create concept map. → Groups present their concept maps. → Individuals make concept maps of new stories.

   a. After students read a story, the teacher guides an all-class concept map.
   b. After the map is finished, she leads a discussion and makes a chart for all to see. The chart tells the students what key elements to consider in making a map.
   c. Each cooperative group of three selects a story with which all members are familiar.
   d. The group reads the story and creates a concept map as the teacher monitors and assists.
   e. Groups present their concept maps. Each group explains the choices it made in organizing its concept map.
   f. More suggestions are added to the chart of elements.
   g. Groups are assigned a new story that members have not read. They repeat steps d–f.
   h. Individuals select a story for independent reading. Each individual makes a concept map of the story.
   i. The class brainstorms a list of other assignments to use with the concept map strategy.

Lesson Example 1: Say It

TARGETED INTELLIGENCE: Verbal/Linguistic

SUPPORTING INTELLIGENCE: Interpersonal

THINKING SKILL: Telling details about a main idea

SOCIAL SKILLS: Listening, Verbal and Nonverbal Communication

CONTENT FOCUS: Language Arts

MATERIALS: Large newsprint, markers

TASK FOCUS: The activity shows correct listening habits and what a person needs to do verbally and nonverbally to be a proactive learner. Social skills can be taught.

PRODUCT: T-charts of listening and nonlistening behaviors

PROBLEM: What happens when people don't listen

ACTIVITY:

Phase I Instructions:

1. Divide students into pairs. Name one A and the other B.

2. Student A thinks of an interesting story that B would like to hear. Student B is instructed to show "proactive listening" with his or her verbal and nonverbal listening habits. (An all-class brainstorm can cue what this means before the activity starts.)

3. A tells the story; B listens intently. Stop after 1 to 2 minutes.

4. Give feedback and describe the "listening behaviors" you noticed.

5. A can continue that story or think of a new one. B is to do everything in his or her power *not* to listen except leave the room. A must keep telling the story no matter what.

6. A tells the story and B doesn't listen for 1 to 3 minutes.

7. When A can't stand it any longer, stop the activity and give feedback of what was observed.

8. Ask A for a comparison and B for feedback.

Phase II Instructions:

1. In groups of three, make T-charts on listening and nonlistening behaviors.

2. Discuss the differences in behavior and feeling.

LISTENING		NONLISTENING	
Looks Like	**Sounds Like**	**Looks Like**	**Sounds Like**
• making eye contact • gestures, or nodding your head in agreement	• acknowledging the conversation by saying "yes" and asking questions • quiet—not interrupting the speaker	• looking away from the speaker, not paying attention • being actively involved in something else	• talking over the speaker • talking to someone else while the speaker is talking

REFLECTIONS:

1. What are the attributes of a good listener?
2. Why is it important to be a good listener?
3. How might you improve your listening behavior?

PRIMARY SCHOOL EXAMPLE: Read a story about what happens when we don't listen. (*Pigs* by Robert Munsch is a great example.) Create a big book story about nonlistening. Pick a favorite character from stories the students have read to be the main character. Brainstorm and make a sequence chart of the stories. Use the sample story you read at the start of the activity to show how groups of three will draw and write one incidence of nonlistening from the story. Provide paper and markers. Coach and monitor as the groups work. When they are done, post the story in sequence around the room and discuss sequence, flow, and other points of interest. Bind the story and save it in the class library.

MIDDLE SCHOOL EXAMPLE: Create an ad campaign to promote good listening. Brainstorm guidelines and criteria for success. Use groups of three. Post the signed ads around the school.

HIGH SCHOOL EXAMPLE: Invite cooperative groups to write video "playlets" for "Saturday Night Live." They must use "nonlistening" as the satire subject. Videotape the plays and have a showing for the class.

Lesson Example 2: The Debate Game

TARGETED INTELLIGENCE: Verbal/Linguistic

SUPPORTING INTELLIGENCE: Interpersonal

THINKING SKILLS: Problem Solving, Reviewing Prior Learning

SOCIAL SKILLS: Debating, Taking Turns

CONTENT FOCUS: Language Arts

MATERIALS: Note paper for each student

TASK FOCUS: Students will review material that they have studied in a unit.

PRODUCT: Review Sheet

PROBLEM: How to listen carefully and not repeat answers

ACTIVITY:

1. Students write down three things they have learned in the unit without letting anyone else see them.

2. Everyone brings a chair, paper with the three items, and pen into a circle.

3. Explain that when a review item is read that is on students' lists they must strike it out. They will stand until all of their items have been said.

4. If one of their items is covered under a broad category, they must delete it. (For example, if "novel" is said and students have the name of a novel the class read, they must delete that entry.)

5. If a specific is given, students may keep their general category (e.g., *Moby Dick* is said. All other novels are kept).

6. If anytime during the game students hear an item that they believe should have already been eliminated, they can signal with an outstretched hand for debate. The first person seen by the teacher with his or her hand up gets to tell the reason why. The student who reads the item gets a rebuttal. No one else speaks.

7. All get to vote to keep or discard an item. If the reader loses the vote, he or she has to give another item.

8. The winner is the last person standing with an item that has not already been identified.

REFLECTIONS:

1. What did we learn about listening with this lesson?

2. How might we use these learnings about listening with other classwork and outside of school?

PRIMARY SCHOOL EXAMPLE: Invite the students to pick characters from favorite stories or games.

MIDDLE SCHOOL EXAMPLE: Focus on a novel, story, or play just read. Students may select characters, events, conflicts, etc., as their items.

HIGH SCHOOL EXAMPLE: Use current events. Students may select stories from magazines, newspapers, or TV.

Lesson Example 3: The Author Game

TARGETED INTELLIGENCE: Verbal/Linguistic

SUPPORTING INTELLIGENCES: Visual/Spatial, Interpersonal

THINKING SKILLS: Creative Problem Solving, Generating Ideas, Sequencing

SOCIAL SKILLS: Listening, Encouraging

CONTENT FOCUS: Language Arts, Biography

MATERIALS: Newsprint, colored markers, game model

TASK FOCUS: Students will become expert on an author that they study in depth.

PRODUCT: Games that students invent

PROBLEM: How to use rules and teamwork

ACTIVITY:

1. Set up the activity for cooperative groups of three. Review cooperative guidelines and roles.

2. Discuss game rules using a familiar game such as basketball or soccer. Make a list of the key game rules.

3. Let students know that they are going to invent a game to teach others about one of their favorite authors.

4. Have each group select the author of focus and the game rules it will use.

5. After they gather all the information about the author that they want to teach in the game, they will brainstorm the game rules they want to use.

6. They will plan the game, name the game, write out the rules, and provide all materials and information that the game players will need.

7. When all games are ready, have groups exchange and play each other's games. You may even want to hold an all-class tournament.

REFLECTIONS:

1. What have you learned about teamwork?

2. How might you improve your teamwork in the classroom?

3. How might teamwork help you outside of school?

PRIMARY SCHOOL EXAMPLE: Select a single author of a favorite book. Tell the class about the author's life and other books he or she has written. Pick a simple game familiar to all such as Duck, Duck, Goose. Make a list of the rules and review the list with the class. Ask the class for ideas to make those game rules fit with the author (e.g., when you ask something about the author, the person who guesses it first gets up and runs around. The person tapped will ask another question). Practice the game with several authors.

MIDDLE SCHOOL EXAMPLE: Teach the class "Spell Sport." The rules are provided below.

> Children divide into teams of about four to nine. Two sets of alphabet cards are provided for each team. The teams line up at the near end of the room; the lettered cards, including a period and exclamation mark, are scattered at the far end of the room. The teacher calls out the name of a sport, or gives clues about the word to be spelled (e.g., played on a mat, two people involved, contact sport, nine-letter word). Each team then has a minute to work out their strategy before running to their set of letters. Each player must pick up a letter and return to the starting line. The whole team then spells the given word by lining up in proper order. (From *The Cooperative Sports and Games Book: Challenge without Competition,* by Terry Orlick, 1978, Pantheon Books, New York.)

After playing that game, make a list of the rules with the class and work in cooperative groups to come up with new games that use information from a favorite author's life. Students must research the author to create the game.

HIGH SCHOOL EXAMPLE: Have groups of three do cooperative research on an author whose work you are reading. Have each group pick a board game to use as the new game model.

Make Your Own

LESSON NAME: _____

TARGETED INTELLIGENCE: Verbal/Linguistic _____

SUPPORTING INTELLIGENCES: _____

THINKING SKILLS: _____

SOCIAL SKILLS: _____

_____

CONTENT FOCUS: _____

MATERIALS: _____

_____

TASK FOCUS: _____

_____

PRODUCT: _____

PROBLEM: _____

ACTIVITY:

_____

_____

_____

_____

_____

_____

_____

_____

REFLECTIONS:

1. _____

_____

2. _____

_____

3. _____

_____

Make Your Own

LESSON NAME: _____

TARGETED INTELLIGENCE: _Verbal/Linguistic_____

SUPPORTING INTELLIGENCES: _____

THINKING SKILLS: _____

SOCIAL SKILLS: _____

_____

CONTENT FOCUS: _____

MATERIALS: _____

_____

TASK FOCUS: _____

_____

PRODUCT: _____

PROBLEM: _____

ACTIVITY:

_____
_____
_____
_____
_____
_____
_____
_____
_____

REFLECTIONS:

1. _____
_____

2. _____
_____

3. _____
_____

Working in This Intelligence, I Am . . .

When I use this intelligence, I am . . .

|—————————————————————————|

very uncomfortable   totally at ease

When I ask students to use this intelligence, I am . . .

|—————————————————————————|

very uncomfortable   totally at ease

In what ways does this shoe fit me personally?

What can I do to polish this shoe for my professional use?

What am I going to do to provide for students in this intelligence?

What to continue	New things to do

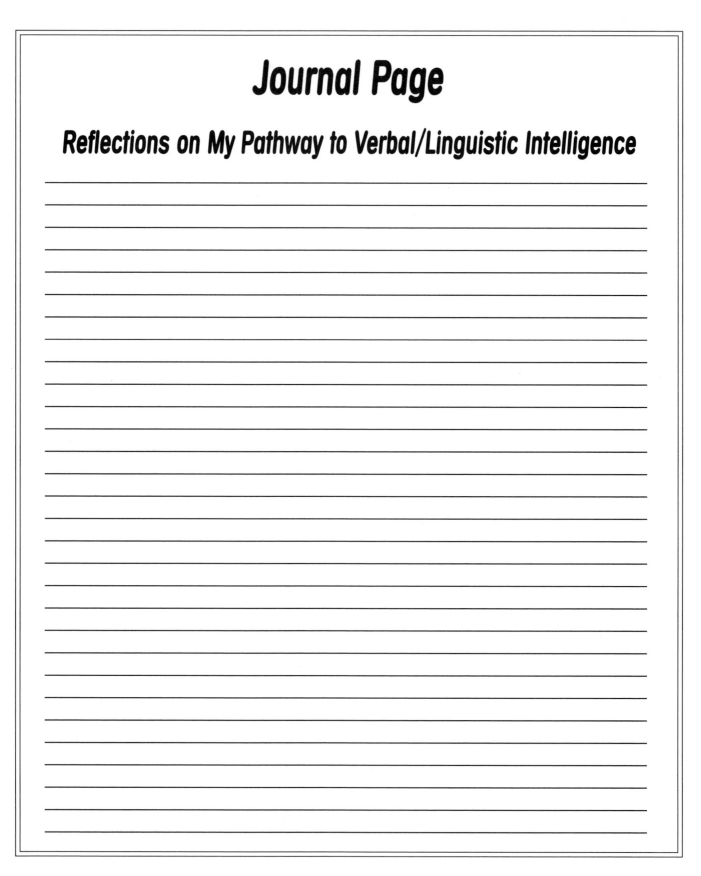

Journal Page

Reflections on My Pathway to Verbal/Linguistic Intelligence

Musical/Rhythmic Intelligence

The drum major's boot is worn as the leader of the beat marches in front of the band. Counting the time with his or her baton, the drum major keeps the band in rhythm as it plays a harmonious tune. The drum major is aware of the sound and the beat; the beat-mind connection.

What Is It?

Musical/rhythmic intelligence is the ability to use the core set of musical elements—pitch, rhythm, and tone, and the acute awareness of sound in one's environment.

If the Shoe Fits... It Looks Like

Bonnie's highly developed intelligence is musical/rhythmic as she is immersed in sound and movement. She is tuned to the sounds and rhythms around her and responds by actions. Hers is a world of melody and beat.

Wearing the Shoe in Life – Career Choices

• Composer	• Singer	• Sound Engineer
• Conductor	• Instrumentalist	• Dancer
• Disk Jockey	• Critic	• Producer

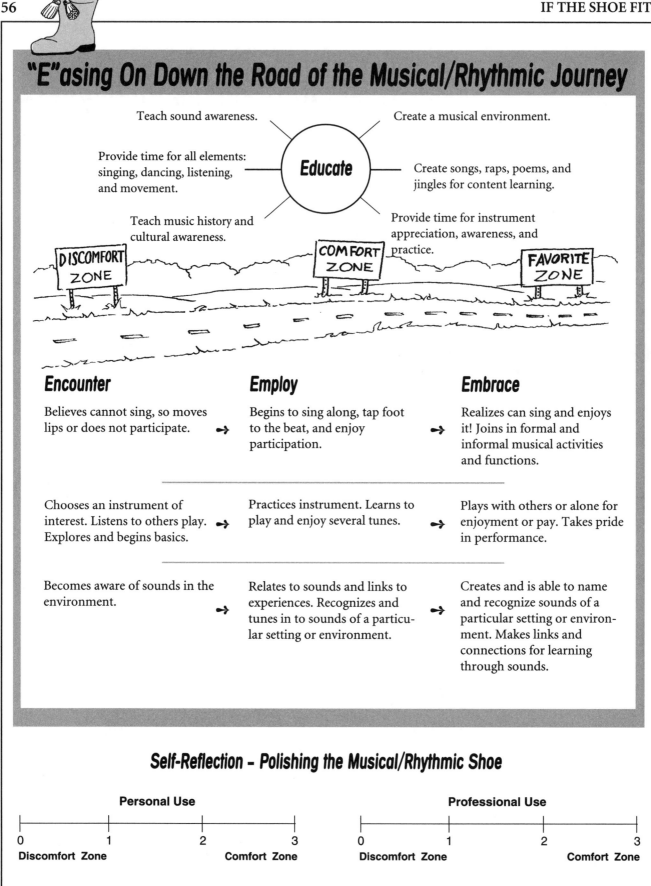

"E"asing On Down the Road of the Musical/Rhythmic Journey

Teach sound awareness.

Create a musical environment.

Provide time for all elements: singing, dancing, listening, and movement.

Educate

Create songs, raps, poems, and jingles for content learning.

Teach music history and cultural awareness.

Provide time for instrument appreciation, awareness, and practice.

DISCOMFORT ZONE　　　COMFORT ZONE　　　FAVORITE ZONE

Encounter

Believes cannot sing, so moves lips or does not participate.

Chooses an instrument of interest. Listens to others play. Explores and begins basics.

Becomes aware of sounds in the environment.

Employ

Begins to sing along, tap foot to the beat, and enjoy participation.

Practices instrument. Learns to play and enjoy several tunes.

Relates to sounds and links to experiences. Recognizes and tunes in to sounds of a particular setting or environment.

Embrace

Realizes can sing and enjoys it! Joins in formal and informal musical activities and functions.

Plays with others or alone for enjoyment or pay. Takes pride in performance.

Creates and is able to name and recognize sounds of a particular setting or environment. Makes links and connections for learning through sounds.

Self-Reflection – Polishing the Musical/Rhythmic Shoe

Personal Use

```
0        1        2        3
Discomfort Zone        Comfort Zone
```

Professional Use

```
0        1        2        3
Discomfort Zone        Comfort Zone
```

In today's world of country music, rock and roll, gospel, heavy metal, rap, big bands, and symphonies, young people are exposed to music of all types. Street music, MTV, rock concerts, tapes and CDs, boom boxes, and Walkman fill their ears with music, music, music. In cars, bedrooms, and sometimes every room in the house, the beat goes on. But how intelligent is this sound?

Our symbol for the musical intelligence is the drum major's boot. The drum major leads the band. The instrument players march along energetically following the drum major's beat. As the drum major leads the parade, he has to be aware of the sounds and the beat. Counting the time with his baton, he keeps the band in rhythm as it plays a harmonious tune.

Like the drum major, the teacher can lead her students in learning to develop the musical/ rhythmic intelligence. In a variety of ways, she can introduce music and rhythm into the classroom. Students can learn about their musical capabilities, use rhythm and sound to master their basic skills lessons, become quite proficient with the voice or a musical instrument, learn to distinguish good music from bad, discover how to appreciate fine music, and, hopefully, for the sake of noise-blasted parents, better develop the musical sensibilities of the next generations.

Unfortunately, most classrooms are quiet. Students get little chance to express themselves with music or to develop their musical/rhythmic intelligence. The traditional "box curriculum" tells teachers that music, if available at all in the school's curriculum, can only take place at the prescribed time slot. Otherwise, no songs are sung, no tunes are hummed, and the beat is silenced.

What Is Musical/Rhythmic Intelligence?

The musical/rhythmic intelligence is the language-related intelligence that starts with the degree of sensitivity one has to a pattern of sounds and the ability to respond emotionally to these sound patterns. As students develop pitch, tone, timbre, and rhythm, they develop this intelligence.

This intelligence has its own rules and thinking structures. These structures are not necessarily linked to other kinds of intelligence. Two common myths are that mathematical students make better musicians and that most musicians are better math students. The author knows from her own experience that the second myth is definitely not true! She can sing but she cannot balance her checkbook! Children, more comfortable than adults with this intelligence, quickly learn words to jingles, raps, and complex songs even when reading or math skills are difficult for them. As they develop the intelligence, children may become adept with singing, playing a musical instrument, or dancing the ballet.

What Is the Developmental Path for This Intelligence?

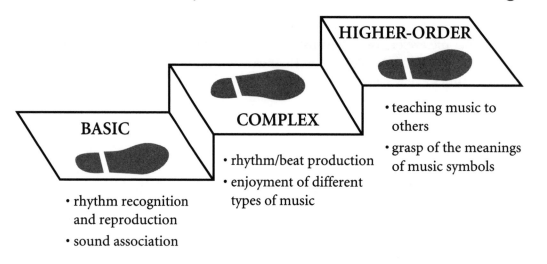

BASIC
• rhythm recognition and reproduction
• sound association

COMPLEX
• rhythm/beat production
• enjoyment of different types of music

HIGHER-ORDER
• teaching music to others
• grasp of the meanings of music symbols

How Is This Intelligence Developed in Other Cultures?

All cultures do not see the same decline in curricular priorities which target this intelligence that we often see in the United States. While our newspapers report one school board after another cutting art and music programs to save the budget, other cultures make music a central part of their young and adult lives. In China, for instance, musical celebrations are annual occurrences in large cities and small towns. The capabilities to sing, play instruments, and dance are nurtured carefully. Every child has the chance to develop the musical/rhythmic intelligence in after-school and Saturday classes. These extended day classes, the equivalent of our child care, give every student, up to the equivalent of our high school, the opportunity to intensively study a program of choice. It is not unusual that the classes in traditional Chinese musical instruments, traditional dance, ballet, modern musical instruments, and choir are the most crowded programs.

In Australia, some aboriginal tribes esteem dance so highly that they use story dances as the main means of resolving interfamily conflicts in the village. When two families argue, perhaps over the rights to a piece of land or the ownership of an animal, the village leaders prepare a ritual dance. The head of each family, bedecked in traditional costume, dances a problem-solving scenario until both parties agree on the solution.

How Can This Intelligence Be Used for Problem Solving?

Students with highly developed musical/rhythmic intelligence may use it to relieve stress, increase academic achievement, or make decisions.

☐ When Mrs. Smith is stressed after a busy day at the office, she puts on the earphones of her pocket tape player for the long bus ride home. As she plays her favorite Mozart opera, her tensions ease, she relaxes, and she walks off the bus feeling energized.

☐ Joe loves jingles. They always help him with his spelling. Given a story to write, he stumbles on a key verb. Is it "recieve" or "receive"? He remembers the jingle, "i before e except after c," correctly spells the verb, and finishes his sentence.

☐ Kate hates silence, especially when doing repetitive tasks. When doing her homework, she turns on the CD player. Although her mother complains about the loudness, Kate manages to complete her tasks with greater speed.

☐ Mary Jo, a bright high school student, gets very uptight before major tests. After several hours of review, she heads off to her dance class where she can lose her anxieties in the concentration of the ballet.

Who Is the Student with This Intelligence?

Bonnie's highly developed intelligence is musical. She is tuned in to the sounds and rhythms around her, and responds by action sometimes. Hers is a world of melody and beat.

This student is immersed in sound and movement. In your classroom she may tap out continual beats with her pencil or foot. She learns all the latest pop tunes and can sing along with any group. She shows interest in playing a musical instrument and may even love to sing in the shower. Individuals who develop this intelligence to a high degree surround themselves with music of all types: blues, jazz, classical, folk, dance, and rock and roll. As listeners, they listen to their favorite symphonies for the fine points of timbre, orchestration, pacing, and tone. As players, they spend long hours practicing favorite pieces that no one else may ever share.

The Comfort Zone: What Helps This Student Learn?

This student thrives during musical/rhythmic activities and games, loves to tell stories rather than read them, and prefers a mnemonic structure when doing basic memory tasks.

Soft background music helps this student keep focused on academic tasks. When music is integrated into the course of study, this student becomes "all ears." When given the chance to create a song or to play an instrument, this student never hesitates. Music and rhythm are the windows of opportunity to this student's motivation.

Students with increased abilities in musical/rhythmic intelligence are extremely responsive to sound and melody. Music has special meaning for these children, as they employ it to assist in their learning. These are the students who are often humming, whistling, or singing while in the midst of other activities. They enjoy rhythmic activities and are more sensitive to voice tones, inflections, tempo, volume, rhythm, style, and delivery. Musical/rhythmic students automatically put concepts to a beat in order to memorize them. It is not uncommon for these children to know the words to many songs, raps, jingles, and poems. Students with a strength in this area do very well in musical/rhythmic activities or games and make great storytellers. They may even walk with a rhythm and frequently rhyme as they talk.

It is important to give musical/rhythmic students the opportunity to move creatively, whistle or hum while working, or tap out a beat. These children need to hear songs, stories, music, and poetry, and perhaps even have the opportunity to hear soft music in the background while learning. Musical/rhythmic students need to hear sounds to express emotion or alter their moods. It is also beneficial for musical/rhythmic students to be very verbal. For example, educators should encourage these students to say information out loud, read out loud, or talk themselves through a task.

The Discomfort Zone: What Hinders This Student?

This student is distracted by random noise, side talking, and harsh sounds. Often brighter than written tests reveal, this student is turned off by written seat work, long repetitive tasks, and complicated writing assignments. Long-winded teacher talk, silent reading period, and sitting still for long periods of time bore this student.

How Do You Catch This Student's Attention in the Classroom?

First, recognize the speech patterns that catch this student. The musical/rhythmic student will tune in to questions such as, "What do you think I am saying?" and "How does this sound to you?" When the student responds, he is likely to say, "It sounds to me like . . ." or "Here is what I'm saying . . ."

Second, plan lessons that start with a musical hook. For example, start with a popular song that fits the lesson topic, such as "Some Like It Hot" to introduce the short story "To Build a Fire" or "The Three Pigs."

Third, make music central to the core of the lesson. For instance, in a study of the Revolutionary War, have students use a Venn diagram to contrast American and English music, conduct a musical pageant, or invent movements to show the meaning of a vocabulary word.

Fourth, use music in the closing activity with an audiotape of a theme-related song, the performance of songs written in the lesson core, or a choral reading.

Fifth, make the classroom climate musical with low background music playing throughout the day.

What Activities Promote Learning With This Intelligence?

- establish a musical environment
- create curriculum songs
- plan musical/rhythmic activities
- create and use songs, raps, cheers, jingles, and poems
- create music mnemonics

- recite choral reading
- offer opportunities to learn about, listen to, and play instruments
- listen to rhythmic sounds and patterns
- listen for tonal patterns
- practice unison recall
- try music and dance of different cultures
- move to the beat

- create dances that illustrate concepts
- practice rhythms
- compose songs
- allow background noises and music
- teach musical symbols

MUSICAL/RHYTHMIC

How Do You Meet the Challenge of the Special Student?

Because a student has difficulty with reading and writing, it does not follow that music will give that student trouble. Very often, this is the intelligence that has developed more strongly. It can become a means to learning in the verbal/linguistic or it can be strengthened on its own. Use the list below for some ideas of how to stimulate the musical/rhythmic intelligence in special needs students.

- Put information into familiar songs, jingles, or beats.
- Give the opportunity to play instruments, sing, or compose music.
- Pull on their strengths through music.
- Assign topics and reading about favorite singers, groups, composers, and types of music.
- Gather research by listening to music and making a report about the music.
- Play background music.
- Use music to demonstrate an idea or theme.
- Integrate the music of a historical period with the literature, history, etc.

How Do You Create an Environment for This Intelligence?

Be conscious in your planning that there are many ways to make music the soul of your classroom climate. In addition to designing lessons with musical components, primary school classrooms can have an exploratory center where students can investigate sounds, tones, instruments, notation, composition, and completed works. In the upper grades, use music and rhythm to make transitions, to relax, to energize after lunch, to change moods, to set the image, feeling, and tone for a new lesson, or to close a unit.

Sound Tapes

RELAXATION

When students come to your class after a high energy activity such as recess, gym, or an assembly, play a soft, slow tape. Invite them to feel the quiet and slide into a relaxed mood.

ENERGIZER

After lunch or late in the day, pick a musical piece that will stir the students and give them energy. Invite them to imagine events suggested by the music. Try Handel's Water Music, Beethoven's *1812* Overture, or the Beatles' "Yellow Submarine."

DRAW A PICTURE

Pick a popular song with vivid images. Invite the students to draw a picture of the song or of the moods and feelings it stirs.

SOUND AWARENESS

Every unit you study may have sounds associated with it. For instance, forest, prairie, and canyon sounds in zoology; home, school, and street sounds in social studies; urban, suburban, and rural voices in sociology.

Sound Centers

WATER SOUNDS

Fill glasses with water to demonstrate that the amount of water determines sound tone (high to low pitch).

HOMEMADE INSTRUMENTS

Make homemade instruments from scrap box materials.

MATCH A PICTURE

Make an audiotape of various instruments being played. Have the students match a picture with the instrument sound.

Choral Readings

POEMS

Pick a poem such as "The Cremation of Sam McGee." Divide it into equal parts and assign a part to groups of three. Let each group practice reading together for a class presentation. Use shorter poems for an all-class choral reading. Present to other classes. Some poems such as "Jabberwocky" allow for different groups taking different parts. For older students, sonnets by Browning and Shakespeare work well for choral readings. For younger students, use nursery rhyme readings by pairs of students.

POPULAR SONGS

Raps are great fun. Have student groups write raps to summarize what they have learned and present the works to the class in a small-group chorus.

JOIN IN

Read a story or a narrative poem to the class. Pick one where there can be a chorus read by the whole class.

Music Centers

HISTORIC MUSIC

Make musical instruments of a historic period or culture. Write new songs, raps, poems, or jingles to fit a historic period or culture.

THEME MUSIC
Play music that fits a theme or unit being studied.

MUSICAL CAREERS
Explore career possibilities in music. Provide reading materials, videos, filmstrips, etc. about specific careers.

Composer	Conductor	Sound Engineer
Musician	Critic	Disc Jockey
Dancer	Teacher	Singer

Lessons From Songs

In the primary grades, adapt favorite stories and nursery rhymes to song. Teach the song to the children and then bridge to other lessons. On the following pages are sample lessons using songs. (If you are a self-conscious singer yourself, ask a colleague to record the song on an audiotape and sing along with the children.)

LULU

Lulu, where are you going?
Upstairs to take a bath.
Lulu, with legs like toothpicks,
And a neck like a giraffe.
Lulu stepped in the bathtub,
Pulled out the plug.
Oh, my goodness!
Oh, my soul!
There goes Lulu down the hole.
Lulu! Lulu! Blub, Blub, Blub, Blub...

Lulu Extension Activities
1. Have students draw a picture of Lulu in the setting where she landed after she went down the drain. Then have them write a story to go with the picture.
2. Use the Lulu song to introduce skinny questions (questions that require only a one-word response).
3. Discuss how students would make Lulu feel welcome if she were a member of their class.
4. Make a big class book of Lulu's adventures. Let each group sketch a page.

(Old camp song, author unknown)

LITTLE PETER RABBIT

Little Peter Rabbit had a flea upon his ear.
Little Peter Rabbit had a flea upon his ear.
Little Peter Rabbit had a flea upon his ear.
And he flicked it 'til it flew away.

Chorus
Glory, glory for the rabbit!
Glory, glory for the rabbit!
Glory, glory for the rabbit!
And he flicked it 'til it flew away.

(NOTE: To the tune of "The Battle Hymn of the Republic"
refrain: Glory, Glory Hallelujah!)

1. Have cooperative groups read a story. For example, *Peter Rabbit* by Beatrix Potter works well. Or you can substitute another book of your choosing. Make up a short and simple song using "Little Peter Rabbit" as a model. In each group, have the child who reads best read to the group. If you have a classroom of "not yet readers," you can read to them before they break into groups to illustrate the scenes and make their own big books about the main character's adventures. When the stories are done, have them make up more verses to sing along as they share the illustrations.
2. Have cooperative groups make a dance to illustrate scenes in the story. Assign each scene in the story to a group. Have the groups perform in sequence.

Little Peter Rabbit Extension Activities
1. Omit words such as "rabbit," "Peter," "ear," or "flea" as you sing the song.
2. Write new verses to the song, stressing syllables, adjectives, nouns, or proper nouns. This might be done in total group language experience or cooperative learning groups. Don't forget those hand motions!
3. Make a class song book with all the new verses, motions, and illustrations.

Such activities develop the verbal/linguistic, musical/rhythmic, and interpersonal intelligences.

VOWELS
There was a teacher who had a class
And they could say their vowels.
A-E-I-O-U, A-E-I-O-U, A-E-I-O-U
And they could say their vowels.
(NOTE: To the tune of "BINGO.")

COLORS
There was a teacher who had a class
And they could spell the colors.
P-U-R-P-L-E, P-U-R-P-L-E, P-U-R-P-L-E
And they could spell their colors.
(NOTE: All color words will fit.)
(NOTE: To the tune of "BINGO.")

STATES
The USA has many states
and we can learn to spell them.
G-E-O-R-G-I-A, G-E-O-R-G-I-A, G-E-O-R-G-I-A
And we can learn to spell them.
(NOTE: All the state names will fit.)
(NOTE: To the tune of "BINGO.")

STATES IN THE USA
There are southern states in the USA
And we can name all of them.
Texas, Louisiana, and Arkansas, Mississippi, and Alabama,
Florida, Georgia, Tennessee, and North and South Carolina.
These are states in the South.
(NOTE: To the tune of "BINGO.")

Extension Activities
1. Write other verses to extend the students' knowledge.
2. Give some of the students simple musical instruments such as wood blocks, a triangle, or a tambourine. Let them take turns learning the beat and accompanying the class.
3. Have cooperative groups illustrate the topics of the song (e.g., draw the state maps or write the vowel letters).

PARTS OF SPEECH

LEADER:	These are the nouns.
GROUP:	These are the nouns.
LEADER:	People, places, things.
GROUP:	People, places, things.
LEADER:	Oranges, apples, bananas.
GROUP:	Oranges, apples, bananas.
LEADER:	These are the nouns.
GROUP:	These are the nouns.
LEADER:	People, places, things.
GROUP:	People, places, things.
GROUP:	People, places, things.

SECOND VERSE: These are the verbs. Our actions words …
THIRD VERSE: These are the adjectives. Our describing words …
FOURTH VERSE: These are conjunctions. Our connecting words …
Continue with all the parts of speech!
(NOTE: To the tune of "Frère Jacques.")

When teaching your theme, have the students name three nouns that relate to the theme. For the next verse, name three action words (verbs) related to those nouns, continue to build each verse of the song around the theme and the parts of speech.

Extension Activities
1. Select stories to read or other favorite songs. Show the story or the words of the song to the class. Invite groups to pick out the parts of speech and sketch the examples.
2. Have the students sit in place and mimic your movements as you lead them in the song.

MAC-A-LENA

REFRAIN: MAC-A-LENA, MAC-A-LENA, RUBENSTINE WALK-A-DIME,
HOKEY POKEY LOCA WAS HER NAME.

(NOTE: Sing refrain after each verse.)

(NOTE: To the tune of "Short'nin' Bread.")

Verses:

1. Draw a circle for her head. Only draw the body part that I have said. Who? (Refrain)
2. She had two hairs on her head. One was curly and the other was dead. Who? (Refrain)
3. She had two eyes in her head. She goes both ways when she's looking ahead. Who? (Refrain)
4. She had one ear on each side. One was narrow and the other was wide. Who? (Refrain)
5. She had a nose on her face. It wasn't very pretty but it took a lot of space. Who? (Refrain)
6. She had two teeth in her mouth. One pointed north and the other pointed south. Who? (Refrain)
7. She had a neck like a ten-foot pole. And right in the middle was a big black mole. Who? (Refrain)
8. She had two arms long as a door. And when she walked they touched the floor. Who? (Refrain)
9. She had two hands with ten fingers. Those long, skinny things were real humdingers. Who? (Refrain)
10. She had a tummy round as a ball. She bounced right back when she took a fall. Who? (Refrain)
11. She had two legs shaped like an S. Oh, my goodness, they were a mess. Who? (Refrain)
12. She had two feet flat as a mat. Oh, I wonder how they got like that. Who? (Refrain)
13. This is the story that has been told about Mac-A-Lena and her heart of gold. Who? (Refrain)

Extension Activities

1. As you sing the song, have the students draw Mac-A-Lena. This is a great activity to teach students how to follow directions.
2. Have the students write and illustrate a story about themselves and Mac-A-Lena sharing a great adventure.
3. Ask students to pretend Mac-A-Lena is the new student in the room and write about a day in school with her.
4. Divide students into pairs. Each partner will draw every other verse. This is developing the musical/rhythmic, interpersonal, and visual/spatial intelligences.

(Old camp song, source unknown)

Lesson Example 1: Mac-A-Lena

TARGETED INTELLIGENCE: Musical/Rhythmic

SUPPORTING INTELLIGENCES: Verbal/Linguistic, Visual/Spatial, Intrapersonal, Logical/Mathematical, Interpersonal

THINKING SKILLS: Following Directions, Sequencing

SOCIAL SKILLS: Communication, Listening, Accepting Self and Others

CONTENT FOCUS: Parts of the body

MATERIALS: Large piece of newsprint, one dark marker

TASK FOCUS: This is a shared drawing. The partners will take turns drawing their part as each verse of the song is sung. They must accept the drawing of the partner and not correct, adjust, or fix it in any way. At the end they will have completed the picture of Mac-A-Lena.

PRODUCT: A picture of Mac-A-Lena

PROBLEM: To draw a picture from a song

ACTIVITY:

1. Divide students into pairs. Name one Student A and the other Student B.
2. Student A gets a large piece of newsprint and B gets a dark marker.
3. Give these directions:
   a. Place the paper lengthwise between the partners.
   b. When a verse is sung, A draws the body part in the song.
   c. All students join in the chorus.
   d. Give the marker to B to draw during the next verse.
4. Make the students aware of the rules.
   a. No body part is to be drawn unless it is sung about.
   b. Swap the marker each time.
   c. When the drawing is complete, put Mac-A-Lena in the habitat or setting of the current unit of study.
   d. Both partners must sign the shared drawing.

REFLECTIONS:

1. What was it like to share the drawing of a picture?
2. Is it easy for you to draw from a song? Why or why not?

PRIMARY SCHOOL EXAMPLE: Now that students have completed the Mac-A-Lena activity and are familiar with following musical directions, ask them to work with a partner to create their own song. Children can pick a favorite animal and write a few short verses that provide directions for drawing that animal. Once their mini-songs are complete they can share them with their classmates.

MIDDLE SCHOOL EXAMPLE: Incorporate music into unit end projects by asking students to complete a musical project that will help them summarize what they have learned about a particular topic. Encourage students to write a jingle, create a dance, compose a rap song, or write a poem on the topic. When the students are ready to perform, distribute copies of their work to the rest of the class.

HIGH SCHOOL EXAMPLE: Incorporate music into several areas of the curriculum such as history or literature. Start the unit with a review of the period's popular music. Have students listen to selected musical pieces and use a matrix to compare the historical music to what they listen to today. Students can bring in a song or two of their own music to represent today's music. After they complete the matrix, they can draw conclusions about the historic period and discuss the similarities and differences between the periods suggested by the songs.

| | Historic Period (1930–40) | | Today | |
	Song 1	Song 2	Song 1	Song 2
Title	"Boogie Woogie Bugle Boy" (Andrews Sisters)	"In the Mood" (Glenn Miller)	"You Can't Touch This" (Hammer)	"Good Vibrations" (Marky Mark & the Funky Bunch)
Type	Big Band Swing/Jazz	Big Band	Rap/Dance Music	Rap/Dance Music
Beat	fast/jazzy	medium to fast	repeats a lot; slow–medium	fast
Words	singing is harmonized	no words	words are "rapped" or chanted	singing and rapping
Instruments	bugle, trumpets horns	orchestra instruments, horns	electronic keyboard, bass, drums	electronic guitar, keyboard, drums
Volume	medium–loud	medium–loud	medium–loud	loud
Topic/Theme	Song is about a guy who plays the horn very well and is in the army	no words or theme— instrumental dance music	his dancing and singing ability	good times, dancing

IRI/SkyLight Training and Publishing, Inc.

Lesson Example 2: The Sound Machine

TARGETED INTELLIGENCE: Musical/Rhythmic

SUPPORTING INTELLIGENCES: Bodily/Kinesthetic, Verbal/Linguistic, Interpersonal, Naturalist

THINKING SKILLS: Decision Making, Synthesis

SOCIAL SKILLS: Cooperation, Shared Responsibility

CONTENT FOCUS: To be selected by the teachers

MATERIALS: Index cards

TASK FOCUS: Students will create the environmental sounds of a particular setting. All must participate because it takes all the parts to work together for the machine to produce the setting.

PRODUCT: A sound machine

PROBLEM: Represent a chosen setting by sounds

ACTIVITY:

1. Divide students into groups of four to seven.
2. Assign roles:
   a. Engineer: Assigns parts.
   b. Checker: Makes sure all members of the group understand timing, motions, and sounds.
3. Decide on setting such as the city, country, farm, jungle, medieval times, etc.
4. Ask for a volunteer to suggest a sound. One sound per person.
5. Decide on motions and movements of the machine.
6. Produce the setting.
7. Practice.
8. Celebrate performance time.

REFLECTIONS:

1. What made the machine work?
2. What would have made it better?

PRIMARY SCHOOL EXAMPLE: Farm Unit: Create a farm machine. The groups decide on their machines. Some suggestions you might give them are animals, farm equipment, farm sounds, etc.

MIDDLE SCHOOL EXAMPLE: Ecology Unit: Create a forest machine in each group. Some suggestions are the polluted forest, the natural forest with no pollution, the forest ranger at work, Smokey the Bear machine, etc.

HIGH SCHOOL EXAMPLE: Study of a Period of History or Culture: Create a machine with the sounds of the time. Choose a significant subtopic such as a place or event and create the machine of the time.

Lesson Example 3: The Beat Goes On

TARGETED INTELLIGENCE: Musical/Rhythmic

SUPPORTING INTELLIGENCES: Bodily/Kinesthetic, Intrapersonal

THINKING SKILLS: Analysis, Awareness of Different Beats

SOCIAL SKILL: Moving in synchronicity

CONTENT FOCUS: Music rhythms

MATERIALS: Audiotape with different types of music with varying beats, streamers for each child

TASK FOCUS: Students will move to the varying rhythms and beats. They will each make their streamers move to the beat.

PRODUCT: A streamer parade

PROBLEM: Dancing to a rhythm

ACTIVITY:

1. Assign each student a personal space.
2. Play the tape and instruct students to move streamers to the beat. Demonstrate.
3. Add additional body movements to this activity if desired.
4. Have a streamer parade.

REFLECTIONS:

1. How comfortable did you feel doing this activity?
2. What made you uncomfortable? Why do you think so?

PRIMARY SCHOOL EXAMPLE: Have a parade of streamers that move to the changing songs and rhythms.

MIDDLE SCHOOL EXAMPLE: Have students create drum beats. Let them choose objects that make a drum beat: two sticks, two spoons, pencil on desk, etc. Play the musical tape.

HIGH SCHOOL EXAMPLE: After studying various types of instruments, form pairs. Each pair will choose one object to create the beat. Rotate to new partners for a new sound. Each keeps his or her original object.

Lesson Example 4: Create the Beat

TARGETED INTELLIGENCE: Musical/Rhythmic

SUPPORTING INTELLIGENCES: Interpersonal, Verbal/Linguistic

THINKING SKILLS: Synthesis, Decision Making, Creative Recall

SOCIAL SKILLS: Consensus, Interdependence, Pride

CONTENT FOCUS: Using songs to learn new information

MATERIALS: Paper, pencils, pens, newsprint, markers

TASK FOCUS: Students in cooperative groups will create a song, poem, rap, cheer, or jingle that teaches something very important for them to know. Learning to a beat helps the student to recall the information as needed.

PRODUCT: A song for a basic skill

PROBLEM: How to write a song that will teach a skill

ACTIVITY:

1. Teach the students The Coin Poem. Say it together.

2. Discuss how sound and beat help students to remember the song.

3. Say it again.

4. Put students into groups of three.

5. Assign roles.
   Checker: Checks to make sure each group member knows his or her part for the performance and keeps time.

6. Give the following instructions: Each group is to create a song, rap, jingle, poem, or cheer that teaches a concept that it has learned. Each member has a part in the final presentation.

7. Display some examples from previous student work, or use the examples provided.

8. Allow 7 to 10 minutes for creation.

9. Provide these guidelines:

   a. If you use a song, use a tune we all know.

   b. Make up original words; not ones already written.

   c. It is important that all group members take part in the performance.

   d. The song must fit the topic we are studying.

10. As soon as a piece is written, the groups need to practice.

11. Each group will present its completed work during show time.

These are some examples of other poems and songs written by teachers to help their students remember important information.

THE COIN POEM
A penny equals just one cent.
A nickel is five pennies spent.
A dime is ten like on your hands.
Twenty-five's a quarter, man.
A dollar is one hundred, son,
with a picture of George Washington.
Now you'll know your money fine
If you remember all these lines.

SONG: Are You Metric?
TUNE: "Frère Jacques"
10 millimeters
10 millimeters
equals one centimeter
equals one centimeter
You need 10 millimeters
You need 10 millimeters
To equal 1 centimeter.

GRAMMAR CHEER
Synonyms, synonyms: that's our game
These are words that mean the same.
Homonyms, homonyms, that's our game
These are words that sound the same.
Antonyms, antonyms, take a hike
These are words that aren't alike.

SONG: When the Adjectives Come Marching By
TUNE: "When the Saints Go Marching In"
Oh when the adjectives come marching by
Oh when the adjectives come marching by
Don't you know their job is to modify
When the adjectives come marching by.
Oh when the adjectives come in to town
Oh when the adjectives come in to town
They'll tell you which one, how much, how many
Everything about a noun.

REFLECTIONS:

1. What did you learn by writing this song?
2. How did the song help you?
3. What other "teaching" songs do you know?

PRIMARY SCHOOL EXAMPLE: Very young children may have a difficult time trying to create a song on their own, even when working in small groups. In this case, modify the activity so that you can create a *class* song. Follow the directions for the Create the Beat activity and discuss how music can help people remember things. Next, as a class, pick a topic from a subject you are studying and create a song about it together. Once the song is complete, allow the students to practice and perform it for another class.

MIDDLE SCHOOL EXAMPLE: Older students are able to complete the activity on their own or in groups. Extend the activity by having the students think of their groups as rock bands. After they have completed their "song," students can design an album cover or poster illustrating the content of their creation. Time allowing, students can also have the choice of creating a video to perform or act out their song.

HIGH SCHOOL EXAMPLE: Incorporate this activity into a review period before an exam. Allow students to work in groups to decide which parts of the material they are having trouble grasping. Once they have picked their topics, they can work together to create a song, poem, or cheer that helps them remember the information. Encourage students to share their group's creation with others. Have students provide copies of their songs for all class members.

IRI/SkyLight Training and Publishing, Inc.

Lesson Example 5: The Music of Mozart

TARGETED INTELLIGENCE: Musical/Rhythmic

SUPPORTING INTELLIGENCES: Interpersonal, Visual/Spatial, Verbal/Linguistic, Logical/Mathematical

THINKING SKILLS: Comparing and Contrasting, Drawing Conclusions

SOCIAL SKILLS: Listening, Responsibility

CONTENT FOCUS: The music of Mozart

MATERIALS: Newsprint and markers, Mozart and Beatles tapes

TASK FOCUS: This is a cooperative task. Use groups of three. Give groups one large sheet of newsprint and one to three colored markers. Play alternating pieces from Mozart and the Beatles. If this is the class' first encounter with Venn diagrams, demonstrate how to use them and walk among the groups to ensure success and answer questions.

PRODUCT: A Venn diagram

PROBLEM: Identify similarities and differences between Mozart and the Beatles

ACTIVITY:

1. Set up your groups of three with a materials manager, recorder, and checker who will make sure that everyone agrees on the ideas put on the newsprint.

2. Find out what the class knows about Mozart and the Beatles. Use the first answers to demonstrate use of the Venn.

3. As the groups listen to the music, have them chart the similarities and differences they hear in the music as well as in their responses.

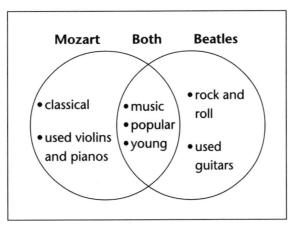

4. After the groups are done, invite several to share with the class.

5. Discuss the similarities and differences of the two music genres.

REFLECTIONS:

1. What have you learned about the music of Mozart? The Beatles?

2. What are their respective contributions to the history of music?

3. How did the times affect their music and vice versa?

PRIMARY SCHOOL EXAMPLE:

1. Teach the students a Beatles song to do in chorus. Present it at parents' night.

2. Have students draw pictures of the images created by the music.

3. Play more Beatles and Mozart music as background to class work for the rest of the month.

MIDDLE SCHOOL EXAMPLE:

1. Have groups select a scene from Mozart's and/or the Beatles' lives. Act them out.

2. Ask students to make posters advertising a concert with each or both performing at the school.

3. Tell students to research the lives of each and expand the Venn diagrams.

HIGH SCHOOL EXAMPLE:

1. Students can research other music that was well known in the time periods of Mozart and the Beatles and expand the Venn before writing a comparative essay.

2. Have students write a short story incorporating Mozart and the Beatles. They can select other pieces by each and identify patterns in their styles.

VARIATION: Use videos or films that show the traditional dances of different cultures. Use the Venns for a comparison/contrast of the movement, costumes, traditions, and music. Assign subtopics for different cooperative groups to research.

Make Your Own

LESSON NAME: _____

TARGETED INTELLIGENCE: _Musical/Rhythmic_ _____

SUPPORTING INTELLIGENCES: _____

THINKING SKILLS: _____

SOCIAL SKILLS: _____

_____

CONTENT FOCUS: _____

MATERIALS: _____

_____

TASK FOCUS: _____

_____

PRODUCT: _____

PROBLEM: _____

ACTIVITY:

_____

_____

_____

_____

_____

_____

_____

REFLECTIONS:

1. _____

_____

2. _____

_____

3. _____

_____

Make Your Own

LESSON NAME: _____

TARGETED INTELLIGENCE: Musical/Rhythmic _____

SUPPORTING INTELLIGENCES: _____

THINKING SKILLS: _____

SOCIAL SKILLS: _____

_____

CONTENT FOCUS: _____

MATERIALS: _____

_____

TASK FOCUS: _____

_____

PRODUCT: _____

PROBLEM: _____

ACTIVITY:

_____

_____

_____

_____

_____

_____

_____

REFLECTIONS:

1. _____

_____

2. _____

_____

3. _____

_____

Working in This Intelligence, I Am . . .

When I use this intelligence, I am . . .

very uncomfortable   totally at ease

When I ask students to use this intelligence, I am . . .

very uncomfortable   totally at ease

In what ways does this shoe fit me personally?

What can I do to polish this shoe for my professional use?

What am I going to do to provide for students in this intelligence?

What to continue	New things to do

IRI/SkyLight Training and Publishing, Inc.

Journal Page

Reflections on My Pathway to Musical/Rhythmic Intelligence

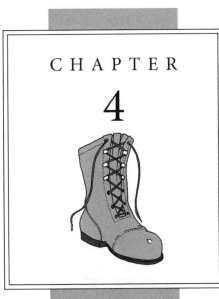

Logical/Mathematical Intelligence

The hiking boot symbolizes the pattern seeker as represented by the laces. The problem-solving and critical-thinking hiker climbs step by step up the challenging path making decisions about direction and survival for food, clothing, and shelter. This is the tough shoe of the abstract thinker.

What Is It?

The logical/mathematical intelligence is the ability to use inductive and deductive reasoning, solve abstract problems, and understand complex relationships of mathematical reasoning and the scientific process.

If the Shoe Fits... It Looks Like

Roy has a highly developed logical/mathematical intelligence. This logical, abstract thinker enjoys calculations, problem solving, critical thinking, interpreting data, categorizing facts, and using technology. As he uses numbers, he is precise and accurate. He relies on the tools of the trade such as calculators and computers.

Wearing the Shoe in Life – Career Choices

- Engineer
- Physicist
- Computer Programmer

- Mathematician
- Inventor
- Astronomer

- Retail Buyer
- Banker
- Economist

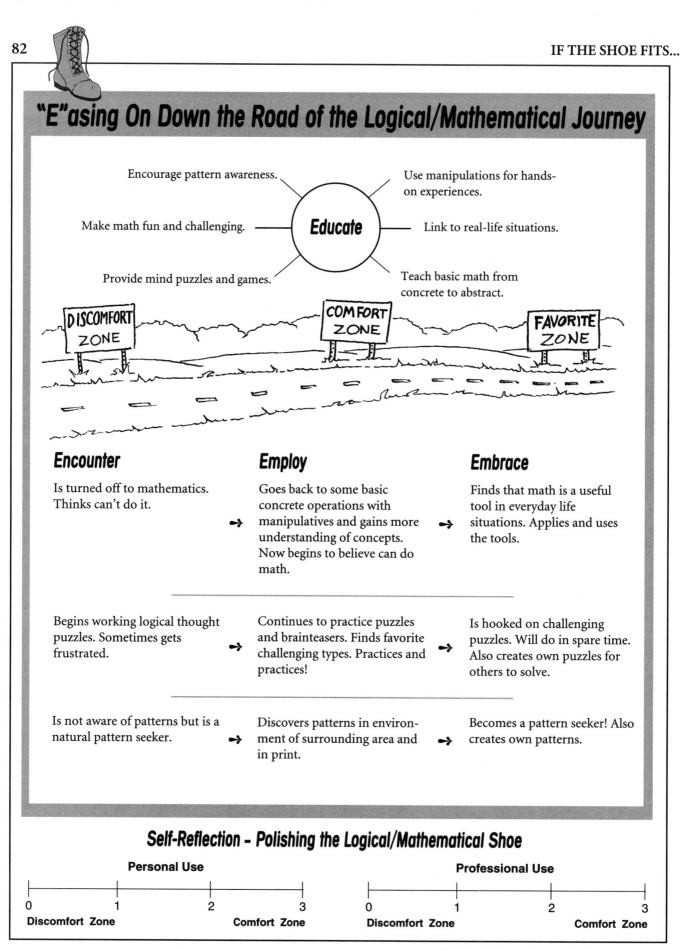

"E"asing On Down the Road of the Logical/Mathematical Journey

Encourage pattern awareness.

Use manipulations for hands-on experiences.

Make math fun and challenging.

Educate

Link to real-life situations.

Provide mind puzzles and games.

Teach basic math from concrete to abstract.

DISCOMFORT ZONE

COMFORT ZONE

FAVORITE ZONE

Encounter

Is turned off to mathematics. Thinks can't do it.

Employ

Goes back to some basic concrete operations with manipulatives and gains more understanding of concepts. Now begins to believe can do math.

Embrace

Finds that math is a useful tool in everyday life situations. Applies and uses the tools.

Begins working logical thought puzzles. Sometimes gets frustrated.

Continues to practice puzzles and brainteasers. Finds favorite challenging types. Practices and practices!

Is hooked on challenging puzzles. Will do in spare time. Also creates own puzzles for others to solve.

Is not aware of patterns but is a natural pattern seeker.

Discovers patterns in environment of surrounding area and in print.

Becomes a pattern seeker! Also creates own patterns.

Self-Reflection – Polishing the Logical/Mathematical Shoe

Personal Use

0   1   2   3

Discomfort Zone   Comfort Zone

Professional Use

0   1   2   3

Discomfort Zone   Comfort Zone

As the globe shrinks and technological highways link the smallest villages in the most remote regions of the world, the logical/mathematical intelligence becomes more and more important.

First, there is the need for highly skilled engineers, programmers, and technicians to work these intricate systems. Second, there is the need for greater user skills to access the networks and to take advantage of what they can do. Now, with the development of INTERNET and other electronic highways, students in Moscow can talk with students in Peoria, Illinois, Puerto Vallarta, Mexico, or Macon, Georgia, via classroom computers.

With new technology comes an ever-increasing demand for greater development of products dependent on highly developed logical/mathematical intelligences. Just as students in the U.S. can use computers and modems to speak more easily with students in other nations, doctors, lawyers, business owners, graphic artists, teachers, and government workers can communicate in the same way. Each year, the information that they can share, much of it aided by technological advances in their fields, becomes more and more complex. And as these advances bring people of different nations closer together, they also raise the level of competition in the world market. Thus, in classrooms around the world, nations are reexamining curriculum in math, science, technology, engineering, and finance so that future workers will keep those nations at the forefront of world trade.

For this intelligence, the hiking boot symbolizes the need for a tough shoe that can keep the hiker climbing the rugged path of competitive technology and scientific exploration. There are many complex and intricate decisions to make. The hiker must be a knowledgeable problem solver, a critical thinker able to analyze information and develop new technological products, while climbing step by step up the challenging path.

The teacher's role in the development of this intelligence starts with the content of mathematics and the sciences. Traditionally, American elementary teachers receive little preparation in these areas. As a result, the science/math curricula have not advanced to meet the demands of the global marketplace. While other nations give priority to mathematical problem solving, critical thinking, the understanding of mathematical principles, and the application of these principles to the fields of accounting, finance, engineering, science, and computer technology, the American curriculum focuses on computation and calculation skills. Any opportunity for advanced mathematical studies is restricted to a small percentage of high school students. For too many, the gates are shut to advanced study. As a result, other nations graduate ten percent or more of their college students with majors in mathematics and the average for American universities stays below one percent. Of these, less than five percent enter the secondary classroom. Worse yet, the largest percentages of elementary teachers have little mathematical training beyond the first two years of college.

When considering teacher preparation for logic, the situation is even more dire. In Europe, formal training in logic has been part of the university tradition since the Middle Ages. American universities typically relegate this study to the philosophy department.

The logic that does come to teachers in training is what they bring through their informal learning. Beyond logic, the preparation in the undergraduate years in the understanding and the pedagogy of critical and creative thinking is even more inadequate with little or no attention to problem solving, reasoning, and applying.

To improve what all students, including the most talented by American standards, are able to do with mathematical problem solving and the scientific, technological, and financial applications of math, there are three important steps for our schools. First, provide more rigorous preparation for future math/science teachers. Second, include intense staff development practices for teachers in mathematics, science, and technology. Programs that are positive experiences for teacher buy-in provide not just information but how to present this information to students. Third, restructure curriculum so that teachers have the time to develop the critical thinking skills and the intellectual dispositions that form the foundation of the logical/mathematical intelligence.

What Is Logical/Mathematical Intelligence?

Although the critical thinking skills of sequencing, analyzing, and estimating are already imbedded in most school curricula, the dispositions of persistence, precision, inquiry, and elaboration are highly desired. What remains are instructional approaches that will bring these to the forefront of classroom time and student use.

The logical/mathematical intelligence is the one to which American schools give the most attention, at least when it comes to standardized testing. It includes the abilities to use inductive and deductive reasoning, solve abstract problems, and understand complex relationships so that the individual can develop products based on mathematical reasoning and use those products with skill.

Beginning with the Greek philosophers, especially Aristotle and Plato, western civilization has given primary attention to the development of this intelligence. Some western cultures such as Germany have carried the formal development of the logical/mathematical intelligence to a high point of refinement in science and engineering. Germany's thirteen-grade curriculum emphasizes rigorous mathematical training.

The logical aspects of this intelligence are built on deductive and inductive reasoning models. Each has a large set of rules to govern the right processes of thinking. From these two models have sprung applied systems of thinking including the scientific process, aeronautical engineering, and space technology.

What Is the Developmental Path for This Intelligence?

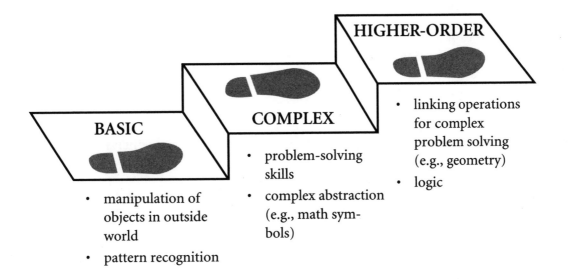

BASIC
- manipulation of objects in outside world
- pattern recognition

COMPLEX
- problem-solving skills
- complex abstraction (e.g., math symbols)

HIGHER-ORDER
- linking operations for complex problem solving (e.g., geometry)
- logic

How Is This Intelligence Developed in Other Cultures?

When this intelligence is mentioned in the international community, the discussion immediately turns to the Japanese, German, and Swiss cultures. Each of these is known for its emphasis on math and science. Schools in these countries use curricula closely aligned with their national educational standards and the business climate. Precision, accuracy, and persistence are touted as core values. Parents in these nations believe that mathematical achievement is the result of hard, disciplined, and persistent work. They strongly believe that this intelligence can develop and that parents, students, and teachers are responsible to work hard and make this happen. Conversely, studies in the United States show that most people believe mathematical achievement is due to natural talent.

In China, mathematics is a tradition that is centuries old. In the early grades, all children learn to count with the abacus. By the time young adults go to work in a retail shop or attend the university, they are advanced users of the abacus. Purchase a bolt of silk in a department store and the clerk's hands will operate with lightning speed to total the amount of the purchase. In restaurants, science laboratories, and shops, the abacus is the universal tool of choice for completing complex calculations needed to solve problems.

How Can This Intelligence Be Used for Problem Solving?

There are few places one can go where mathematical problem solving and logical reasoning are not important.

☐ Tomasina needs to buy a new car. She goes to three dealers and prices the same model. At each dealership, she is offered a different base price, different extras, plus some special deals. She listens patiently to each offer and goes home where she can compare the three. She makes a problem-solving matrix so that every detail lines up.

☐ Ralph's special assignment in the accounting office is to make a new accounts receivable package that will tie into inventory control for the entire company. He researches the available software programs and picks the one most compatible to the other programs the company already uses.

☐ Mary Ellen wants to go with her friends to an amusement park. She knows that her mom will not like the idea. Mary Ellen decides to make a list of reasons why it is a good idea for her to go.

☐ Jose is saving up money to buy a new bicycle. He knows the price and the tax. He knows how much he has saved. All he has left to do is estimate the balance and the time it will take to complete his savings.

Who Is the Student With This Intelligence?

Roy has a highly developed logical/mathematical intelligence. He is good at calculations, problem solving, critical thinking, interpreting, categorizing facts and information, and using technology.

This is a student who is a persistent problem solver and a lover of numbers and logic. Rather than getting stuck on the details of math facts, he relies on the tools of the trade: the abacus, the slide rule, the calculator, and now the computer. Because he has an understanding of numbers, this student is able to use these tools to solve complex mathematical problems. As this student reasons with numbers and logic, he is precise and accurate, carefully thinking and rethinking how to go about solving a problem. Numbers, number theory, and logical reasoning fascinate this student. He talks about the beauty of numbers and loves to explore the possibilities for using numbers in new and different ways.

The Comfort Zone: What Helps This Student Learn?

This student likes "a place for everything and everything in its place." His book bag and desk are neat and orderly. Given a computer, he grabs the serious games like "Oregon Trail" or "Carmen San Diego." He works the program, calculating each step and recalling what decisions he made at each juncture. Each time he replays the game, he thinks about the decision trail and eliminates past mistakes that led nowhere. He becomes very strategic in his thinking as he conquers more and more of the electronic game.

It is not long before he jumps to spreadsheets and prediction charts. He uses the tools of the computer trade to solve problems. For memory, he relies on mnemonics. For reasoning, he calls on charts and graphs that help him interpret data. Often, he is a sequential thinker, proceeding step by step through a problem, seeking a pattern, investigating alternatives with thoughtful questions, and staying with the challenge until the solution is found. A look back at his notes reveals a precise and orderly outline of his observations and his reflections.

The Discomfort Zone: What Hinders This Student?

This student finds it difficult to work in chaos and confusion. When a teacher rambles through a lesson without providing the big picture, a clear objective, or connections between ideas, this student gets very uncomfortable. Workbooks with endless, repetitive, and nonchallenging blanks to be filled bore this student. Poorly structured cooperative groups with hitchhiking, off-task talking, and constant low-level goals motivate this student to take over the group, do all the work, and complain about the unfair responsibility for carrying the others. When this student is given a mundane learning task lacking challenge, he will question, "Why are we doing this?" When forced to memorize without an explanation of the connection between this task and the "big picture," or when he is rushed through tasks without a chance to understand rationales or to use problem-solving tools, he will eventually shut down. Without an opportunity to estimate, find patterns, calculate, reason or interpret, he would just as soon gaze out the window.

How Do You Catch This Student's Attention in the Classroom?

First, remember the challenge phrases for this student. "I have a special challenge for you"; "I have a tough problem for you to reason out." You may also ask this student such questions as: "How would you solve this?"; "How would you interpret this idea?"; "What is your understanding of_____?"; "What do you think an expert would say about_____?"

Second, provide this student with access to the high-tech tools. If you have a computer in your classroom, assign this student to monitor its use. He may also enter nonconfidential data for you, tutor other students on its use, lead a group that is going to write letters to students in another country, use the computer to do high-challenge research, or solve a complex math problem the class is working on. If you don't have a classroom computer, locate one in the school, community library, or local business and arrange for the student to do challenging projects.

Third, when you structure lessons, be sure that you provide the big picture and the objective. Throughout the lesson, invite this student to tell you and the class how each task fits with the big picture. If the response is off target, make the connection. It will help this student if you use a concept map on the blackboard to connect the details of the lesson to the main idea. Constantly refer to the map as the lesson proceeds.

Fourth, plan your lessons to include challenge assignments. To practice math problem solving, use cooperative groups, but with a tight structure (roles, guidelines, common goal, materials, etc.). Let this student serve as the checker in the cooperative group. Have each student solve the problem alone before the checker tests each answer and helps all come up with the best answer. After guided practice in the cooperative groups, assign this student to a homogeneous cooperative group that will take on a challenge problem while you assist the other students with more guided practice. Use this same pattern in the other subject areas. Make sure that the challenge problem calls for the new group members to analyze how they solved the problem and to draw generalized conclusions about their approach to problem solving.

What Activities Promote Learning With This Intelligence?

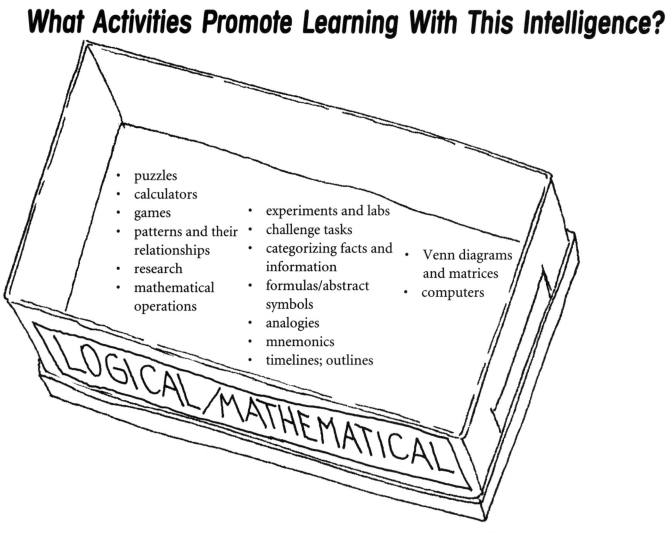

- puzzles
- calculators
- games
- patterns and their relationships
- research
- mathematical operations
- experiments and labs
- challenge tasks
- categorizing facts and information
- formulas/abstract symbols
- analogies
- mnemonics
- timelines; outlines
- Venn diagrams and matrices
- computers

LOGICAL/MATHEMATICAL

IRI/SkyLight Training and Publishing, Inc.

How Do You Meet the Challenge of the Special Student?

This is the second intelligence that challenges many special needs students. As with the verbal/linguistic, the challenges may come as much from the boring methods used to teach the subject as by the students' difficulties in learning the approach.

- Use pictures, movement, objects, and musical beats to understand concepts.
- Make learning to count fun with games, activities, and objects.
- Work on problem solving. Set up problems that require manipulatives before any computation is brought in. Show the reasons for computation.
- Start with authentic applications or uses of math (bank statements, grocery store receipts, etc.). Set up a micro-society with a bank and money, grocery stores and checks, etc.
- Start a company. Make a product to advertise and sell in the school. Plan a field trip with the earnings.
- Teach students how to use calculators.
- Use computer math games for practice and problem solving. ("Oregon Trail" is great for math!)
- Sell stock for the class company and use the stock market to teach math.

How Do You Create an Environment for This Intelligence?

A valuable aid for this student is a well-ordered and sequenced lesson design. This design starts with an anticipatory set. The set lets this student get his mind ready for what is going to happen and to make connections with prior knowledge and the big picture. Next, the design calls for a lesson objective. This lets the logical/mathematical thinker put the lesson in place and lay out a step-by-step target. When this objective is framed with an explicit outcome, this student is ready. Next comes the demonstration or modeling that helps the student see a best example of what will be learned, and then the guided practice. Along the way, the teacher checks for understanding to ensure that the student is making the connections and seeing the relationships.

Although the logical/mathematical student warms easily to lessons taught with orderly and rational design, is it fair to say that it benefits all students? The answer is both yes and no.

There are those educators who would say dogmatically that this design, united with a strong lesson outcome and aligned with course and curricular outcomes, is the only way to guarantee success for all students. Such a position is unsupported by any sound learning theory and certainly unsupported by any solid effects research. Within the perspective of the theory of multiple intelligences and the constructivist notion of learning, direct instruction lesson design is a tool, most helpful for facilitating the academic success of those students with a strongly developed logical/mathematical intelligence. This lesson design is also beneficial for those students who have not yet developed the logical/mathematical intelligence. Thus, for all students the lesson design can be a helpful means to an end. It is not, however, the be-all and end-all for promoting academic success in the classroom. In this light, it is important that a teacher use direct instruction lesson design judiciously as a tool with specific uses at specific times. Its overuse and misuse, as is evident in many classrooms, is a sure-fire way to kill the development of the logical/mathematical intelligence even in the most motivated students.

You can make math and science a stimulating, interesting, and fun time. "Math does not have to bore," says Disney Math Teacher of the Year, Pat Taylor. In Pat's nontracked geometry classroom, students were mixed in heterogeneous, cooperative groups. Each lesson began with a problem connected to a mathematical thinking skill such as estimating. The problem was posed as a question about a concrete application of a theorem. After a question such as, "How can you estimate the circumference of a glass?" was answered in the hands-on demonstration, Pat provided the students with manipulatives and information for making mathematical solutions. Working in cooperative groups, the students measured circles and used the math formula. It was Pat's job at this point to guide the practice with advice, correction, and encouragement. After checking the students' ability to solve the problem with manipulatives and to explain the procedures, she regrouped the students by ability. In the new groups, students worked on pen-and-pencil algorithms. As she gave special assistance to the "not yet" group and its basic challenge example, the other groups worked on challenge examples commensurate with their mathematical abilities. Students from Pat's classes report on a regular basis that her approach, which begins with hands-on problem solving, uses cooperative groups, and focuses on the thinking skill applications, is "fun, interesting, difficult, and a place where math is real."

Chemistry students in Palatine, Illinois, make similar comments about their teacher, Sally Berman. On any given day, students may find themselves faced with one of Sally's interdisciplinary lessons. Students especially love Sally's "mole" lesson. As she helps them understand how to calculate a mole (in chemistry, the molecular weight of a substance expressed in grams), Sally also teaches her students how to use moles to count everything from beans to nuts, and when, how, and where to use mole-counts in chemistry experiments. Her students design and sew moles (the animal) with pun-names like "Mole-be Dick," celebrate "Mole Day," and write poems and stories about moles.

The Mnemonic Devices

The shoe box for this intelligence includes mnemonics. Mnemonics are techniques for improving one's memory by using certain formulas, usually consisting of a key phrase or word. Students often use mnemonics to memorize information, setting up patterns and associations. For example, a pianist might remember the phrase "Every Good Boy Does Fine" to identify the notes on the lines of the treble staff as E, G, B, D, and F. For the spaces, the pianist might use the word "FACE" to read the notes F, A, C, and E. Another example of a mnemonic device is the word "HOMES" used by geography students to remember the five great lakes: Huron, Ontario, Michigan, Erie, and Superior. To remember the number of days in each month, people often recite the well-known poem, "Thirty days have September, April, June, and November . . . ."

Graphic Organizers

Three graphic organizers, the attribute web, the Venn diagram, and the question matrix promote the analytic thinking essential to the development of this intelligence. (Please note: all graphic organizers help develop the Visual/Spatial Intelligence. In this case, these three organizers are shared between Logical/Mathematical and Visual/Spatial Intelligences.)

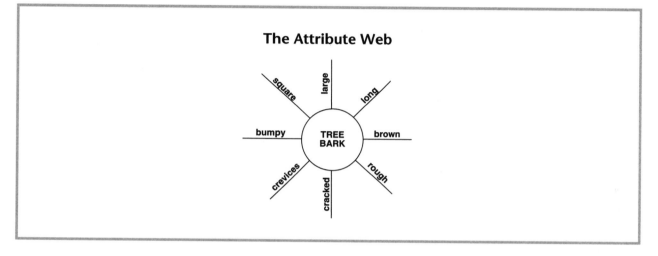

Primary Example: Give students pieces of tree bark. On the board draw a giant web. Invite the students to describe the colors, shapes, texture, and size of the bark. Add the words to the web.

Middle School Example: Put students in cooperative groups. On a sheet of newsprint, assign each group a different geometric form. On the same sheet, the group is to construct a web indicating the shape, color, uses, purposes, size, angles, etc., of its form.

High School Example: Put students in cooperative groups. Assign each student a nearby building (or a photo of a building). On a sheet of newsprint each group will web the various geometric forms they see in the architecture.

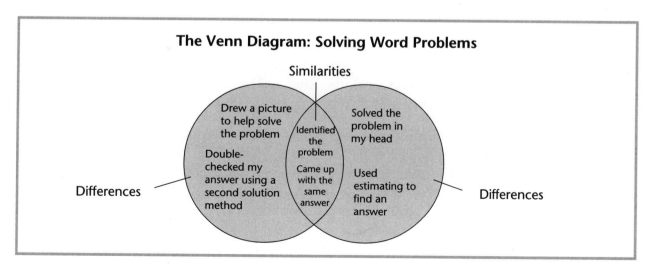

Primary School Example: Provide pairs of students with two samples from a similar scientific group (two clam shells, two oranges, two spiders). Have them study the samples and construct a Venn diagram showing the similarities and differences.

Middle School Example: Provide students with a word problem that allows different problem-solving approaches. Invite the students to select two approaches they think will work and construct a Venn showing the similarities and differences in using those approaches.

High School Example: Provide pairs of students with two spreadsheet programs. Have them investigate the programs and prepare a Venn diagram illustrating the similarities and differences.

The Question Matrix

QUESTION	North America	Asia	Africa
What is the size?			
What is the shape?			
What is the average temperature?			
What is the population?			

Primary School Example: Construct a question matrix on three patterns students can form with pattern blocks. On the board, write the names of the patterns across the top of the matrix. In the left-hand column, ask the questions: what? when? where? how? After pairs have made each pattern, invite the children to fill in the boxes. When all the boxes are filled, ask the children to tell you how the patterns are alike and different.

Middle School Example: Construct a matrix on the continents. On the board, write the names across the top. In the left-hand column, ask about the size, shape, average temperature, special geographic features, time zones, and population. After you have studied each, invite the class to fill in the matrix. Use the completed matrix to start comparative essays.

High School Example: Form cooperative groups. Show them how to construct a matrix on laws of physics. Across the top, they will enter three to five laws studied in your course. In the left column, they will write five key questions to ask about the attributes of the laws. After the matrices are made, exchange them among the groups. The new group will complete the matrix before returning it to the creator group for correction and reaction.

Learning Centers

MATHEMATICS

Fill this center with math manipulatives, brain teasers, puzzles, challenge problems, math games, objects to classify and seek patterns, and research assignments. Label all materials "start up," "tough," and "high challenge." Supply a calculator and a computer with math games and math problem-solving software.

SCIENCE

Fill this center with hands-on experiments that fit the science unit you are teaching. Simple objects such as seeds, dried flowers, animal pictures, leaves, etc., will reinforce attributing and classifying. Supply a computer with science simulations that fit your curriculum. Provide graphic organizer-based assignments to extend skills in classifying and attributing.

CAREERS

Fill this center with books, pictures, and articles about careers in math, science, technology, research, engineering, and finance.

COMPUTERS

Fill this center with computer games, robotic kits, and other math-science simulations.

Lesson Example 1: Connections by Shape

TARGETED INTELLIGENCE: Logical/Mathematical

SUPPORTING INTELLIGENCES: Interpersonal, Intrapersonal

THINKING SKILLS: Forced Relationships, Analysis

SOCIAL SKILLS: Communicating, Listening, Following Directions

CONTENT FOCUS: Geometric Shapes

MATERIALS: Bags and contents

TASK FOCUS: This is a hands-on activity that will help students make connections (via similar features) among geometric shapes.

PRODUCT: A list of similarities and differences

PROBLEM: How to distinguish similarities and differences

ACTIVITY:

1. Ask students to bring a brown bag containing three objects that represent themselves. Each object must have a unique geometric shape. They are not to show the objects to anyone until math time.
2. Match pairs, assigning students A and B.
3. Student A pulls one object out of the bag and explains it. Student B chooses something that is similar in shape. B tells why he or she brought this object.
4. The two decide how the objects are alike.
5. They continue the same way with Student B beginning the next round, and so forth.
6. When all three objects are out, have the pairs decide how all six are alike and what their common relationships are.
7. Have students make and sign a list of similarities and differences.

REFLECTIONS:

1. What new thing did you learn about geometric shapes?
2. Which objects were easiest and most difficult to name the relationships?

PRIMARY SCHOOL EXAMPLE: Each person chooses a favorite shape from a pile you provide and puts it in a bag. The whole class or small groups can assist with the relationships. Then do the activity as it is written above.

MIDDLE SCHOOL EXAMPLE: After the students have discussed all items, they can make forced relationships among unlike items in the collection. For examples, "How is a book like a pin?" "How is a bar of soap like a shoe?" "How is a chair like a pencil?"

HIGH SCHOOL EXAMPLE: In the bag, place examples of three different geometric patterns. Use these for the comparison items.

Lesson Example 2: Pattern Hunt

TARGETED INTELLIGENCE: Logical/Mathematical

SUPPORTING INTELLIGENCES: Verbal/Linguistic, Interpersonal

THINKING SKILLS: Reasoning, Problem Solving, Evaluating

SOCIAL SKILLS: Quiet Voices, Orderly Movement, Following Directions, Working With Teams

CONTENT FOCUS: Geometric Patterns

MATERIALS: Writing element, worksheet, an assigned area to go on the hunt

TASK FOCUS: Students will look for patterns all around them on buildings, in books, in nature, and in poetry. We are natural pattern seekers. This activity tunes students into the patterns around them.

PRODUCT: Pattern worksheet

PROBLEM: How to find patterns

ACTIVITY:

1. Group students in threes.
2. Assign roles.
   a. Materials Manager: Gets a worksheet and recording pencil.
   b. Timekeeper: Keeps tabs on group members and paces them through activity.
   c. Checker: Constantly checks for accuracy and what is needed next until worksheet is complete or time is up.
3. Read over the Pattern Worksheet and explain these rules to the class.
   a. Locate each set pattern/blocks.
   b. Tell where you found it.
   c. Sketch the pattern on the worksheet.
   d. Letter the pattern sequence (e.g., ABA–ABA–ABA).
4. Assign a time limit for students to be back in their desks with as much of the worksheet completed as possible.

REFLECTIONS:

1. How many patterns did you find?
2. Which was the most difficult to find?
3. Where else do you see patterns?

PRIMARY SCHOOL EXAMPLE: Expose students to more work with patterns by allowing them to create their own patterns with beads and string. Obtain a large number of beads in all shapes, colors, and sizes. Let each child have a piece of string on which he or she can create his or her own pattern with the colored beads. Once all students are finished, ask them to share their patterns with the class.

MIDDLE SCHOOL EXAMPLE: Modify the lesson for middle school students by asking them to search out patterns (1) in the classroom, (2) in or on a building across the street, (3) on the clothes of someone in the classroom, and (4) in a picture. Ask students to describe or sketch the patterns that they find and record the location.

HIGH SCHOOL EXAMPLE: Alter the lesson for high school students by asking them to find patterns (1) in graphics, (2) in nature, (3) on someone in their cooperative group, and (4) in all of their group members' names.

Pattern Worksheet

NAMES OF GROUP MEMBERS: _____

_____

Date: _____

Pattern	Location	Sketch
A B A	leaf-tree-leaf	
A B B		
A B B C		

IRI/SkyLight Training and Publishing, Inc.

Lesson Example 3: Silver Bells With Rap

TARGETED INTELLIGENCE: Logical/Mathematical

SUPPORTING INTELLIGENCES: Verbal/Linguistic, Visual/Spatial, Interpersonal

THINKING SKILLS: Analysis, Decision Making, Defining Attributes, Observation

SOCIAL SKILLS: Following Directions, Communicating Verbally and Written

CONTENT FOCUS: Attributes

MATERIALS: Wrapped candy silver bells (two for every student), worksheets, pencils

TASK FOCUS: Students will find the similarities and differences of two objects and give enough information in writing for others to distinguish the difference.

PRODUCT: Venn diagram

PROBLEM: How to compare and contrast

ACTIVITY:

1. Assign partners and give each pair two pieces of wrapped candy.
2. Instruct them to name each piece of candy.
3. Assign the roles.
   a. Checker checks answers.
   b. Recorder writes on the data sheet.
4. Show the pairs how to draw a Venn diagram.
5. With each piece of candy in a Venn spot, they are to list the unique characteristics of each and put one common attribute in the center section.
6. They will now move the candy off of their A and B positions. Rotate groups. When the next group comes, they are to read the attributes and determine A and B and add one new common attribute to the center section.
7. The checker from the previous group goes back and checks to see if the new group was correct.

REFLECTIONS:

1. How many common attributes did you agree on?
2. How easy or difficult was it to find differences?

PRIMARY SCHOOL EXAMPLE: For other variations, do this lesson with crackers or colored marbles.

MIDDLE SCHOOL EXAMPLE: Have the students go on a nature hunt. Each group of four will find the natural objects (stones, flowers, leaves) it will use. When they start, each pair will have similar objects of the same type to observe.

HIGH SCHOOL EXAMPLE: Use chemical compounds or botany slides.

Lesson Example 4: Coin Play

TARGETED INTELLIGENCE: Logical/Mathematical

SUPPORTING INTELLIGENCES: Visual/Spatial, Intrapersonal

THINKING SKILLS: Analysis, Problem Solving

SOCIAL SKILLS: Listening, Following Directions

CONTENT FOCUS: Math problem solving

MATERIALS: Ten coins of the same size, a blank overhead transparency for each pair

TASK FOCUS: These activities are designed to stretch the mind and facilitate problem solving.

PRODUCT: Problem-solving technique

PROBLEM: How to solve a coin puzzle

ACTIVITY 1:

1. Pair students.

2. Each pair gets ten coins or circles of the same size.

3. Place the coins in the following design on the overhead projector.

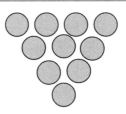

4. Tell students that they must try to move one coin at a time in only three moves to end up with this shape.

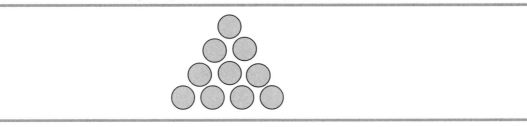

5. Allow time for students to solve the puzzle. The solution is provided below.

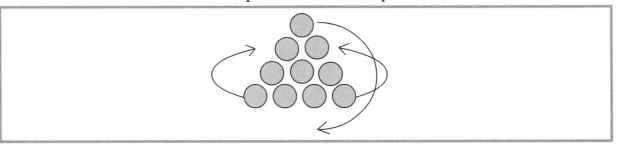

IRI/SkyLight Training and Publishing, Inc.

ACTIVITY 2:

1. Each student needs six coins that are the same size.
2. Show this arrangement on the overhead.

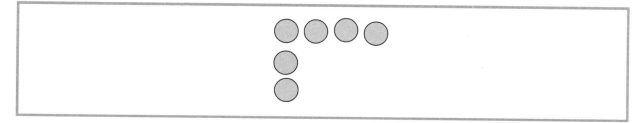

3. Now arrange the coins so that each row has three coins, using all six coins.
4. Allow solving time, and then show the trick. (One coin is placed on top of another.)

ACTIVITY 3:

Have each pair make up a problem with coins and get another pair to solve it.

REFLECTIONS:

1. What were the steps in your thinking as you solved the problems?
2. How well did you follow directions?
3. What was difficult about making your own problem?

PRIMARY SCHOOL EXAMPLE: Let students familiarize themselves with manipulatives by providing them with a variety of differently shaped blocks: triangles, diamonds, squares, etc. Ask students to rearrange the pieces to create different geometric shapes. Have students examine how many different shapes they can create with the pieces and have them draw and record their solution each time.

MIDDLE SCHOOL EXAMPLE: After students have completed this lesson, ask them to think about their own problem-solving strategy. Have the pairs discuss how they approach a problem by answering some of these questions: How did you know you were on the right track? Does drawing a problem seem to help you, or do you do something impulsively and evaluate it later? Do you think about the problem before starting to solve it, or do you like to talk about a problem first? Explain to students that thinking about their own problem-solving process can help them become better problem solvers.

HIGH SCHOOL EXAMPLE: Ask students to check the library for brainteasers and logic problems. Each student must first find one problem, present it to the class, allow time for the rest of the class to figure it out, and present the solution.

Lesson Example 5: Kidney Bean, Jelly Bean

(A lesson from *Catch Them Thinking in Science*, by Sally Berman)

TARGETED INTELLIGENCE: Logical/Mathematical

SUPPORTING INTELLIGENCES: Interpersonal, Visual/Spatial

THINKING SKILLS: Observing, Checking for Accuracy

SOCIAL SKILLS: Sharing, Clarifying

CONTENT FOCUS: Biology

MATERIALS: Kidney beans, jelly beans, newsprint, markers, blindfolds

TASK FOCUS: Using the think-pair-share strategy, ask students to list the five senses and describe specific information that each of the senses can give about an object. Map their answers on the board, overhead, or newsprint.

PRODUCT: Accurate observation

PROBLEM: Object differentiation

ACTIVITY:

1. Divide students into groups of three. Each group needs an **observer** who will use the five senses to make observations; a **recorder** who will write down the observations; and a **guide** who will time the activity. Let the group know when it is time to rotate roles, and check with the group members for agreement on the accuracy of observations at the end of the round.

2. The first-round guide is the person who lives closest to school. The first-round observer sits to the right of the guide. The first-round recorder is the third group member.

3. Be sure that all groups know who has which role for the first round.

4. The activity will take place in three initial rounds and three final rounds. Roles rotate one person to the right with each new round.

5. The objects to observe are a kidney bean and a jelly bean. Each observer is to make as many observations about the objects as possible in one minute. The recorder and the guide may not help the observer.

6. Check for accuracy in understanding the instructions. Have a student repeat them.

7. Tell the first-round observers to come to your desk for three kidney beans and three jelly beans. They are to perform their observations on one bean of each kind. The others are used in the succeeding rounds.

8. When all groups have their beans, start the initial round.

IRI/SkyLight Training and Publishing, Inc.

9. At the conclusion of the three initial rounds, signal for silence. Tell the students that they are now going to check the accuracy of their observations. The observer in each final round will receive a new kidney bean and jelly bean. The observer will then be blindfolded and will have one minute to examine the new beans and eat the one that he or she believes is the jelly bean. The observer will instantly know whether his or her observations were correct or not.

10. The roles will rotate as before. There will be three final rounds. Each group will keep score of the successful identifications—how many final-round observers correctly select the jelly bean.

11. Check for accuracy in the instructions.

12. Do the final round.

REFLECTIONS: Ask students to respond to the following questions in their logs:
1. How did you know you had the jelly bean?
2. What might you do differently next time?
3. What did you learn about observing with all of your senses?

Have students share their answers with their group.

PRIMARY SCHOOL EXAMPLE: Collect fifteen to twenty ordinary objects or articles one might find around the house or classroom (e.g., keys, chalk, scissors, eraser). Place these objects in front of the students for one minute and tell them to concentrate on the objects. Encourage the students to think of the objects in terms of all their senses, not just sight. Remove the objects so the students cannot see them anymore. Now ask the students to visualize the objects and record as many of the articles as they can remember.

MIDDLE SCHOOL EXAMPLE: Have students work in groups to create their own observation exercises that the rest of the class can complete. Make sure that the groups incorporate the use of the five senses in their observational activity. Allow time for groups to complete each other's activities and discuss them.

HIGH SCHOOL EXAMPLE: Develop your students' observation skills further with another exercise entitled, "Hide in Plain Sight" (from *Catch Them Thinking in Science*, by Sally Berman). For this activity, you need a small- to medium-sized stuffed animal that you will hang some place in your classroom. This should be done before students enter the room. Each day you will move it to a new location and keep track of each location. Tell students that you are, at the moment, checking their observation skills. Inform them that they have five days in which to figure out how you are doing this. They can write you a note when they have discovered the test and record their daily observations about the test. On the sixth day, announce that the test is over and have one student explain what the test was. Have students check the accuracy of their observations as you read off your list of the locations.

Make Your Own

LESSON NAME: _____

TARGETED INTELLIGENCE: _Logical/Mathematical_____

SUPPORTING INTELLIGENCES: _____

THINKING SKILLS: _____

SOCIAL SKILLS: _____
_____

CONTENT FOCUS: _____

MATERIALS: _____
_____

TASK FOCUS: _____
_____

PRODUCT: _____

PROBLEM: _____

ACTIVITY:
_____
_____
_____
_____
_____
_____
_____
_____

REFLECTIONS:

1. _____
_____

2. _____
_____

3. _____
_____

Make Your Own

LESSON NAME: _____

TARGETED INTELLIGENCE: Logical/Mathematical _____

SUPPORTING INTELLIGENCES: _____

THINKING SKILLS: _____

SOCIAL SKILLS: _____

_____

CONTENT FOCUS: _____

MATERIALS: _____

_____

TASK FOCUS: _____

_____

PRODUCT: _____

PROBLEM: _____

ACTIVITY:

_____

_____

_____

_____

_____

_____

_____

_____

REFLECTIONS:

1. _____

_____

2. _____

_____

3. _____

_____

Working in This Intelligence, I Am . . .

When I use this intelligence, I am . . .

|———|

very uncomfortable   totally at ease

When I ask students to use this intelligence, I am . . .

|———|

very uncomfortable   totally at ease

In what ways does this shoe fit me personally?

What can I do to polish this shoe for my professional use?

What am I going to do to provide for students in this intelligence?

What to continue	New things to do

Journal Page

Reflections on My Pathway to Logical/Mathematical Intelligence

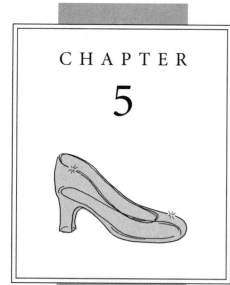

CHAPTER

5

Visual/Spatial Intelligence

Cinderella's glass slipper represents the world of imagination and creativity. The images reflected on the glass symbolize the images one sees behind one's eyelids. The way one sees the world in the "mind's eye" is that personal view of the world as pictured in one's mind.

What Is It?

The visual/spatial intelligence is the capacity to perceive the visual world accurately and to be able to recreate one's visual experiences. It involves the ability to see form, color, shape, and texture in the "mind's eye" and to transfer these to concrete representation in art form.

If the Shoe Fits... It Looks Like

Kay, our doodler, is visual/spatial. She is creative and sees her work in terms of pictures and colors. She invents in order to learn and will see complex visual and spatial relationships, abstract geometric patterns, and renderings of impressions of common objects.

Wearing the Shoe in Life – Career Choices

- Sculptor
- Engineer
- Painter

- Sailor
- Designer
- Architect

- Artist
- Graphic Designer
- Layout Editor

"E"asing On Down the Road of the Visual/Spatial Journey

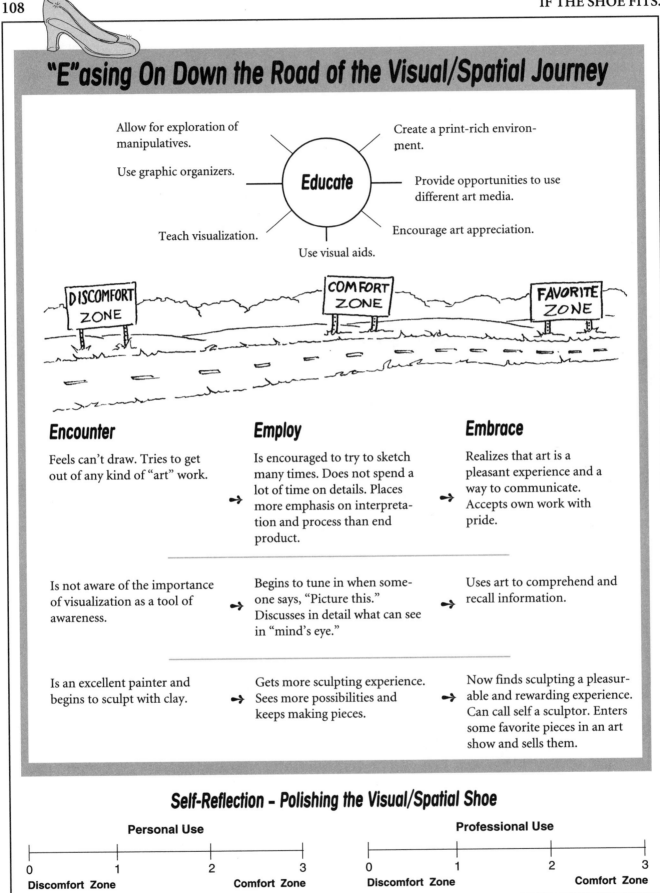

Allow for exploration of manipulatives.

Use graphic organizers.

Educate

Create a print-rich environment.

Provide opportunities to use different art media.

Teach visualization.

Encourage art appreciation.

Use visual aids.

DISCOMFORT ZONE

COMFORT ZONE

FAVORITE ZONE

Encounter

Feels can't draw. Tries to get out of any kind of "art" work.

Employ

Is encouraged to try to sketch many times. Does not spend a lot of time on details. Places more emphasis on interpretation and process than end product.

Embrace

Realizes that art is a pleasant experience and a way to communicate. Accepts own work with pride.

Is not aware of the importance of visualization as a tool of awareness.

Begins to tune in when someone says, "Picture this." Discusses in detail what can see in "mind's eye."

Uses art to comprehend and recall information.

Is an excellent painter and begins to sculpt with clay.

Gets more sculpting experience. Sees more possibilities and keeps making pieces.

Now finds sculpting a pleasurable and rewarding experience. Can call self a sculptor. Enters some favorite pieces in an art show and sells them.

Self-Reflection – Polishing the Visual/Spatial Shoe

Personal Use

0   1   2   3

Discomfort Zone   Comfort Zone

Professional Use

0   1   2   3

Discomfort Zone   Comfort Zone

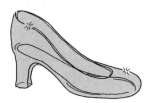

Two of the most beautiful gardens in the world are located in Southern Europe. The first, created by Monet as a living palette, is in Giverny, France; the second is in the Dominican Monastery (now a hotel) on the eastern coast of Sicily in the mountainsides of Taormina. Each in its own way celebrates the visual/spatial intelligence.

When Monet left Paris for the French countryside, he built his studio at a farmhouse in Giverny. One of his monumental tasks was to dam a small stream and create the flowered garden and ponds made famous in his work. Some would argue that even his great paintings of the Japanese bridge, the rowboats, the flowered trellis, and other scenes painted here never matched the color explosion of the garden itself. Even today, as if it were a centuries-old natural phenomenon, no camera can capture the spray of color, the subtle curves, and the intricate designs that amaze the eye. Although it may be true that "beauty is in the eye of the beholder," it is also true that beauty is Monet's garden.

On the eastern shore of Sicily, the island of flowers climbs the steep mountainsides to the village of Taormina. Here is located the brightly cultivated garden of the Dominican Monastery Hotel. Using the basic design of an English knot garden, the caretakers have blended a riot of color with the ancient architecture. Giant geraniums reach up to touch cascading bougainvillea as rich purples and bright reds blend with sunny yellows and clear whites. Over seventy varieties of flowers and plants, each placed in the perfect spot to catch the eye, wave in the gentle winds.

Both gardens suggest the sharpness and sensitivity of their creators' visual/spatial intelligence. This intelligence, represented by Cinderella's glass slipper, involves the ability to see form, color, shape, and texture in the "mind's eye" and to transfer these to a concrete representation: a painting, a sculpture, an architectural rendering, a flower arrangement, or a garden. Cinderella's slipper suggests first the world of fantasy and imagination that the visual artist creates. It also suggests the transfer the artist makes to share his or her inner vision with the world.

In the back-to-basics movement, the visual arts have taken many hard blows. Classroom art instruction is often eliminated because it is seen as a frill. Museums are forced to struggle for funds and art students struggle even more to avoid the traditional starvation.

What Is Visual/Spatial Intelligence?

This intelligence begins with a sharpening of the sensorimotor perceptions of the world around us. The eye discriminates color, shape, form, texture, spatial depth, dimensions, and relationships. As the intelligence develops, eye-hand coordination and small muscle control enable the individual to reproduce the perceived shapes and colors in a variety of media. The painter, sculptor, architect, gardener, cartographer, drafter, graphic designer, and house painter all transfer the images in their minds to the new object they are making or improving. In this way, visual perceptions are mixed with prior knowledge and experience, emotions, and images to create a new vision for others to experience.

What Is the Developmental Path for This Intelligence?

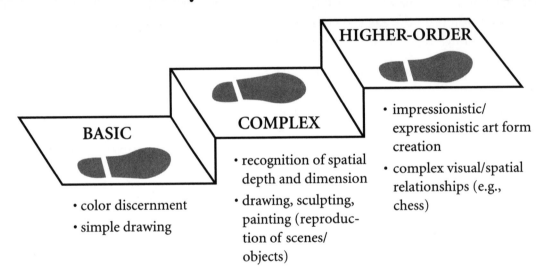

BASIC

- color discernment
- simple drawing

COMPLEX

- recognition of spatial depth and dimension
- drawing, sculpting, painting (reproduction of scenes/objects)

HIGHER-ORDER

- impressionistic/expressionistic art form creation
- complex visual/spatial relationships (e.g., chess)

How Is This Intelligence Developed in Other Cultures?

Some of the earliest history is reported to us through picture stories found on cave walls. Through these pictures, we get mental images of a time long forgotten.

The children of southwest Texas and Mexico have a culture enriched by a heritage of patterns, designs, and colors. The crafts of pottery, tapestry, painting, clothing, and architecture reflect the natural colors and shapes of the region. From an early age, these children see the harmony of the visual arts with the natural setting. Fantasy, reality, and humanity are blended into visual traditions handed from adult to child.

Perhaps no single period of history better represents the flowering of the visual/spatial intelligence than the Florentine Renaissance. Within a century, Michelangelo and Raphael led hundreds of artists and architects to create a city dedicated to the visual arts. Centuries later, visitors to Florence, Italy, are awed not only by the quantity and quality of the work by famous masters, but also by the plethora of fine work that the craftspeople and the less famous artists created. Today, legions of workers, carefully trained in the visual arts, are needed year after year to restore all the fine work created in a time span of one hundred years.

In China, it is the architecture that stands out. While many Americans are familiar with the unique architecture of Imperial China, they are often surprised at the massive yet finely detailed buildings. Although the great palaces are now museums showing the history of China, the traditions of lacquer-painted screens, ceramic sculptures, and sumai painting are carried on in every small town and village.

How Can This Intelligence Be Used for Problem Solving?

The developed "mind's eye" allows for many types of problem solving.

☐ Mary lost her mother's best ring. She remembered wearing it to a wedding on the previous weekend. When panic started to set in, Mary turned to her visual memory. First, she relaxed. Then, she concentrated on retracing her steps from the time of the wedding to the present. Halfway through the mental journey, she saw herself taking off the ring to wash the dishes. When she went to the kitchen, she found the ring on the window sill next to the sink.

☐ Dave, a potential Olympic qualifier in the 400-yard freestyle, readied himself for his morning workout. He sat by the pool and let his legs dangle in the water. He closed his eyes and focused on the back of his eyelids. On this miniscreen, he saw himself step to the blocks, leap with the starter's gun, and glide through the water. At each turn, he switched to slow motion, watching himself approach the wall, flip, and push out.

Lap by lap he followed himself through the ever-rougher water. In the corner of the screen, he watched the clock tick off the seconds. In the last lap, he saw himself right on pace. He quickened his stroke, dashing home .15 of a second ahead of his best previous time. He touched the wall and relaxed.

With the visual workout done, Dave stood and readied himself for the dive. His goal, to knock .15 of a second from his best time, reflected in the water.

☐ Leonard, a civil engineer, was puzzled by the uneven and marshy terrain. The architectural renderings for the bridge set the main abutment directly into the marsh. His twenty-three years of experience raised warning flags. He could visually recall the fate of the Ogedenton Bridge. He flipped on the computer and booted the CAD-CAM disk. In a few minutes, it showed him a design alternative he knew was safe.

☐   Joanna knew her problem. She opened her journal and sketched the problem-solving tree. It was a graphic organizer she had learned to use in social studies class. As she visualized each barrier, she wrote it on the chart. When she got to solutions, she sketched a picture of each one. No worry about being a Michelangelo, but the sketches gave her clarity. By the time she finished the last sketch, she knew how she was going to solve her problem.

Who Is the Student With This Intelligence?

Kay, our doodler, is visual/spatial. She is creative, seeing the world in terms of pictures and colors. Her doodling may actually be the channel through which she internalizes what is being said. Her shoe looks like Cinderella's slipper because of her creative imagination. She invents in order to learn.

Have you encountered a student who makes color distinctions that most people do not see? The student with the strong visual/spatial intelligence makes these distinctions, sees nontraditional patterns, and can translate these to subtle designs in a favorite medium. In the early development stages, this student is as comfortable with crayons "in the lines" as with "freehand" but with a color sense that makes you wonder. In the early teens, the student picks several media to experiment with designs. As readily as some youngsters pick up a book or turn on the TV, this youngster will concentrate for long periods on sketches, renderings, drawings, and designs. In the completed works, you will see complex visual and spatial relationships, abstract geometric patterns, and renderings of impressions of common objects.

The Comfort Zone: What Helps This Student Learn?

This student loves a picture-rich classroom environment. Brightly colored bulletin boards illustrating key ideas, photos, posters with pithy sayings, mobiles, and other visual strategies stimulate her interest. The use of colored cartoons on overheads illustrating key lecture points, video demonstrations, learning centers with slides, picture collections, and filmstrips reinforce lesson objectives. Given the opportunity to summarize or explain lesson concepts, this student loves the opportunity to draw pictures, assemble collages, or make mobiles.

The Discomfort Zone: What Hinders This Student?

When the visual student is overloaded with long print passages and little graphic design, she gets discouraged. Likewise, she finds it difficult to describe and to communicate with words. Long writing assignments as the means to detail ideas frustrate her. Without the opportunity to express thoughts and feelings in images, she tends to become silent.

How Do You Catch This Student's Attention in the Classroom?

The easiest hook for this student is the verbal cues you give. Before starting a task, ask the class to think about, reflect on, imagine what it would be like if, picture, or pretend. Describe a situation that is related to the concept that will center your lesson. For instance, to start a lesson on George Washington at Valley Forge, begin with, "Take a minute to see yourself in a ragged tent. Outside, the snow is piled high and the cold winds are blowing. Your shoeless feet. . . ."

When providing reflective time so the students can see themselves in the situation, it is important to use wait-time. Wait-time is the three seconds to a minute between the end of your cues and the start of the student responses. It is essential for the visual/spatial student's development to have the time to see the details of color, shape, arrangement, and so on.

Adding the think-pair-share strategy to wait-time will help even more. In the "think" stage, ask the students to draw what they "imagine" or "picture." After waiting two or three minutes, ask the students to talk with a partner about their sketches for a few moments before you ask for volunteers to share their sketches with the entire class. For this variation of think-pair-share, be sure to encourage the strong visual students to share and receive recognition from the entire class.

Graphic organizers are a special plus for visual/spatial development. Concept and right-angle thinking maps that show connections and relationships are especially beneficial in helping these students organize their thoughts. Encourage the visual/spatial learners to serve as recorders in cooperative groups so they can feel as well as see what they are drawing. Let them sketch the organizer to match the concept. For example, Venn diagrams don't have to be overlapping circles. For a comparison of two continents, the Venn can be the outlines of the continents; for a study of two geometric shapes, the recorder can elect to use those shapes as the Venn. Idea trees and concept maps are two additional pro-visual organizers. In the journal, encourage visual/spatial development by allowing pictures, sketches, symbol thinking, and graphic organizers appropriate to the task.

How Do You Meet the Challenge of the Special Student?

Often the child who has difficulty expressing with words finds it easy to express in pictures and sketches. Yale's Robert Sternberg has indicated that the "person who expresses is the person who learns." Before there was written language, there was pictorial expression. The makers of those early story paintings as well as the many great artists who have pictured their understandings remind us that "a picture is worth a thousand words."

- Select graphic organizers to help these students picture their ideas. Concept maps are especially telling.

- Invite students to make comic strips and storyboards to tell a story.
- Assign students to make picture ads to sell an idea learned in a subject.
- Encourage pictures in the students' journals.
- Have students sketch a picture of a vocabulary word's meaning and teach from the picture.
- In groups, assign the student with artistic talent to make the visuals.

What Activities Promote Learning With This Intelligence?

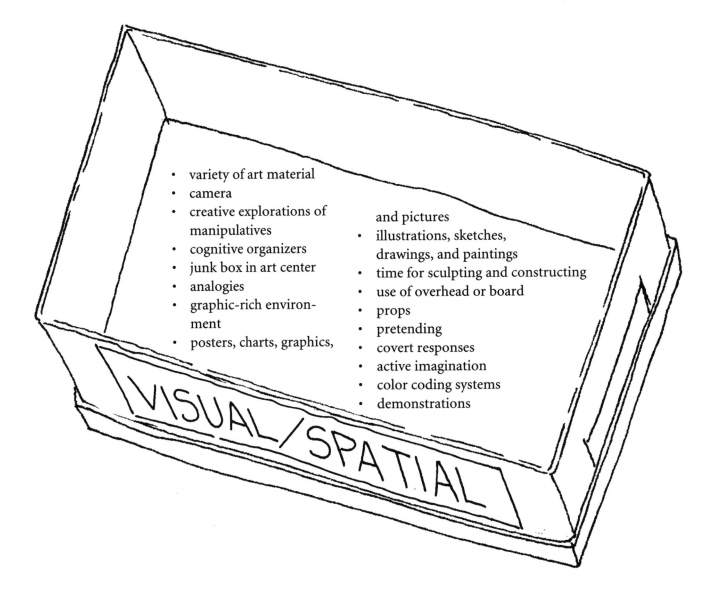

- variety of art material
- camera
- creative explorations of manipulatives
- cognitive organizers
- junk box in art center
- analogies
- graphic-rich environment
- posters, charts, graphics, and pictures
- illustrations, sketches, drawings, and paintings
- time for sculpting and constructing
- use of overhead or board
- props
- pretending
- covert responses
- active imagination
- color coding systems
- demonstrations

VISUAL/SPATIAL

How Do You Create an Environment for This Intelligence?

The visual/spatial environment starts with the classroom walls. Remember that color, design, and pattern stimulate the development of this intelligence. A random bombardment of visual elements is as disastrous as bland and blank walls. Start with a visual/spatial plan by asking yourself these questions: What color scheme do you want to use? How will you coordinate the bulletin board, posters, mobiles, and other visual objects by color and pattern? How often will you change the schema? How will you use your plan as a teaching tool to help students develop their visual/spatial acuity and better appreciate design and pattern? If you are a person with an undeveloped visual intelligence, who in the school or community can help you with your design? Can you go so far as to add student murals or murals by a local artist on your classroom walls?

It is helpful to acclimate your students to visual reflections. In addition to times when the students use the journal for print responses, encourage a sketch or drawing at least once a week. To help the students develop their visual responses, allow ample reflection time after your prompts. At times you may wish to guide them through a visual journey with a character from a book, a historic figure, a scientist working in the lab, an artist in the studio, or a parent at work. As you guide them with prompts through this "movie in the mind's eye," allow ample wait-time for the students to construct the picture and paint in its details. After the mental journey, invite pairs to share what they created. Encourage the students to be as vivid and detailed as they can. For those who struggle or can develop only skimpy outlines, discuss the elements of visual and spatial perception and invite other students to share how they filled in the details.

Use activities that enable students to develop their visual and spatial capabilities. These activities will also take vocabulary and reading comprehension out of the mundane and the "does it count for a grade?" syndrome.

PICTURE A FLOWER

In this activity, invite the students to picture a flower. After several minutes, ask them to sketch the flower and share the sketch with a neighbor. At first, many will sketch a different flower from the one they pictured. They will protest that they made the first flower too complicated. On the next round, tell them that they will have to sketch the flower before you tell them to picture it. In this case, the discussion is likely to reveal that they started with a simple picture in the reflection and then added details on the sketch. Continue discussion in multiple rounds, perhaps with different objects for them to picture and sketch. The students will gather ideas from each other and improve how they see and how they sketch.

IMAGE EXERCISES

The visual and spatial skills of students need as much attention as any other. Integrate image exercises into lessons in other areas of the curriculum. Name an object (person, place, or thing) that leads into a lesson about which the students will have prior knowledge. (For example, if you are doing a unit on city life, in the primary grades, ask urban students to picture city life and sketch the picture.)

RECALL THE EVENT

After a video or film or at the end of a lesson, invite students to picture the event as they remember it, sketch the memory, and share the sketch with a partner. (For example, from a video about pollution, ask middle grade students to picture one example that they recall, sketch it, and share it.)

VISUAL VARIETY

In *The School as a Home for the Mind* (1991), Arthur Costa describes this practice for visual imagery. First, have each student draw a two-inch frame. Next, they are to listen to all directions before starting again. Say, "in the center of the frame, draw a circle, a square, and a triangle. All figures should be inside the circle and only the triangle should be empty." After the students finish, have them compare and discuss the variations and why they think there are differences.

SEE AND SKETCH

After you teach a procedure, invite students to recall the steps in the task. They should watch themselves doing the task. After they are finished with the visual review, have them use a sequence chart to sketch the steps and compare the results with a partner. (For example, in a high school chemistry class, see and sketch the steps in setting up a safety experiment.)

READY TO WRITE

Before students do a writing task, have them picture from prior knowledge what they will write about and sketch the images (a familiar spot, doing a familiar task, directions for a trip, friendship, a character in a story, feelings about a poem read). Use pairs or trios for a discussion of the pictures before the students write.

SAY A WORD

Pick a word or phrase such as family vacation, favorite food, best friend, most liked book, most disliked TV character, pets, job, or future. Allow time for reflection, sketches, and pair-sharing.

PICTORIAL VOCABULARY

In *Blueprints for Thinking in the Cooperative Classroom* (Bellanca & Fogarty, 1991), the authors introduce the portmanteau vocabulary. In this cooperative jigsaw, three students divide up three portmanteau words, learn the definitions, sketch a picture of the definitions, and teach the definitions to the other group members.

MORE PORTMANTEAUX

Do like Lewis Carroll did in *Jabberwocky*. Invent words for the students to sketch and teach. Once students get the idea for making these words or you find a collection of modern variations in your local bookstore, your students will have many fun chances to develop their pictorial language skills.

KEY WORDS

In a lesson, pick out six to nine key words. Give each student two to three index cards and crayons. After the students look up definitions in a dictionary or you review them in a choral response mode (for the primary classroom), each will draw his or her representation of the words and then teach them to the group. Monitor the groups to ensure accuracy and to avoid misteaching. After the teaching is done, allow time for checking and reviewing before you give individual quizzes.

GALLIMAUFRIES

In this linguistic/visual lesson, teach students to understand the different uses of language through visual/spatial connections. Start with a word such as *gallimaufry* (definition: a hodge-podge or jumble). Name examples of *gallimaufries* and ask the students to picture the meaning of the word from the examples.

"I have a kitchen drawer that is one of my *gallimaufries.*"

"The top of my desk here in the classroom gets to be a *gallimaufry* at the end of the day."

"A teenager's room where you have to walk through carefully so as not to step on anything is a *gallimaufry.*"

After several examples, ask the students to draw a *gallimaufry* they know (not your examples), share the sketch, and tell what part of speech it is. Share with the class the meaning of the word. Have a student look the word up in the dictionary to verify its meaning.

PICTURE SHOW ON A PAGE

Visual/spatial learners often have trouble with reading comprehension. The words never connect just right. For this type of learner, the chance to make a picture is beneficial. For book reports, sequencing historic events, lab experiments, or math procedures, have the students draw a sequence of pictures as the key way to express their ideas. Use a sequence chart with pictures only, invite students to make a master sketch that you display or ask them to interpret in a conference with you, or follow the sketches with a cooperative group-sharing or with a writing task.

VISUAL CUES

Young learners can develop their own visual cuing system to help them remember key elements of a task.

FIVE-FINGER BOOK REPORT

As students make an oral book report, they can refer to the tips of their fingers. Each finger represents an element: character, setting, plot, ending, and favorite part.

PARTS OF A LETTER

What are the five details? (Use the fingers again.) What is the main idea? (Use the palm.)

SENSE SHARPENERS

To help students sharpen their sense of sight and attention to visual detail, use these activities for prewriting and discussion.

Crayon Capers

Give pairs of students boxes of crayons. Have them arrange the colors in a spectrum and discuss the differences within the basic color families.

Feelings for Color

Give trios of students three crayons with a wide range of colors. Ask them to decide what feelings they associate with each color. Have them make a group story built around the feeling and the color or have each make a sketch with one color.

Flower Facts

Give each pair a single flower to examine. Have them use a triple T-chart with the headings of Color, Pattern, and Shape. Under each column they are to record and/or sketch in each column as many of the details they can observe.

The T-chart		
Color	Pattern	Shape
orange	long thin petals surrounding the center	circular
pink	rounded layered petals	bulb-like
red	tiny petals attached to stems	triangular

Picture Detail

Give trios of students a web chart and a copy of a painting or photo. Have them study the picture for its detail and record the most minute details on the web.

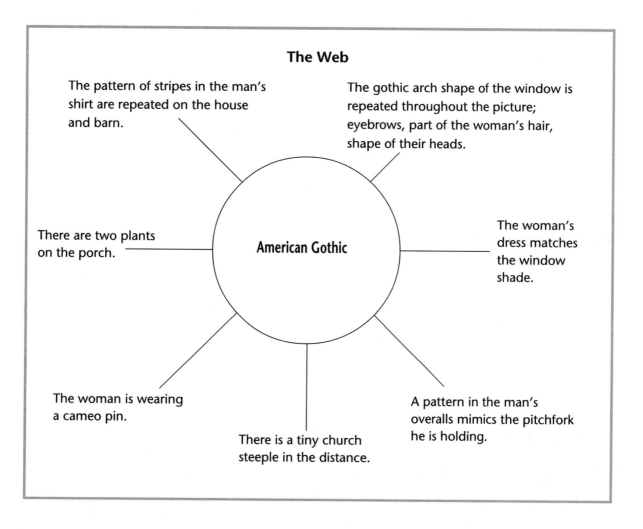

The Web

The pattern of stripes in the man's shirt are repeated on the house and barn.

The gothic arch shape of the window is repeated throughout the picture; eyebrows, part of the woman's hair, shape of their heads.

There are two plants on the porch.

American Gothic

The woman's dress matches the window shade.

The woman is wearing a cameo pin.

There is a tiny church steeple in the distance.

A pattern in the man's overalls mimics the pitchfork he is holding.

Object Observation

Give each student a natural object (rock, leaf, etc.). Invite the students to look for shadings of color, patterns, and designs. Have the students sketch the details.

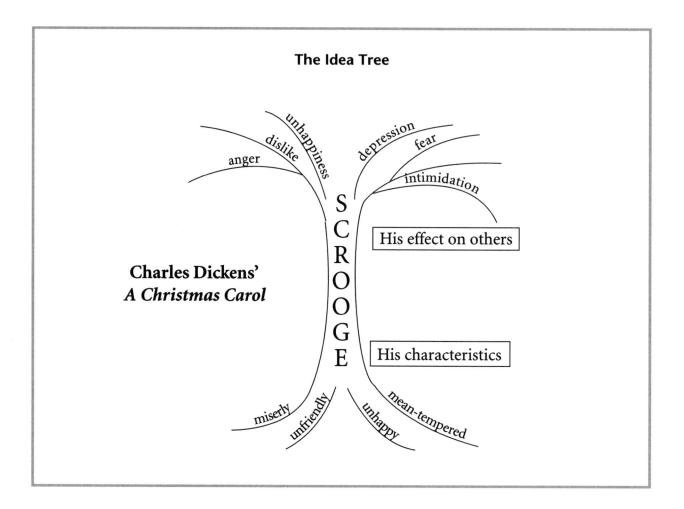

The Idea Tree

Charles Dickens'
A Christmas Carol

THE IDEA TREE

Invite the students to sketch a tree with roots, trunk, and branches. (For advanced users of the idea tree, you may add leaves and fruit.) As students read a novel, study a historic period, examine a culture, or investigate a scientific problem, they can fill in the idea tree. (In primary grades, you may sketch the tree on the board and fill it in with an all-class discussion or just rely on invented words.) For instance, in language arts, the main character's name could appear on the trunk; the character's traits on the roots; and the effects he or she had on the other people on the branches.

IRI/SkyLight Training and Publishing, Inc.

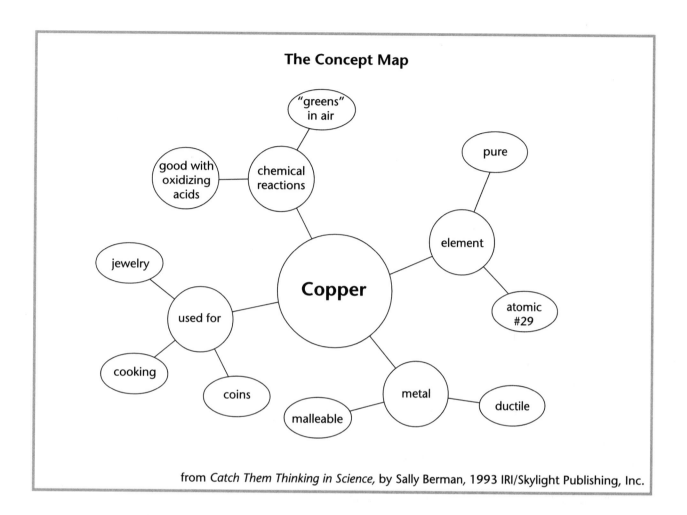

The Concept Map

from *Catch Them Thinking in Science,* by Sally Berman, 1993 IRI/Skylight Publishing, Inc.

THE CONCEPT MAP

Tony Buzan first introduced the concept map to business in his book, *Use Both Sides of Your Brain* (1977). Since then, many have adapted his ideas and the map is known by many names. For the visual/spatial organizer, the concept map is a convenient tool to show idea relationships via color, symbol, and design. The best concept maps are made in large notebooks or journals with multicolor pencils (each color shows a basic strand of thought), have circle connectors which show symbols rather than words, and have ample blank space to develop additional thoughts on the page.

TOWN MAP

Invite the students to make a map of their town. Put the school or the home in the center circle. Demonstrate with your own map first.

PROBLEM-SOLVING MAP

Encourage students to make a map of math problem-solving methods learned throughout the year. At the end of each method, allow time for cooperative sharing of maps.

LITERATURE MAP

Have the students make a map of a novel or play that the class is reading. Each night, students can add to their maps in their journals as they read assigned chapters. On the blackboard, make an all-class map as you discuss the assigned readings.

VISUAL/SPATIAL CENTERS

Set up a center with various types of media supplies. Each week change the task. Some weeks you may want to adapt many of the activities described above for use in the center. Other weeks, set up the center for free exploration of a media.

A CAREER CENTER

Provide pictures, video, print materials, and sample work of artists, draftsmen, clothes designers, pilots, navigators, architects, craftspeople, sculptors, interior decorators, graphic artists, advertising directors, and magazine designers.

SOAP SCULPTURE STUDIO

Provide bars of soap and dull table knives. Set up examples of famous, simple structures such as a pyramid or an obelisk. Encourage students to carve their own.

COMPUTER CENTER

Provide flight simulation, navigation, and simple graphic design software.

ARTIST IN RESIDENCE

Many states provide funds for an artist in residence. Local college artists may be able to provide special programs on a short-term basis for an internship. In your community, take advantage of the many talented people who have hobbies they can share or teach. Think of the unusual such as flower arranging, interior design, clothes design, landscape architecture, pottery, or graphic design. Encourage these local artists not only to share samples of their work, but also to set up an activity to have the students experience the creative act.

VISUAL PROJECTS

Have students work together to make historical diagrams, science projects with display backgrounds, advertising campaigns for subjects they are studying, mobiles and collages that reflect key concepts of a unit, and editorial cartoons on current issues.

Lesson Example 1: Story on a Rope

TARGETED INTELLIGENCE: Visual/Spatial

SUPPORTING INTELLIGENCES: Verbal/Linguistic, Intrapersonal

THINKING SKILLS: Analysis, Decision Making

SOCIAL SKILLS: Listening, Ownership and Accountability

CONTENT FOCUS: Language Arts

MATERIALS: 5 x 7 index cards, crayons or markers, book with chapters to read aloud, yarn or string to hang from ceiling

TASK FOCUS: The teacher reads a story each day as one child draws it.

PRODUCT: A drawing

PROBLEM: How to represent a story with a drawing

ACTIVITY:

1. Read a chapter of a book.
2. Assign a student to be the "reporter for the day." As you read, have the child draw the main ideas of the chapter. The child can choose how he or she wants to draw. The reporter is the only one with paper for drawing.
3. After the chapter is done, the child shares the drawing.
4. The artist receives a hurrah from the class.
5. The sketch is stapled or taped to the yarn or string, one per chapter.
6. At the end of the book, all the sketches are stapled in a class book, and words may be added.

REFLECTIONS:

1. As the student depicts the story in pictures, check for comprehension of the main idea, as well as for details.
2. Ask the artists/reporters of the day to describe their favorite aspect of the drawing and why they picked certain colors.
3. Ask the class to retell the story from the drawing.

PRIMARY SCHOOL EXAMPLE: Obtain a book of children's poetry and review it for poems that are especially descriptive. When you have chosen one, tell students that you will read it aloud to them while they close their eyes and visualize the poem. Read slowly, giving children ample time to absorb the words and think about them. When you are finished reading, ask students to draw what they visualized, paying special attention to details.

MIDDLE SCHOOL EXAMPLE: Instruct cooperative trios to read a short story. After the story, they are to create a comic strip with thought and speech balloons that depict a version of the story that might take place in their town. Color and post the stories signed by each member of the group.

HIGH SCHOOL EXAMPLE: Have groups of students research a period in American history. They can select a typical or important event from that time and create a series of sketches or cartoons about their selection.

Lesson Example 2: Pictured Predictions

TARGETED INTELLIGENCE: Visual/Spatial

SUPPORTING INTELLIGENCES: Verbal/Linguistic, Intrapersonal, Interpersonal

THINKING SKILLS: Interpretation, Prediction, Analysis

SOCIAL SKILLS: Respect Others, Active Listening

CONTENT FOCUS: Reading Comprehension

MATERIALS: Worksheets, crayons or markers, pencils

TASK FOCUS: Students will develop the valuable comprehension skills of prediction by drawing conclusions.

PRODUCT: Drawing or sketch

PROBLEM: Making predictions

ACTIVITY:

1. Choose a selection to read aloud. The selection should be one that builds high anticipation of what will happen next and is very descriptive.

2. See the Prediction Worksheet on the next page for an example.

3. Read the title, show the cover, or read the first segment. Let the students make a prediction as to what the story is about by looking at a picture or the book cover.

4. As you read, students will draw a picture of the facts they hear.

5. At each step, call for a new prediction and the rationale.

6. Continue reading the story in this manner. When you are finished, the chart should show in the left-hand column the predictions, and on the right-hand side, the story in pictures.

7. Pair the students to share the right-hand side for a review of the story.

REFLECTIONS:

1. What are the important questions to think about when reading a prediction story?

2. How did the sketches help you?

3. How else might you use these techniques?

PRIMARY SCHOOL EXAMPLE: Use the story *Flat Stanley* by Jeff Brown.

1. Read the title, show the cover, and read the first page. Ask students to:

   a. Sketch how they think Stanley becomes flat.

   b. Predict what will happen next and tell why.

2. Read the next section and ask students to:

   a. Sketch the details of his adventure.

   b. Predict what will happen next and tell why.

3. Read the next section and ask students to:

a. Sketch the details of how he becomes a hero.

b. Predict what will happen next and tell why.

4. Read the next section and ask students to:

a. Sketch how he becomes a normal boy again.

b. Predict what will happen next and tell why.

Prediction Worksheet

Name:_____

Story: _____

Predictions	Facts
1.	1.

MIDDLE SCHOOL EXAMPLE: Pair students for this activity. Use the story *Heckedy Peg* by Audrey Wood. Ask students to:

1. Predict what the children are going to want from the market.

2. Draw what they want.

3. Predict what happens when the mother leaves.

4. Sketch what happens.

5. Predict what the children do when Heckedy Peg throws the pipe to the floor and shouts, "Now I've got you."

6. Sketch what happens.

7. Predict how the mother gets her children back.

8. Sketch how she gets them back.

9. Predict what they do to Heckedy Peg.

10. Sketch what happens to her in the end.

HIGH SCHOOL EXAMPLE: A variety of authors lend themselves to this activity. An excellent author to use is Edgar Allan Poe (*The Tell-Tale Heart* or *The Cask of Amontillado*). Follow middle school example.

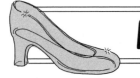

Lesson Example 3: Create-A-Creature

Biology teacher Bob Kapheim from York High School in Elmhurst, Illinois, coined this phrase for an activity he invented to teach principles of classification. The activity, borrowed from *Blueprints for Thinking in the Cooperative Classroom,* has many components that facilitate the development of visual/spatial intelligence.

TARGETED INTELLIGENCE: Visual/Spatial

SUPPORTING INTELLIGENCES: Interpersonal, Logical/Mathematical, Naturalist

THINKING SKILL: Classifying

SOCIAL SKILL: Cooperation

CONTENT FOCUS: Biology

MATERIALS: Newsprint, markers, science textbooks

TASK FOCUS: Students will classify critical attributes of insects and invent a new insect.

PRODUCT: A classification chart and a PMI chart

PROBLEM: Learning to correctly classify

ACTIVITY:

1. Distribute a die to each lab group and tell the students that these will help them in today's lesson. Show the Three-Story Intellect model and explain that students will follow through the three stages to learn about classifying in a lab called "Create-A-Creature." (See page 248 for the Three-Story Intellect model.)

2. Using lab groups of three members, assign and define the roles:
   Researcher: Finds the information in the text.
   Recorder: Charts the information.
   Illustrator: Draws, diagrams, and labels the creature with the designated attributes.

3. To gather information, distribute a copy of a blank Create-A-Creature matrix to each lab group. Using the text, have student groups complete the matrix by choosing possible variables.

	A	B	C	D	E	F
	Body Symmetry	Segmentation	Form of Locomotion	Sensory Organs	Support Structures	Body Covering
1	radial	2 body segments	fins	antennae	soft bodied	skin-hair
2	bilateral	none	none	eyes, ears, and nostrils	shell hinged	scales
3	bilateral	many segments	legs	tentacles	bony skeleton	feathers
4	radial	3 body segments	6 legs	antennae	cartilaginous skeleton	scales
5	bilateral	none	wings	compound eye	shell carried	skin-hair
6	radial	2 body segments	2 legs	eyes, ears, and nostrils	exoskeleton	scales

CREATE-A-CREATURE—CLASSIFICATION LAB

Lesson courtesy of Bob Kapheim.
IRI/SkyLight Training and Publishing, Inc.

4. Once the grids are complete, have students roll the dice. For each roll, have them circle the corresponding square in each column of the grid. For example, for the first column the toss might be 4. Students would circle the fourth item in first column (radial). For the second column, if the toss is 2, they are to circle the second item (none). Continue with the tosses until all columns have a circled item.

5. To process the information, have students predict what they might do next. Students should figure out that the next step is to synthesize the various elements by creating a creature designed by the circled items.

6. Have students follow these Create-A-Creature directions:

   a. Illustrate the new creature.

   b. Label the diagram with all the designated attributes.

   c. Name the creature appropriately.

   d. Have all group members sign the sheet.

   e. Display the creatures on the bulletin board.

7. To apply the information during the next lab period, have student groups select a creature other than their own. Using the labeled attributes on the diagram and referencing the text for the classification procedure, the lab groups should classify the creature according to formal scientific methodology. Once the creatures are classified in the appropriate manner, have the groups return the creature diagrams to the originators.

REFLECTIONS: For affective processing, use a PMI to talk about the pluses and minuses students felt about the lesson.

PMI	
What I liked [**P**luses (+)]	I liked the creativity.
What I didn't like [**M**inuses (-)]	It took a long time.
My questions or thoughts [**I**ntriguing (?)]	I wonder what my creature will look like.

PRIMARY SCHOOL EXAMPLE: Start by asking the students to think of two animals that they know well. Make a list of the combinations they provide (dog and cat, rabbit and cow). Give each pair of students a sheet of drawing paper and ask them to draw what the new animal would look like if they combined the two (an example will help). After they have drawn the animal, they can name it by combining the two original names (e.g., rabbow) and tell what sound it makes, how it moves, its color, and what it is used for. On the board put a matrix that shows the two original animals and the new animal in the left-hand column and the headings for sound, movement, color and use across the top. Fill in the matrix with one of the ideas. For older primary students, give them a matrix similar to the one on the board so they can fill in their own. After all share, provide clay and paint for them to make their own sculptures. Set up a museum in the hallway with all the new animals named.

Animals	Sound	Movement	Color	Use
Cow	moo	walks and runs	black and white patches	gives milk
+ Rabbit	+ none	+ hops, jumps, and runs	+ white	+ makes a good pet
Rabbow	moo	can jump high and run fast	black and white patches	good farm animal

MIDDLE SCHOOL EXAMPLE: Brainstorm a list of characters from current TV shows. Next, list the six most important characters in a novel just read by the class. Divide students into groups of three. Have each group add up its members' ages, divide by two or three, and round off to the nearest whole number. They will use the result to identify the two characters to be compared. The first digit will give them the character from TV; the second digit will give them the character from the novel.

For example, a group of three students adds up their ages: $12 + 12 + 13 = 37$. Then they divide by 3 to get 12.3 and round to 12. The first digit (1) refers to the number 1 person on their TV character list, and the second digit (2) refers to the second person on the novel character list.

Each group will then use a Venn diagram to identify the similarities and differences between the two characters. They are to combine the differences to create a new character who has none of the similarities. They will name the new character, draw a full-figure sketch, and include on the character at least three objects that symbolize his or her most important traits. Invite groups to post the finished sketches and to describe the character to the class.

HIGH SCHOOL EXAMPLE: Follow the instructions for "Create-A-Creature." Brainstorm with the class the seven most important characteristics that distinguish cultures and use these to label the top columns.

After the random selection of the traits by the cooperative groups, each group is to name the culture, to write a descriptive essay about the culture and to make one artifact that would be typical of the culture. Display and share the cultures.

Make Your Own

LESSON NAME: _____

TARGETED INTELLIGENCE: Visual/Spatial _____

SUPPORTING INTELLIGENCES: _____

THINKING SKILLS: _____

SOCIAL SKILLS: _____

_____

CONTENT FOCUS: _____

MATERIALS: _____

_____

TASK FOCUS: _____

_____

PRODUCT: _____

PROBLEM: _____

ACTIVITY:

_____

_____

_____

_____

_____

_____

_____

_____

REFLECTIONS:

1. _____

_____

2. _____

_____

3. _____

_____

Make Your Own

LESSON NAME: _____

TARGETED INTELLIGENCE: _____Visual/Spatial_____

SUPPORTING INTELLIGENCES: _____

THINKING SKILLS: _____

SOCIAL SKILLS: _____

_____

CONTENT FOCUS: _____

MATERIALS: _____

_____

TASK FOCUS: _____

_____

PRODUCT: _____

PROBLEM: _____

ACTIVITY:

_____

_____

_____

_____

_____

_____

_____

REFLECTIONS:

1. _____

_____

2. _____

_____

3. _____

Working in This Intelligence, I Am . . .

When I use this intelligence, I am . . .

very uncomfortable   totally at ease

When I ask students to use this intelligence, I am . . .

very uncomfortable   totally at ease

In what ways does this shoe fit me personally?

What can I do to polish this shoe for my professional use?

What am I going to do to provide for students in this intelligence?

What to continue	New things to do

Journal Page

Reflections on My Pathway to Visual/Spatial Intelligence

CHAPTER 6

Bodily/Kinesthetic Intelligence

What shoe could possibly represent the bodily/kinesthetic learner better than the athletic shoe? The wearer is a picture of grace and skill in movement, using the body to express thoughts, actions, and emotions. Those wearing the sports-minded shoe are proactive learners—the doers.

What Is It?

The bodily/kinesthetic intelligence enables us to control and interpret body motions, to manipulate physical objects, and to establish harmony between the mind and the body.

If the Shoe Fits... It Looks Like

Joan tunes in to the world through touch and movement. She enjoys sports and physical movement, has a keen sense of direction, and a sense of timing when moving her body. She is full of energy and is a proactive learner.

Wearing the Shoe in Life – Career Choices

- Actor
- Coach
- Athlete
- Inventor
- Physical Therapist
- Martial Artist
- Acrobat
- Juggler
- Dancer

"E"asing On Down the Road of the Bodily/Kinesthetic Journey

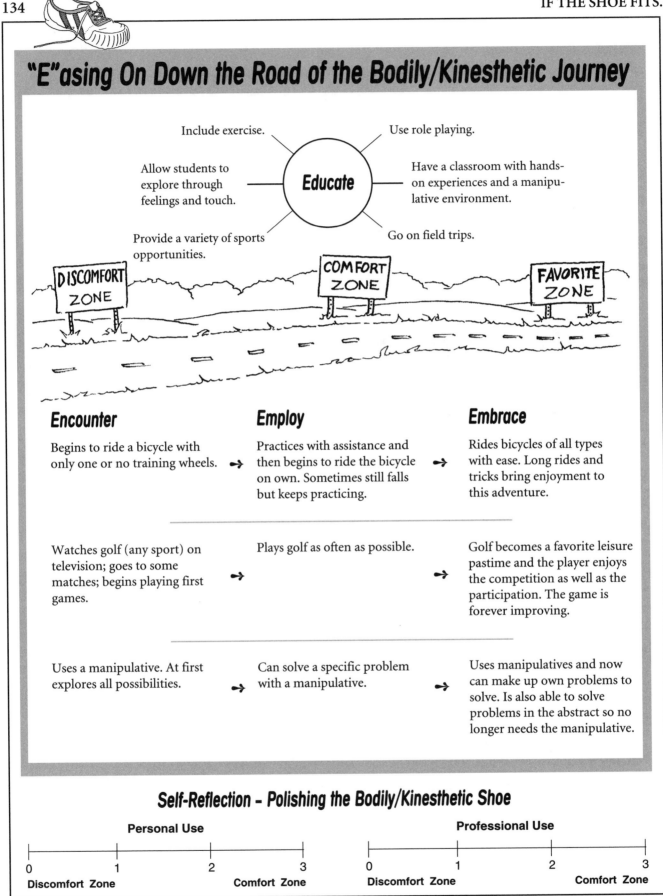

Include exercise.

Use role playing.

Educate

Allow students to explore through feelings and touch.

Have a classroom with hands-on experiences and a manipulative environment.

Provide a variety of sports opportunities.

Go on field trips.

DISCOMFORT ZONE

COMFORT ZONE

FAVORITE ZONE

Encounter

Begins to ride a bicycle with only one or no training wheels.

Employ

Practices with assistance and then begins to ride the bicycle on own. Sometimes still falls but keeps practicing.

Embrace

Rides bicycles of all types with ease. Long rides and tricks bring enjoyment to this adventure.

Watches golf (any sport) on television; goes to some matches; begins playing first games.

Plays golf as often as possible.

Golf becomes a favorite leisure pastime and the player enjoys the competition as well as the participation. The game is forever improving.

Uses a manipulative. At first explores all possibilities.

Can solve a specific problem with a manipulative.

Uses manipulatives and now can make up own problems to solve. Is also able to solve problems in the abstract so no longer needs the manipulative.

Self-Reflection – Polishing the Bodily/Kinesthetic Shoe

Personal Use

0   1   2   3

Discomfort Zone   Comfort Zone

Professional Use

0   1   2   3

Discomfort Zone   Comfort Zone

IRI/SkyLight Training and Publishing, Inc.

The athletic shoe that symbolizes this intelligence comes in a multitude of forms, each tailored to a specific sport. In today's world of aerobics, fitness, wellness, new sports and games, and the sports TV market, the athletic shoe represents the active "mind-body" connection. Individuals developing their bodily/kinesthetic intelligence have an infinite selection of shoe types. There are athletic shoes for jogging, running, walking, aerobics, tennis, paddle ball, basketball, and touch football.

When budget cuts occur, formal physical education programs go the way of music and art. Students are left without any fitness and wellness opportunities, other than what a classroom teacher might invent to fill the gaps. Even where there are physical education programs, the emphasis is often misplaced. Students may spend a large amount of the time in free play with little attention to wellness or to fitness. For wellness, a program that does not provide knowledge, skill, and attitude development in disease prevention (cancer, diabetes, stroke), personal health care (weight control through positive eating and exercise), stress management, abuse prevention (drugs, alcohol, tobacco), good nutrition, and the quality of life, is cheating children.

Fitness is an important part of wellness. By understanding how physical exercise, conditioning, and sports are connected, the student learns to take control of his or her body and to develop lifelong attitudes. When the program is presented in a fun and challenging way, students form a solid foundation for wellness attitudes in later life. In many schools, physical activity is relegated to the gym or to highly skilled competitive teams. Only the best athletes get the special treatment. However, when a school has a goal to help all children learn wellness principles and practices, it is contributing to the bodily/kinesthetic intelligence development of all. It is the role of the teacher to encourage all students to develop the attitudes and the skills for maintaining a healthy body and mind. When the school has a formal physical education program, the classroom teacher works in a supporting role. When it doesn't, it is important to integrate the wellness program across the curriculum

What Is Bodily/Kinesthetic Intelligence?

This is the intelligence that enables us to control body motions, to manipulate physical objects, and to establish harmony between the mind and the body. The Spartans of ancient Greece built their culture around the importance of the body, its looks, and its performance. In modern times, the Olympics carries on that tradition in formal competition between the best athletes of different nations.

It is a mistake, however, to think that the development of this intelligence is limited to the athletic world. Imagine a surgeon without the fine small-motor control to perform an intricate heart operation or a plane navigator who cannot fine-tune his instruments. How would you like a porch built by a carpenter who can't hit the head on a nail? Would you hire a plumber who can't straighten pipes with a wrench?

Marcel Marceau is an example of an individual with a highly developed bodily/kinesthetic intelligence. With his body, the mime can create many different personalities: the bully, the recluse, and the clown. He can suggest the mountain climber, the butterfly, waves cresting, or the concepts of good and evil or freedom and bondage with equal facility. More amazingly, he can create a number of these illusions simultaneously.

What Is the Developmental Path for This Intelligence?

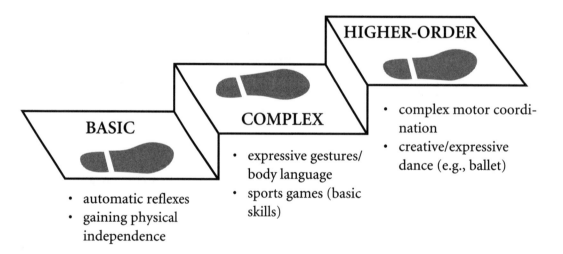

HIGHER-ORDER
- complex motor coordination
- creative/expressive dance (e.g., ballet)

COMPLEX
- expressive gestures/ body language
- sports games (basic skills)

BASIC
- automatic reflexes
- gaining physical independence

How Is This Intelligence Developed in Other Cultures?

When it comes to sports, the former East Germany and many of the Eastern European countries lead the world, often to the point of excess, in the systematic preparation of young people for international sports competition. The best young prospects in international sports such as gymnastics, ice hockey, or figure skating are taken from their families to live and train at sports schools.

Virtually every country of the world participates in international competitions. The sports selected can reflect the culture, natural environment, or geographic location. The Scandinavian countries are strong in such sports as ice hockey, cross-country skiing, and white-water kayaking. Nigeria produces great long-distance runners. China excels in gymnastics. The Alps countries of France, Switzerland, Austria, and Italy dominate downhill skiing.

The United States, by its size, diverse population, and intense interest in sports, thrives in many different international events. However, in the eyes of the world, the U.S.A. stands for excellence through professional sports. Before and after the regular seasons, U.S. football and baseball teams play exhibition games in Europe and the Far East. NBA basketball broadcasts are sold worldwide and the star players are familiar to young people of all nations.

When thinking about wellness programs, Australia and Japan stand in the forefront. Australia is recognized for its community-based health programs. Japan is the pioneer in the introduction of formal wellness programs to the workplace.

How Can This Intelligence Be Used for Problem Solving?

At first a person might think of fighting, wrestling, or war games as the problem-solving examples for this intelligence. No way! There are more sophisticated and positive examples.

☐ James was assigned to design a new office building. To get his perspective, he visited the site and walked off the area. He went back to his studio and used Lego blocks to manipulate the ways the new building would fit the site.

☐ When Susan's students have difficulty with math problem solving, she brings out manipulatives so that the students can move the objects and see themselves solving the problem. At other times she encourages her students to stand and "be" the problem. Her favorite strategy for helping students judge distance is to have the students role play being a ball thrown from point to point.

☐ Harold was institutionalized most of his adult life and declared "mentally retarded." He could not direct his own movement, actions, or speech. Doctors claimed he had learned all that he possibly could. Yet, he learned to type at a computer keyboard with someone holding his hand. He typed out things that he heard in conversations while nurses and doctors worked around him.

Who Is the Student With This Intelligence?

Joan has a highly developed bodily/kinesthetic intelligence. When a ball is thrown to her, she reacts well, judging distance and maneuvering to be at the right place at the right time.

This is a student who tunes in to the world through touch and movement. She enjoys sports and physical movement, has a keen sense of direction, and a sense of timing when moving her body. She has finely tuned small-motor skills that allow her to take small objects apart and reassemble them, weave, and sculpt. When asked to solve abstract problems, she prefers to start with manipulatives. When asked to express herself, she enjoys role playing, creative dramatics, mime, and simulations. In cooperative groups, she appreciates the freedom to stand as the group works. Unconsciously, her energy may start her leg swinging or her foot tapping. Exercise breaks, energizers, and stretches can help release her energy.

The Comfort Zone: What Helps This Student Learn?

When this student is in a classroom where she can move at will, stand and stretch when bored, and select her spot for quiet work, she is in her comfort zone. To enhance this zone, the teacher can celebrate classroom successes with hurrahs (physical energizers), provide a variety of manipulatives for mathematics, plan role plays and simulation to teach concepts, and assign appropriate roles in the cooperative groups (such as materials manager, traveler) that absorb energy.

The Discomfort Zone: What Hinders This Student?

When a learner is in the early developmental stages for this intelligence, she may be easily distracted by the movement of others in the class, bothered by others sitting too close, and sitting too long. After a physical activity, she needs extra time to settle down. As she gains control over her physical energy, long lectures where she must "sit and git," dead time in the classroom, and quiet reading time will still give her difficulty. Isolating her in a carrel or sending her to another room will only alienate her.

How Do You Catch This Student's Attention in the Classroom?

The easiest way to capture this student is to plan lessons that begin with a physical demonstration of the objective. In math, join this student with other movers and shakers (not the political kind) to be the numbers or letters. Make a human equation so they can demonstrate moving across. In reading, have her prepare a role play to introduce a story. In science, let her hold the materials needed for the lab demonstration.

These same strategies work in the middle and at the end of the lesson. In addition, try some of these ideas. Make her the "traveler" in cooperative groups so she can compare her group's answers with others. In math, she can be the materials manager who handles and moves the manipulatives, gets the supplies, and records the data for her cooperative group. In language arts, have her produce a play. In social studies, give her an observation checklist or video camera to record how her classmates are practicing their social skills or working as a team. Make her chief class encourager who leads class "hurrahs" and stretch breaks.

IRI/SkyLight Training and Publishing, Inc.

What Activities Promote Learning With This Intelligence?

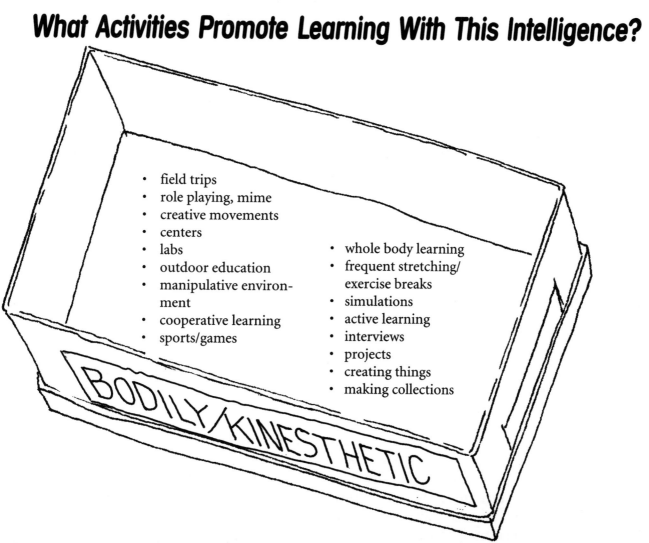

- field trips
- role playing, mime
- creative movements
- centers
- labs
- outdoor education
- manipulative environ- ment
- cooperative learning
- sports/games
- whole body learning
- frequent stretching/ exercise breaks
- simulations
- active learning
- interviews
- projects
- creating things
- making collections

How Do You Meet the Challenge of the Special Student?

Many special needs children have developed a tactile sense. Although all students learn concepts better when they can start with the concrete experience, "hands on" is a must for this special needs child.

- Practice writing and numbers in salt trays, pudding, or shaving cream.
- Learn spelling through mime and dance.
- Start mathematical concepts with work using manipulatives. Master the understanding in the manipulatives before going to the abstractions.
- Role play characters from stories, history, current events, and science.
- Set up animal care labs in the classroom.
- Do hands-on science experiments.
- Play cooperative games.
- Build objects that reflect concepts.
- Take field trips to museums for science, to famous buildings for geometry, to the zoo for biology.

How Do You Create an Environment for This Intelligence?

Rather than isolate this student for her high energy, make use of high-activity lessons throughout the curriculum.

CREATIVE DRAMATICS

These activities cause this kinesthetic learner to feel the roles, the setting, the problem, or the character. Such activity stimulates all students to put information in long-term memory. Creative drama can show a historic person, character in a story, cultural value, or walk-through of the action in a story.

Enact creative "what ifs." "Pretend you are the wind." "Pretend you are the chair." When the students are "being" the wind, the chair, or a character, they tune information more accurately through experience.

WHOLE BODY MOVEMENTS

When exercise and stretch breaks are scheduled periodically, it helps to tone down energy flow and guide the kinesthetic learner back to the curriculum. Stress breaks help to revitalize the body and prepare it for more receptive learning.

A MANIPULATIVE ENVIRONMENT

In today's classroom, teachers are using more and more manipulatives for hands-on learning. The bodily/kinesthetic learner needs to experience abstractions, feel them, move them, and manipulate them. An effective teacher gives students manipulatives to practice, learn, and discover concepts, to measure, to form patterns, and to design. The hands-on work produces better results than worksheets and lectures. When the student seems to have grasped the concept in the concrete, there is nothing wrong with moving to the abstract.

COOPERATIVE GAMES

Physical games that include developing several intelligences help the kinesthetic child bridge energy into development of the other intelligences.

Logical/Mathematical

Numbers Together Children play this game with two partners. Ask if they can make a certain number with their bodies. How they do it is up to them, just as long as all three students are a part of the numbers.

Interpersonal

This Is My Friend This game is useful for getting to know children's names and helping the children get to know one another's names. The game begins with the children sitting in a circle holding hands. One child starts the game by introducing the person on his left to the rest of the group: "This is my friend John." When he says his friend's name, he raises his friend's hand in the air and keeps it there for the rest of the game. His friend then introduces the person on his left in the same way and raises her hand. This continues until everyone has been introduced and all hands are in the air, with everyone still holding hands with the friend who introduced him and the friend he introduced.

Visual/Spatial

Paint-In This activity improves children's eye-hand coordination and vertical jumping abilities in a situation involving group cooperation. The children are divided into groups of four, preferably of varying heights. Outlines of various geometric shapes are drawn on paper and taped to a wall at a level slightly higher than the children's arms reach, making it necessary for them to jump in order to mark the drawing. The children are asked to dip their index fingers into a pot of thick paint, select a point on the outline of the drawing, jump up, and mark this point with their painted finger. By taking turns jumping and marking, the team eventually covers the entire outline of the shape. Each group works cooperatively as the children who can jump higher become responsible for marking the higher limits of the drawing, and the children who cannot jump as high fill in the sides and the base line of the figure. This paint-in approach can be modified to introduce the fundamental concepts of printing (e.g., making the circles and lines which will eventually form letters).

Health Projects

Food can awaken the creative genius in everyone. Colors and shapes may be learned through nutritious foods.

Health Projects

Art ideas
- Collage of good and bad food
- Collage of only good food
- Collage of labels from foods—good and bad
- Still-life drawing of fruit
- Still-life drawing of vegetables
- Decoration with toothpicks and vegetables
- Decoration with peanut butter, raisins, and popcorn rice cakes
- Pumpkin carving and decorating

Make posters promoting good foods and discouraging junk foods. A poster put on the soft drink machines might read as follows: "Warning: Each can contains nine teaspoons of sugar!" Other ideas for posters are: drugs, alcohol, a "Say YES" Campaign, a "Say NO" Campaign, and addiction.

Health Projects continued

Stamp Out Junk Food Campaign
- Lunch Club
- Breakfast Club
- Nutritious Snack Break
- No Vending Machines
- Nutritious Snack Birthday Parties
- Popcorn Parties
- Language Arts - Consumer Ed - Writing Projects

Write to various food manufacturers for labeling information. Set up a little intra-classroom competition. Assign groups of four. Each group writes to a food company of their choice. The address can usually be found on the label. The first letter inquires about exact ingredients. When the company responds, and the group finds extra sugars, salts, preservatives, etc., they write back to the company to inquire about the reason for the undesirable foodstuffs. Each group presses the food companies for answers. The groups have to work together to plan their own strategies. The first group to come up with an acceptable answer from their chosen food company reports to the class and wins a little prize of an apple or bag of popcorn. This can also be done on a schoolwide basis, using each classroom as a group or each grade level as a group.

Field Trips to Take
- Apple orchard
- Cider factory
- Outdoor market
- Neighbor's garden with fruit trees or vines
- Farm
- Health food store
- Pumpkin patch
- Flour mill

Music
Have student composers and lyricists work on songs about good food and perform them for other classes. Talk about the words. Have students make up a medley of junk food jingles. You can use the same tunes from popular commercials, but change the words to reveal the hidden nutritional and environmental liabilities of too much junk food.

(Health Projects activity is from *Early Stars,* by Susan Archibald Marcus and James Bellanca, p. 152–153.)

Lesson Example 1: Walk-A-Story

TARGETED INTELLIGENCE: Bodily/Kinesthetic

SUPPORTING INTELLIGENCES: Visual/Spatial, Interpersonal

THINKING SKILLS: Analysis, Decision Making

SOCIAL SKILL: Responsibility for a group role

CONTENT FOCUS: Literature (a story of choice)

MATERIALS: Large sheets of poster board, markers

TASK FOCUS: The purpose of this activity is to sequence the story by walking through and retelling it.

PRODUCT: A Big Book

PROBLEM: How to sequence a story

ACTIVITY:

1. Arrange students in groups of three
2. Assign the roles: *Materials Manager:* Gets any materials needed for group.
   Recorder: Writes down notes during brainstorming time.
   Leader: Keeps discussion productive, on task, and all members of the group involved.
3. Assign a scene to each group.
4. Have groups paint or create assigned scenes from the story on a large sheet of paper or posterboard.
5. Have each group write about the scene on its paper.
6. Put the sheets on the floor in sequence. Students walk from sheet to sheet telling the story to a partner.
7. Create an all-class "Big Book" by putting all the sheets together.
8. Check how well students carried out their roles.

REFLECTIONS:

1. What did you learn about your story sequence?
2. How did walking through the story help?
3. What did you like best about your contribution to the whole story?

PRIMARY SCHOOL EXAMPLE: Use a story that learners have heard several times so that they are familiar with the sequence. Record on a tape recorder each group's reading of its scene. When the Big Book recording is done, put it in the listening center as a read-along.

MIDDLE SCHOOL EXAMPLE: Have students construct a timeline or a sequence of events of a fictitious story or factual event. As students choose scenes to capture on their poster, let them sign up so that you will not have repeats and you will have all the important events of the story.

HIGH SCHOOL EXAMPLE: When studying a complete unit, go back over important happenings, details, and/or events. Brainstorm a list on the board with the whole class. Let each group sign up for one part of the unit. Have groups present their parts orally.

Lesson Example 2: Feelings in My World

TARGETED INTELLIGENCE: Bodily/Kinesthetic

SUPPORTING INTELLIGENCES: Visual/Spatial, Verbal/Linguistic, Intrapersonal, Naturalist

THINKING SKILLS: Analysis, Interpretation, Body Interpretation, Awareness of Feelings

SOCIAL SKILLS: Self-Reflection, Following Directions

CONTENT FOCUS: Science

MATERIALS: Paper, markers

TASK FOCUS: This activity builds the realization of the connection between the parts of the body that we associate with the things we do, people around us, and the world in which we live.

PRODUCT: Completed self-drawings

PROBLEM: How to understand the connection of self to others

ACTIVITY:

1. Everyone needs paper and markers.
2. Each person will draw themselves in the middle of the paper. They may use a stick figure.
3. As you call out a word, have students write the word around the figure.
4. Ask students to draw a line from each word to the part of the body where they associate feelings about this word.
5. Examples of words to use are: school, home, children, pets, Saturday, vacation, hobby, loved one, role model, car, shopping, ferris wheel ride, past, present, future, decision, and friends.

REFLECTIONS:

1. What was the association you liked best?
2. What did you discover about yourself with these associations?

PRIMARY SCHOOL EXAMPLE: Have students lie on newsprint and trace their bodies.

MIDDLE SCHOOL EXAMPLE: Make this a physical activity without a sketch. Use groups and let one student in each group be the subject.

HIGH SCHOOL EXAMPLE: Use a character from history or literature. Have a visually talented student sketch the character.

Lesson Example 3: Act the Word

TARGETED INTELLIGENCE: Bodily/Kinesthetic

SUPPORTING INTELLIGENCES: Verbal/Linguistic, Intrapersonal, Interpersonal

THINKING SKILL: Synthesis

SOCIAL SKILLS: Accountability, Communication

CONTENT FOCUS: Vocabulary

MATERIALS: Words whose meaning can be acted out. (See the next page for a list of sample words.)

TASK FOCUS: This activity allows teachers to review vocabulary words by using body motions and movements while saying the word and the meaning.

PRODUCT: Definitions of new words

PROBLEM: To learn vocabulary words through movement

ACTIVITY:

1. Assign cooperative groups of three.
2. Assign the roles.

   Actors: Each member of the group.

   Coach: Makes sure that all group members know the words.

   Director: Distributes the words and decides the order of the words to be introduced.

3. Begin the activity by having the director distribute the words.
4. Each member learns the words assigned and decides on the best action to teach the word to the group.
5. Each team member teaches his or her words. As a word is taught all members should do the motion while saying the word and the meaning over and over.
6. The coach has each member review all of the words for a final check.
7. Have the class stand in a circle. The teacher calls out a word and the students do the learned action while saying the word and the meaning.

REFLECTIONS:

1. Which words did you learn most easily?
2. How did this strategy help you learn the words?
3. How else might you use this strategy?

PRIMARY SCHOOL EXAMPLE: Allow students to practice acting out a series of grade-appropriate vocabulary words. Invite another class to view the performance. After each word is performed, allow student guests from the other class to tell what word was demonstrated.

MIDDLE SCHOOL EXAMPLE: Extend this type of activity to incorporate other areas of study. In a charades-like game, have students act out scenes, topics, or characters from their history books or literature classes with the rest of the students guessing what action they are performing. For example, students can act out the signing of the Declaration of Independence, the Boston Tea Party, or Paul Revere's historic ride.

HIGH SCHOOL EXAMPLE: Ask students to use their own creativity to apply this technique of acting out vocabulary words, scenes from literature, and topics from history to science and math. Can they work in groups to explain the laws of physics, math theorems, or chemical reactions? Set aside class time for students to pick a subject for the rest of the class by "performing." Make sure students explain their performances and discuss how actions helped to make concepts clearer to them.

Sample Bodily/Kinesthetic Vocabulary Words To Act Out

Word	Definition
asthenia	loss of strength; bodily weakness
descry	to discover or spy with the eye
desist	to cease; stop
detonate	to explode with a loud noise
gambol	to skip about joyfully; frolic
ichthyology	the study of fishes
imperious	domineering; overbearing
jollify	to make or be jolly
magnanimous	great minded; generous
mollify	to soothe, calm
obviate	to meet and dispose of; to remove
oppugn	oppose, as by argument; attack or resist
pule	whine, whimper
rallentando	slowing down gradually
salvo	round of applause
tweedle	to produce tunes
vermiculate	to mark with wavy lines
vociferous	noisy; loud
vulpine	foxy; cunning; like a fox
yammer	shout, yell; talk persistently

Lesson Example 4: Kapheim's Musical Molecules

TARGETED INTELLIGENCE: Bodily/Kinesthetic

SUPPORTING INTELLIGENCES: Musical/Rhythmic, Logical/Mathematical, Naturalist

THINKING SKILL: Comparison

SOCIAL SKILL: Collaborative movement

CONTENT FOCUS: What is a molecule?

MATERIALS: Three musical tapes with different tempos

TASK FOCUS: Students will be asked to move to music.

PRODUCT: Test/quiz of words

PROBLEM: To learn definitions through movement

ACTIVITY:

1. Tell students what a molecule is and what happens in its different forms (solid, liquid, gas).

2. To help them remember, assemble the entire class in a circle with tightly locked arms. Instruct them to move together as you play a slow, heavy dirge. Ask them to identify the molecular state (solid).

3. Have the groups spread out. Let them hold hands at arm's length. Play a waltz and invite them to swing and sway. Identify the state (liquid).

4. Have each person stand alone. Play a rock song. Tell them to dance freely. Identify the state (gas).

5. When all of the students sit down, check for the definitions.

REFLECTIONS:

1. Explain each of the terms danced.

2. How did movement help you to learn and remember the terms?

PRIMARY SCHOOL EXAMPLE: There are many word groups a primary teacher can put to music. For instance, pair long vowel words against short vowel words. Invite students to move accordingly (long steps vs. hops).

MIDDLE SCHOOL EXAMPLE: In beginning study of a new language, use music and movement to teach accentuation.

HIGH SCHOOL EXAMPLE: In chemistry class, have students study molecular structure by "acting out" a molecule. For example, assign two students to be hydrogen and one to be oxygen to form a water molecule (H_2O).

Make Your Own

LESSON NAME: _____

TARGETED INTELLIGENCE: _Bodily/Kinesthetic_____

SUPPORTING INTELLIGENCES: _____

THINKING SKILLS: _____

SOCIAL SKILLS: _____

_____

CONTENT FOCUS: _____

MATERIALS: _____

_____

TASK FOCUS: _____

_____

PRODUCT: _____

PROBLEM: _____

_____

ACTIVITY:

_____

_____

_____

_____

_____

_____

_____

_____

REFLECTIONS:

1. _____

_____

2. _____

_____

3. _____

_____

Make Your Own

LESSON NAME: _____

TARGETED INTELLIGENCE: Bodily/Kinesthetic _____

SUPPORTING INTELLIGENCES: _____

THINKING SKILLS: _____

SOCIAL SKILLS: _____

_____

CONTENT FOCUS: _____

MATERIALS: _____

_____

TASK FOCUS: _____

_____

PRODUCT: _____

PROBLEM: _____

ACTIVITY:

_____

_____

_____

_____

_____

_____

_____

_____

REFLECTIONS:

1. _____

_____

2. _____

_____

3. _____

_____

Working in This Intelligence, I Am . . .

When I use this intelligence, I am . . .

very uncomfortable   totally at ease

When I ask students to use this intelligence, I am . . .

very uncomfortable   totally at ease

In what ways does this shoe fit me personally?

What can I do to polish this shoe for my professional use?

What am I going to do to provide for students in this intelligence?

What to continue	New things to do

IRI/SkyLight Training and Publishing, Inc.

Journal Page

Reflections on My Pathway to Bodily/Kinesthetic Intelligence

_____

_____

_____

_____

_____

_____

_____

_____

_____

_____

_____

_____

_____

_____

_____

_____

_____

_____

_____

_____

_____

_____

_____

_____

_____

_____

_____

_____

_____

_____

_____

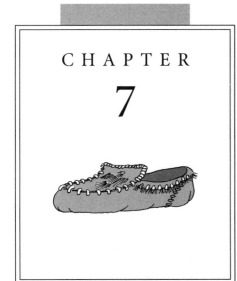

CHAPTER 7

Naturalist Intelligence

The moccasin represents the Native American working the raw land and setting up one's environment for living.

What Is It?

The naturalist intelligence is the ability to use the sensory input from nature to survive; to get the most from one's environment. This involves surviving, adapting, using, and labeling one's world of nature. This is man's scientific world of nature.

If the Shoe Fits... It Looks Like

Miles, our science wizard, enjoys the study of nature. He is in tune with little things such as bugs, and is concerned about his environment. Miles adapts well in his environment and is intrigued by nature.

Wearing the Shoe in Life – Career Choices

- Botanist
- Veterinarian
- Hiker

- Scientist
- Oceanographer
- Geologist

- Gardener
- Park Ranger
- Zookeeper

"E"asing On Down the Road of the Naturalist Journey

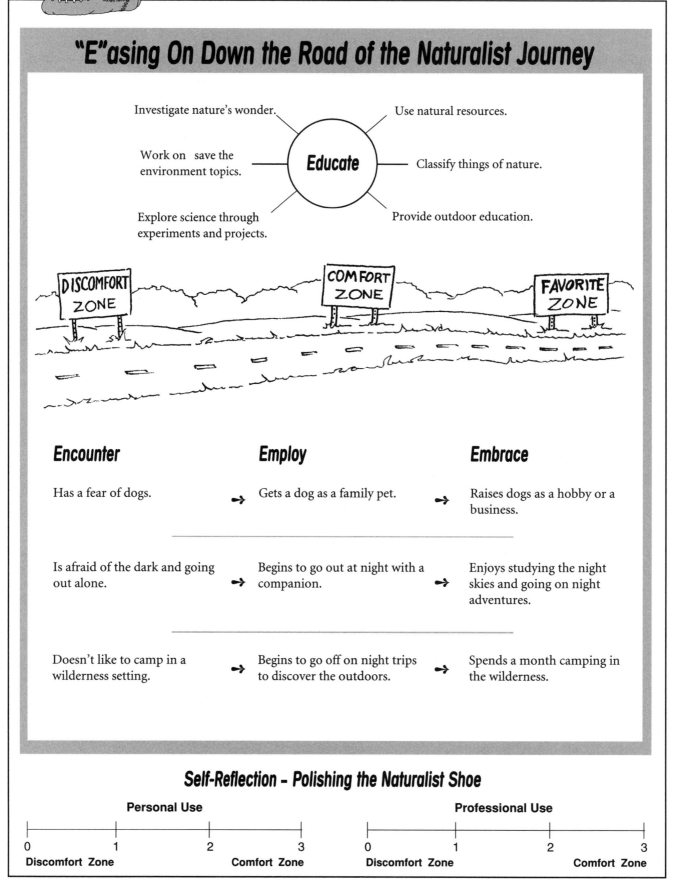

Investigate nature's wonder.

Use natural resources.

Work on save the environment topics.

Educate

Classify things of nature.

Explore science through experiments and projects.

Provide outdoor education.

DISCOMFORT ZONE

COMFORT ZONE

FAVORITE ZONE

Encounter

Has a fear of dogs.

Is afraid of the dark and going out alone.

Doesn't like to camp in a wilderness setting.

Employ

Gets a dog as a family pet.

Begins to go out at night with a companion.

Begins to go off on night trips to discover the outdoors.

Embrace

Raises dogs as a hobby or a business.

Enjoys studying the night skies and going on night adventures.

Spends a month camping in the wilderness.

Self-Reflection – Polishing the Naturalist Shoe

Personal Use

```
0        1        2        3
Discomfort Zone          Comfort Zone
```

Professional Use

```
0        1        2        3
Discomfort Zone          Comfort Zone
```

In the summer of 1995, Gardner introduced to the public the naturalist as a new intelligence. He defined the naturalist as one's ability to adapt and survive in one's environment—the relationship of man and nature. This also includes one's intuitive sense for adapting and surviving as one makes decisions.

The Native American moccasin is the shoe chosen to represent this intelligence. This is the author's tribute to the tribes coming to a new land and making a home for their families. As they adapted to the land, they made good use of their surroundings to provide the basic needs of life—food, clothing, and shelter. By the establishment of the tribes, rituals, and laws, theirs was a feeling of belonging and ownership.

Some well known examples of people whom have made specific contributions to our society because of their strength of this intelligence are Charles Darwin, Jacques Costeau, John Glenn. Very recently, Captain Scott O'Grady was able to survive in Bosnia off the greenery and the bugs of the land before his rescue. When asked how he survived under such terrible circumstances, he said it was by trial and error. He also stated that he had learned something about it in school, but he really learned survival in that environment through the experience.

In schools our science, geography, environmental studies, and social studies curriculum are some of the places where we, as educators, are preparing students to adapt to tomorrow's world, as well as get along in today's world.

What Is Naturalist Intelligence?

This is the intelligence that enables us to use the information we gather through our senses. It is most useful in our natural environment. It helps us become comfortable in nature. It enhances our ability to survive in our world by being better able to discriminate and recognize differences among nature's offerings.

What Is the Developmental Path for This Intelligence?

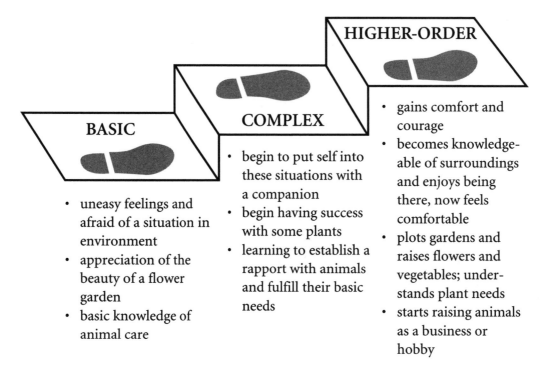

BASIC
- uneasy feelings and afraid of a situation in environment
- appreciation of the beauty of a flower garden
- basic knowledge of animal care

COMPLEX
- begin to put self into these situations with a companion
- begin having success with some plants
- learning to establish a rapport with animals and fulfill their basic needs

HIGHER-ORDER
- gains comfort and courage
- becomes knowledge-able of surroundings and enjoys being there, now feels comfortable
- plots gardens and raises flowers and vegetables; under-stands plant needs
- starts raising animals as a business or hobby

How Is This Intelligence Developed in Other Cultures?

There are Polynesian islanders who move in boats from island to island by knowing and understanding the ocean currents. They pass this knowledge down from generation to generation.

Native Americans took this strange land and survived by pulling together as a tribe to establish shelter and provide food and clothing to the tribal members.

There are sections of the world that have certain animals in the wild that man has to learn to live with. For example, Australians must coexist with kangaroos and their habits; the people in Alaska need a true understanding of their bear neighbors to successfully share the environment.

How Can This Intelligence Be Used for Problem Solving?

In the world of nature, there are many, many opportunities to use problem-solving techniques.

☐ Matthew has always enjoyed the outdoor life of camping and hiking in the wilderness. He maps out his adventures as often as possible. Sometimes when traveling on a new path he uses his intuitive sense to decide which way to go. He says to himself, "This feels right."

☐ When Rosa is highly emotional about a situation or a problem, by holding, stroking, and caressing her cat, Tiger, she can seem to think more clearly and tackle the problem. She takes care of Tiger and is responsible for his survival and understands his needs well. He provides a calming, stress-relieving outlet through the touch and feel of the body warmth and fur.

☐ In biology lab when experimental studies are assigned, Lee is the person the students in the class want for their lab partner. He understands and enjoys the problems and questions of science. By observing nature, Lee learns answers to apply elsewhere in his studies.

Who Is the Student With This Intelligence?

John has a highly developed naturalist intelligence. He enjoys being outdoors and relating to nature. Taking care of his environment is a high priority. Whether sailing, fishing, or walking in the woods, or hiking in the mountains, he explores his natural surroundings and feels at home.

This is a student who is an explorer, experimenter, and wonderer. He loves an adventure. Because of his understanding and enjoyment of nature, a variety of factual science and social studies information gives him quality enjoyment time. Also he relates well to animals and likes the responsibility of taking care of raising a pet.

The Comfort Zone: What Helps This Student Learn?

This student enjoys using his naturalist intelligence and is comfortable around things of nature. His favorite shoes could be hiking boots for enjoying the outdoor life. He has a highly developed curiosity and an inquiring mind. Animals are a source of comfort to this person.

With the highly developed curiosity also comes a strong intuitive sense "to know something is about to happen." This type of student often feels he should take a particular path, or senses that something is right or wrong.

This is the student who often carries a frog or rock in his pocket, would pick up a snake, or lead a nature hike. When this student goes on a trip to the beach, he will bring things back to the classroom—like plants, flowers, live animals, shells.

Science is a favorite subject. Usually this student would learn more if he could sit by a window or go to the outdoor classroom very often. Units of study, videos, nature books, and books about animals, explorers and travelers, plants, living things, the body and how it works, life of different times and different places excite this learner. This is the "back-to-nature" learner.

Environmental concerns, such as saving the rain forest, animal extinction, and pollution are areas that interest this inquisitive, exploring mind.

The Discomfort Zone: What Hinders This Student?

This is about survival and fitting in one's environment. If students do not feel they belong and are accepted, they will not do well in this learning setting. Each person learns differently. A brain is as unique as a fingerprint, so by planning curriculum around the different intelligences there will be areas of discomfort as well as comfort. Remember, everyone's ways of learning are forever changing. So, if people are challenged, they learn. Because some hours of the school day may be boring or frustrating to the learner their learning is hindered.

How Do You Catch This Student's Attention in the Classroom?

Students with a strong naturalist intelligence must have their physical needs met in order for academic learning to take place. For example, a naturalist student learns best when comfortable in the surrounding environment.

Asking students how they learn best, what they like and dislike, and their interests helps to design curriculum to meet individual needs.

Many students enjoy hands-on experiences with nature, such as going outdoors for lessons, walks, and experiences. Field trips appeal to our naturalist intelligence because we go out and see, explore, and discover our living world.

Living with and observing classroom animals and participating in the care of these animals add to the understanding of living things. Watch which students the animals gravitate toward and enjoy being with the most.

Science experiments and projects catch everyone's attention as they explore the world of nature and living things. Stepping through the scientific process teaches a procedure road map for thinking.

This intelligence deals with five ways to understand, relate to and survive in one's environment. The first way to catch the student's attention is to create a comfortable and nonthreatening environment. This is where one can take risks, have successes, make mistakes, be accepted by others, and feel a part of the working classroom team.

A second way is to create the outdoor classroom to study living and nonliving things in the environment. To feel and touch nature is learning to relate and live with it. Nature trails, field trips, outdoor gardens, and labeling of nature all make the outdoors a learning place.

Third, bring the outdoors inside the classroom. This can be done by housing and studying classroom pets, making and caring for terrariums and aquariums. You can begin by experimenting, sorting, classifying, and studying collections of nature items such as leaves, rocks, shells, etc.

You can bring in nature tapes, CDs, videos, and factual books and reference books to research the things around us.

Fourth, use computer programs with the multimedia to make nature come alive. They can make factual information more interesting and exciting.

A fifth way to catch attention is to create times for science experiments that explore, discover, and explain the problem solving of the wonderments of nature.

What Activities Promote Learning With This Intelligence?

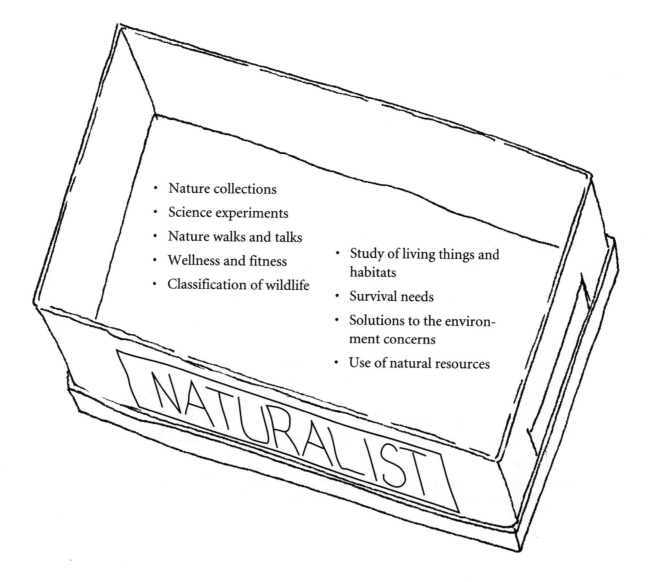

- Nature collections
- Science experiments
- Nature walks and talks
- Wellness and fitness
- Classification of wildlife

- Study of living things and habitats
- Survival needs
- Solutions to the environment concerns
- Use of natural resources

How Do You Meet the Challenge of the Special Student?

First of all, consider the individual differences in the world of survival in a classroom. These physical needs, when met, provide a more open door for learning. The student strong in the visual/spatial intelligence may be happier doodling during a read-aloud to help comprehension. A person can doodle by drawing pictures of what the teacher is reading. Other times, they might draw a picture of something else that relates to the subject. Are they conceptualizing or day-dreaming? To discover this, ask a specific question from the information you are reading. If the student can answer the question correctly, then the doodling is assisting in the comprehension of the material.

Students' bodily gestures, such as a nervous twitch, sometimes get in the teacher's way, and one has a tendency to tell the student to stop. A wiggling leg or hair-twirling are two examples often seen in classrooms. Watch when this is happening. Students often do this unconsciously when they are concentrating. If another student is not being disturbed by this, let it continue as a natural outlet.

Classroom animals enjoy being cuddled by students. Many times a child with a behavioral problem can calm down and change to appropriate behavior by rubbing, loving, and taking care of an animal. It has a rewarding, calming effect.

Sometimes changing one's environment helps to recharge the mind. Outdoor experiences that teach stimulate a learner's interest.

The special needs students often do not fit into the school environment—either socially, physically, or academically. Through the naturalist intelligence, one learns survival and adaptation skills to meet their needs.

- Discuss with the student the location for the most appropriate comfort to work, get along socially, and work most effectively in the classroom. For example, where do they need to sit to do their best work?
- Give students responsibility so they know they have a part in the everyday running of the classroom. Examples would be to feed the class animal, check on their safety, water the class plants, or chart class plant's growth and upkeep needs.
- Praise when doing right. Establish rules and be consistent with their follow through.
- Find out what their likes and dislikes are.
- Make science, geography, and other environmental studies come alive with hands-on, pro-active learning.
- Provide assignments of project-based learning for studies of interests and long-term research to be done.

How Do You Create an Environment for This Intelligence?

Much of the science curriculum of today's classroom teaches to this intelligence. Also every country, culture, period of history studied in social studies teaches how our civilization has evolved and explores human existence and how humans make the most of their environment. Human survival through history and adaptability to environments of different cultures have a major influence on our lives today.

The settings of a story explain the environments of the story. The feeling one gets that "they are there" when reading a story is part of exploring one's naturalist intelligence.

You can provide nature studies through a variety of ways.

FIELD DAYS

When studying about a certain topic, going to the actual place gives the experience of being there and living it.

OUTDOOR TRAILS

Labeling and cutting paths is an effective project for a school to undertake. This provides a place that is easily accessible for students to further understand and identify with their environments. The outdoor classroom gives an exciting new type of learning experience.

OUTDOOR GARDENS

Whether flowers or vegetables are grown in these beauty spots, they provide an opportunity to see and study plant life.

CLASSROOM PETS

The type of classroom pet needs to be chosen with care. The students need to take on the responsibility of caring for the animal as much as possible for a true learning experience to happen. Some suggestions for classroom pets are birds, gerbils, or fish. Those that could be caught and become temporary pets that later go back to nature are turtles, snakes, ants, lizards, tadpoles, toads or frogs, and spiders. All sizes of aquariums, jar terrariums and cages are excellent houses for these class pets. Plotting data in daily logs or on charts teaches and shows information that challenges and excites students about learning.

CLASSROOM SURVIVAL

Establishing classroom rules and being consistent helps students know the expectations of the teacher. This is a huge part of adjusting to the classroom environment. There are students who really struggle with following the rules of the classrooms. There are others who follow the rules to the letter.

GETTING ALONG WITH OTHERS

Feeling a part of an environment and being accepted into the group is important for an effective learning environment.

RESOURCES

Factual materials available for study such as computer programs, factual books about nature, famous explorers, and different lands and culture studies are very valuable.

Lesson Example 1: Chambers of the Heart

TARGETED INTELLIGENCE: Naturalist

SUPPORTING INTELLIGENCES: Bodily/Kinesthetic, Visual/Spatial

THINKING SKILLS: Analysis, Sequencing

SOCIAL SKILLS: Following Directions

CONTENT FOCUS: Way the blood flows through the four chambers of the heart

MATERIALS: Large piece of paper

TASK FOCUS: This movement activity teaches an important concept during a unit on the human circulatory system. After learning how blood flows through the heart, students are able to draw a diagram using the information.

PRODUCT: Bodily sequenced motions; diagram of the four chambers and the blood flowing through

ACTIVITY 1:

1. Demonstration by the teacher.
   a. Say Right Atrium—Make an A with your right hand in the air.
   b. Say Right Ventricle—Make a V with your right hand down at waist.
   c. Say Flow to Lungs—Cross arms over chest.
   d. Say Left Atrium—Make an ^ with your left hand in the air.
   e. Say Left Ventricle—Make a V with your left hand down at waist.
   f. Say Out—Take hands and point to both sides outwardly.
   g. Practice several times as a group.

ACTIVITY 2:

1. When the class understands the bodily motions, have them draw a diagram of the way the blood flows through the heart.
2. Color code with a color assigned to each chamber.

REFLECTIONS:

1. Discuss drawings with a partner for review and more practice.
2. Which way will you best remember this data and the bodily motions or the drawing? Why?

PRIMARY SCHOOL EXAMPLE: Go on the school blacktop and fix the diagram. Have a blue and red ball for students to toss as the path blood flows through the heart.

MIDDLE SCHOOL EXAMPLE: Have students put the bodily activity to a beat. Have them create a song, poem, jingle, or rap that teaches the sequence.

HIGH SCHOOL EXAMPLE: Have a study of different diseases of the heart. Draw pictures of different problems and write how they affect the flow of blood through the heart.

Lesson Example 2: The Amazing Brain

TARGETED INTELLIGENCE: Naturalist

SUPPORTING INTELLIGENCES: Bodily/Kinesthetic, Visual/Spatial

THINKING SKILLS: Sorting, Classifying, Analysis

SOCIAL SKILLS: Respect for Others, Sharing Materials

CONTENT FOCUS: Using colors to see diversity among people

MATERIALS: Eight colors of thin wire

TASK FOCUS: Students will make a model of their brain to show they have all eight intelligences, and that they are smart in different ways.

PRODUCT: A model of a brain

PROBLEM: How I learn the best and what my areas of weaknesses and strengths are. Shows "how one is smart."

ACTIVITY:
1. Each person decides on the areas of strength and weaknesses of the eight intelligences.
2. Assign an intelligence to each color of wire. Cut wire of different lengths—represent strong areas with long pieces, weak areas with short pieces.
3. Each person selects their eight pieces of wire according to their brain makeup.
4. Take the wire and make a round ball of wire intertwining the wire to show how their brain is connected.
5. Display the "brains" to celebrate differences.

REFLECTIONS:
1. Discuss with a partner what this shows about each other. How does this affect actions, decisions, and life itself?
2. How and why were the different lengths of wire selected?

PRIMARY SCHOOL EXAMPLE: Make a huge model of a brain of a teacher or famous storybook character. Discuss the different kinds of smarts, varying the length of the wire.

MIDDLE SCHOOL EXAMPLE: Students make journal entries about their own brain models and what they tell about:
1. the way they learn and solve problems
2. the choices they make in after-school activities and time

HIGH SCHOOL EXAMPLE: Think about the future career choices one has by studying strengths of the brain.

Lesson Example 3: Puzzle Pieces

TARGETED INTELLIGENCE: Naturalist

SUPPORTING INTELLIGENCES: Visual/Spatial, Verbal/Linguistic, and Intrapersonal

THINKING SKILLS: Analysis, Evaluation

SOCIAL SKILLS: Understanding Self

CONTENT FOCUS: Psychology

MATERIALS: Writing implement and paper

TASK FOCUS: The activity shows the learner's brain as they learn and use intelligences in daily life. It shows that a brain is unique and everyone has three to four areas of strength.

PRODUCT: A picture of each learner's brain drawn by the learner.

PROBLEM: It is not how smart we are; but how we are smart. Find three or four areas of strengths and weaknesses at this time of life.

ACTIVITY:
1. Draw the shape of a head on the piece of paper.
2. As each intelligence is defined, draw the puzzle piece that represents the use of this intelligence.
3. When complete, reflect on what this reveals about the learner.
4. Share some reflections with a partner, then with the class.

REFLECTIONS:
1. How does this show a picture of me in my day-to-day life?
2. How do I use these intelligences in my daily life?
3. What are my areas of strengths? How do I use them?
4. Ask if others see you the same way.

PRIMARY SCHOOL EXAMPLE: By taking surveys, students let educators know how they think best and what their preferences are for learning. Tom Armstrong called these "the eight kinds of smart." They are art smart, people smart, music smart, self smart, math smart, sports smart, nature smart, and word smart. Take a survey among students to find which of these each student has.

MIDDLE SCHOOL EXAMPLE: Students can sculpt a brain out of plaster of paris or clay.

HIGH SCHOOL EXAMPLE: After the brain puzzle is drawn, relate information about talents to help choose career focus options. With a partner, draw each other's brain and compare. Learners get a good view of how someone else perceives them.

Make Your Own

LESSON NAME: _____

TARGETED INTELLIGENCE: Naturalist _____

SUPPORTING INTELLIGENCES: _____

THINKING SKILLS: _____

SOCIAL SKILLS: _____

_____

CONTENT FOCUS: _____

MATERIALS: _____

_____

TASK FOCUS: _____

_____

PRODUCT: _____

PROBLEM: _____

ACTIVITY:

_____

_____

_____

_____

_____

_____

_____

_____

REFLECTIONS:

1. _____

_____

2. _____

_____

3. _____

_____

Make Your Own

LESSON NAME: _____

TARGETED INTELLIGENCE: _Naturalist_____

SUPPORTING INTELLIGENCES: _____

THINKING SKILLS: _____

SOCIAL SKILLS: _____

_____

CONTENT FOCUS: _____

MATERIALS: _____

_____

TASK FOCUS: _____

_____

PRODUCT: _____

PROBLEM: _____

ACTIVITY:

_____

_____

_____

_____

_____

_____

_____

_____

REFLECTIONS:

1. _____

_____

2. _____

_____

3. _____

_____

Working in This Intelligence, I Am . . .

When I use this intelligence, I am . . .

|——|

very uncomfortable   totally at ease

When I ask students to use this intelligence, I am . . .

|——|

very uncomfortable   totally at ease

In what ways does this shoe fit me personally?

What can I do to polish this shoe for my professional use?

What am I going to do to provide for students in this intelligence?

What to continue	New things to do

Journal Page

Reflections on My Pathway to Naturalist Intelligence

_____
_____
_____
_____
_____
_____
_____
_____
_____
_____
_____
_____
_____
_____
_____
_____
_____
_____
_____
_____
_____
_____
_____
_____
_____
_____
_____
_____
_____
_____

Intrapersonal Intelligence

The warm, comfortable bedroom slipper represents one's reflective time to learn about oneself in a quiet, cozy peaceful spot of one's own choosing. One who wears this shoe well enjoys time alone and feels peace to identify goals, strengths, and areas to improve.

What Is It?

Intrapersonal intelligence is the ability to form an accurate model of oneself, and to use that model to operate effectively in life. It is the ability to know oneself and assume responsibility for one's life and learning.

If the Shoe Fits... It Looks Like

Rose, our thinker, enjoys her own world of daydreams and yet astounds us with her insight and interpretation. She needs time to reflect, think, and complete self-assessments that help her take control and be responsible for herself. She feels confident about herself.

Wearing the Shoe in Life – Career Choices

- Explorer
- Researcher
- Author

- Psychologist
- Philosopher
- Theologian

- Inventor
- Computer Expert
- Elite Athlete

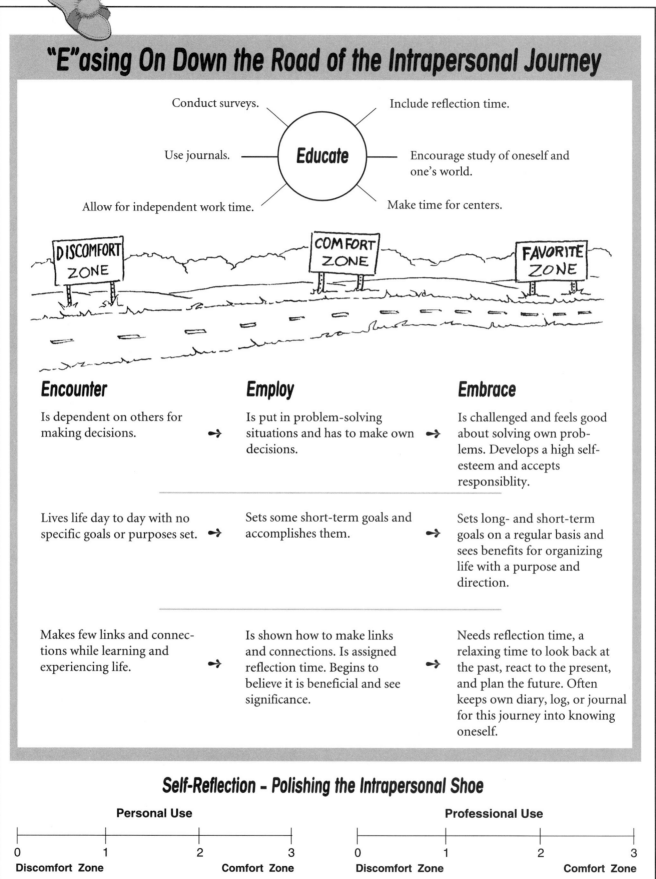

"E"asing On Down the Road of the Intrapersonal Journey

Conduct surveys.   Include reflection time.

Use journals. — **Educate**

Encourage study of oneself and one's world.

Allow for independent work time.   Make time for centers.

DISCOMFORT ZONE   COMFORT ZONE   FAVORITE ZONE

Encounter

Is dependent on others for making decisions.

Lives life day to day with no specific goals or purposes set.

Makes few links and connections while learning and experiencing life.

Employ

Is put in problem-solving situations and has to make own decisions.

Sets some short-term goals and accomplishes them.

Is shown how to make links and connections. Is assigned reflection time. Begins to believe it is beneficial and see significance.

Embrace

Is challenged and feels good about solving own problems. Develops a high self-esteem and accepts responsiblity.

Sets long- and short-term goals on a regular basis and sees benefits for organizing life with a purpose and direction.

Needs reflection time, a relaxing time to look back at the past, react to the present, and plan the future. Often keeps own diary, log, or journal for this journey into knowing oneself.

Self-Reflection - Polishing the Intrapersonal Shoe

Personal Use

0   1   2   3
Discomfort Zone   Comfort Zone

Professional Use

0   1   2   3
Discomfort Zone   Comfort Zone

IRI/SkyLight Training and Publishing, Inc.

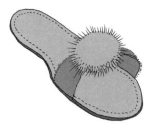

From the time the ancient Greek philosopher, Aristotle, wrote "Know thyself" to the day Biff Loman said about his father, Willy, in *Death of a Salesman*, "The man didn't know himself," there has been a growing understanding of the intrapersonal intelligence. Today, everyone from Olympic hopefuls to medical doctors learns to harness the power of the mind and find the pathway to peak performance.

Being able to reflect and understand oneself comes with the time to find a quiet, cozy spot while wearing the shoe symbol for this intelligence, the warm, comfortable bedroom slipper. This shoe fits the intrapersonal intelligence because it represents the human need to feel a part of our family, our society, our culture, and our world. We like to feel needed, loved, and included. Through quiet reflection, we learn to examine what we are doing to belong and to contribute to the human condition.

It is the classroom teacher's role to make a time and safe place for each child to reflect and analyze his or her learning goals, strengths, areas needing improvement, place in the classroom society, achievements, and reaction patterns. Because the intrapersonal intelligence is the most private, the teacher must strive to create a risk-free environment that encourages the students' reflections but does not invade their privacy.

What Is Intrapersonal Intelligence?

This is the intelligence that enables learners to take greater responsibility for their lives and learning. Too few students, Gardner suggests, know that they can take responsibility for their learning, especially when they find themselves in schools that base recognition on external motivation.

This intelligence requires that students have the time to think, reflect, and complete self-assessments that will help them take control and be responsible for their learning choices. It is the responsible student who is most able to access full intellectual potential.

What Is the Developmental Path for This Intelligence?

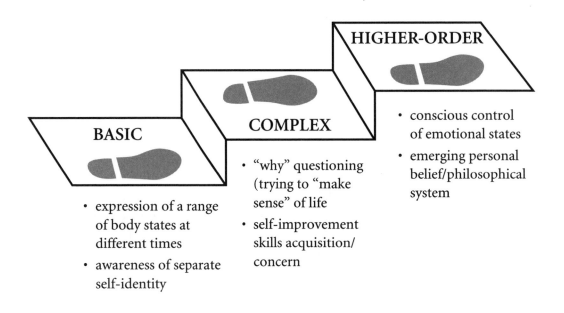

HIGHER-ORDER

- conscious control of emotional states
- emerging personal belief/philosophical system

COMPLEX

- "why" questioning (trying to "make sense" of life
- self-improvement skills acquisition/ concern

BASIC

- expression of a range of body states at different times
- awareness of separate self-identity

How Is This Intelligence Developed in Other Cultures?

Although many eastern cultures value the development of the inner self, it is in China where one can most easily notice the emphasis on intrapersonal development in the schools. In the classroom, there is considerable attention given to developing mental concentration and using that concentration in all areas of study including the arts, sciences, and physical development.

In New Zealand, pioneering work in whole language instruction has filtered through the schools. The New Zealand schools lead the world in the institution of the intrapersonal approach to reading. Reflective journals, metacognition, integrated thinking skills, and process writing are integral parts of their approach.

Reflecting somewhat the influence of trends in the business world, some American classrooms make use of goal-setting strategies and formal instruction in problem-solving and thinking skills. The goal-setting strategies help the student plan areas of academic improvement, assess progress, and revise the plan. The problem-solving approach, designed to raise student performance, and the thinking skills curriculum, designed to better prepare students for the world outside of school, have linked many American schools to the development of metacognition not only in reading, but in all subject areas.

How Can This Intelligence Be Used for Problem Solving?

Persons strong in this intelligence have little difficulty with reflective problem solving. They may make snap judgments in emergencies, but given time, they will make solid decisions.

☐ Kim hated thunderstorms. When she moved from Seattle to the Midwest, it wasn't long before summer storms caused her to shake with fear. For several days she thought about this challenge. Every time she thought of a new solution, she wrote it in her notebook. She weighed the consequences carefully before deciding to keep a set of earplugs in her desk.

☐ Each morning before he started his daily jog, Brian pulled out his journal. He reviewed his times from the previous day and wrote his daily goal.

☐ Allison was having a difficult time with her math. At her counselor's suggestion, she started a record of her mistakes. Each week she charted the common errors. After three weeks, she was ready to discuss the chart with her math teacher.

Who Is the Student With This Intelligence?

Our intrapersonally intelligent child is Rose, who seldom participates in class discussions or social activities. She seems to live in her own world of daydreams and yet astounds us with her insight and interpretation.

The student with a strong intrapersonal intelligence knows herself, recognizes her own strengths and limits, and holds high expectations to improve and challenge herself. Her lifestyle is often described as balanced as she pays close attention to her physical, psychological, and academic well-being. Because she is goal centered and a reflective problem solver, she sees herself as productive and in control of her learning and life. When faced with contradictory information or inadequate facts, she perseveres in getting the information she needs to complete a task. She is confident that her successes are a direct result of her efforts, planning, and persistence.

The Comfort Zone: What Helps This Student Learn?

This student thrives in a classroom where self-determination is encouraged. This classroom would provide many choices in what, when, where, and how to learn. Exploratory center time is well balanced with individual reading time, the opportunity to work in cooperative groups, time for personal reflection, and the chance to plan and chart individual learning tasks. The teacher is perceived as a helper, guide, and support person who makes time for private conversations with students. Each student in this classroom has an individual learning plan framed by personalized goals for the development of a targeted intelligence. The students record and track their own work in double-entry journals where they write their own thoughts and read the teacher's replies. Any student in this classroom has ample time to work alone, reflect alone, or be alone.

The Discomfort Zone: What Hinders This Student?

Standardized tests, direct instruction, lock-step textbook coverage, daily schedules, harsh punishments of other students, sweeping rules, and teacher-directed activities with no reasons why, make this student very uncomfortable.

How Do You Catch This Student's Attention in the Classroom?

This student responds to questions that allow wait-time for serious reflection. The teacher asks the question and then gives the class three to ten seconds to think about an answer. The teacher doesn't answer her own questions or ask questions that need only a one-word answer. Instead, the questions sound like, "How would you feel if. . . ?" or "What would you do in a similar situation?"

What Activities Promote Learning With This Intelligence?

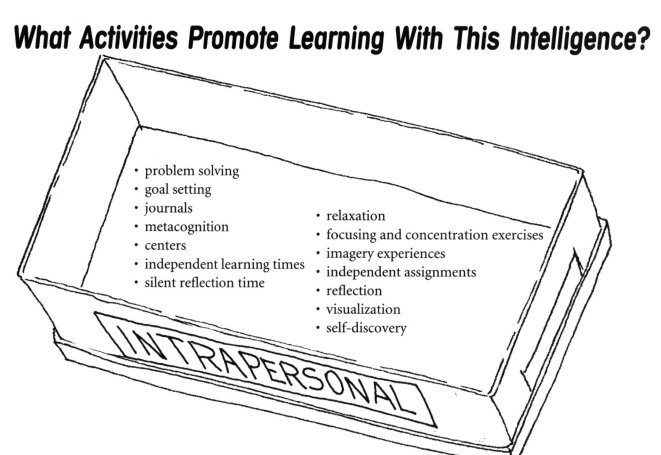

- problem solving
- goal setting
- journals
- metacognition
- centers
- independent learning times
- silent reflection time

- relaxation
- focusing and concentration exercises
- imagery experiences
- independent assignments
- reflection
- visualization
- self-discovery

INTRAPERSONAL

IRI/SkyLight Training and Publishing, Inc.

By individualizing assignments, the teacher can structure reflective questions before, during, and after the task for journal entry. For instance, an algebra assignment might sound like this: "We have just completed a study of unit three. Each of you may select five problems from the end of the chapter. Before you start to work, I want you to review your journal entry from yesterday. Review your goals for doing math homework. After you finish the problems, write a paragraph evaluating your work in light of your goals."

Give many free time opportunities for journal reflection. Provide such lead-ins as, "What am I learning?" "How does this apply to me?" "How can I use this?" "How will this affect me?" "What are my hopes for the future?"

Encourage goal setting. At the start of the school year, teach the A-B-C method. "What is my goal? Is it Achievable? Is it Believable? Am I Capable of reaching this goal?" Add more questions as the year progresses. Have the students start and end each week with new goals and assessment entries in their journals.

How Do You Meet the Challenge of the Special Student?

When special needs children are isolated from their peers, labeled, and made the brunt of jokes, their hurt feelings are no less real. Having the chance to understand their feelings is very important for all children.

- Help students organize a journal. Give a daily "lead-in" and encourage pictures as well as words (see p. 159-162).
- Do goal-setting activities with the students. Pick a weekly social, personal, or academic goal and encourage the students to pick a solution.
- Teach personal problem solving. Give the students "real-world" problems and show them alternative solutions.
- Have students identify their strengths.
- Use sequence charts to help students plan step-by-step solutions to a real-life problem.

How Do You Create an Environment for This Intelligence?

Start with the physical layout of the classroom. Set up a quiet corner in the classroom. Each quiet corner should have a comfortable chair and/or pillows and a carrel. Separate it by a screen from the activity of the classroom. Stock it with reading and writing materials. Post a simple set of guidelines calling for quiet. (This space can also serve as your reading center.) Other posters might show the goal procedure or advocate peak performance ("Be all you can be," "Excellence is a state of mind," "We are great and getting greater").

Surveys

Early in the school year, provide interest surveys, such as the samples provided on the next few pages. These will help you coach development of the intrapersonal intelligence with goal setting and reflection. They also make good starters for journal entries.

Sample Survey: Interests

NAME_____ DATE_____

1. I like to read _____ .
2. I watch television approximately _____ hours per day.
3. My favorite type of TV show is _____ .
4. My two most favorite shows are _____
   and _____ .
5. My favorite type of music is_____ .
6. I listen to music while I_____ .
7. My favorite singer or group is _____ .
8. I study best when _____ .
9. My favorite study spot is _____ .
10. I like to visit _____ .
11. My idol/hero is _____because _____ .
12. In the future I would like to _____ .

Sample Survey: School Interests

1. Learning is fun and interesting to me when _____ .
2. The one thing I do the best at school is _____ .
3. Give traits or characteristics of the best teacher: _____ .
4. My favorite subject is _____ .
5. My hardest subject is _____ .
6. The subject I like the least is _____ .
7. I can learn the most when _____ .
8. One thing that really bothers me about school is _____ .
9. I would like to learn more about _____ .
10. My favorite place/spot at school is _____
    because _____ .
11. I like people who _____ .
12. Ten years from now I want to be _____ .

Sample Survey: Looking At Feelings About School

1. Today I feel _____ .
2. Most of the time I feel _____ .
3. School makes me feel _____ .
4. Cooperative group time makes me feel_____ .
5. Center/lab time makes me feel _____ .
6. Test time makes me feel_____ .
7. Most teachers make me feel _____ .
8. Reading makes me feel_____ .
9. Writing makes me feel _____ .
10. As I group up I feel _____ .
11. My classmates/peers make me feel _____ .
12. _____ makes me feel _____ .

Sample Survey: Use of Multiple Intelligences

1. A sport I can play is _____ .
2. When my favorite music plays I _____ .
3. I doodle. Yes ___ No ___

   When (if yes)? _____ .

   What do you draw (if yes)? _____ .
4. When I picture "red," I see _____ .
5. When I give instructions for someone to get to someplace, I _____ .
6. In my spare time, I like to _____ .
7. I like to be alone when _____ .
8. I keep a journal or diary even when not assigned at school.   Yes_____ No_____
9. I learn best by _____ .
10. When I have a decision to make or a problem to solve I _____ .
11. I have a habit of _____ .

Journals (as presented in Fogarty & Bellanca, 1989)

A journal is much like a footprint. Both are uniquely personal impressions that mark one moment in time. Although the footprint may disappear with the wind, the journal cements the thought-filled page for all time.

By planning for youngsters to process their thinking in written form, teachers ultimately have at their disposal a versatile and valuable teaching tool.

Taking advantage of the teachable moment, students process reflectively by logging their thinking. They catch the freshness of first impressions; jot down the milieu of ideas swarming in their heads; explore for understanding; analyze for clarity; synthesize into personal meaning; apply functionally; judge worth; and make the critical connections between new data and past experience.

Writing in the journal may take many forms. It may be a narrative, a quote, an essay, jottings, a drawing, a cartoon, a diagram, webs or clusters, a soliloquy, a riddle, a joke, doodles, an opinion, a rebuttal, a dialogue, a letter, a flow chart, or just an assortment of phrases and ideas.

The entries may be reflective, evaluative, questioning, personal, abstract, introspective, cynical, incomplete, revealing, humorous, communicative, thoughtful, poetic, rambling, formative, philosophical, or none of the above. There are no right or wrong ways to do the journal. It's just a journal of one's thinking—whatever that thinking may be. It's a personal record of the connections being made within the framework of the student's cognitive capacities and experiences.

A TIME TO THINK

The few minutes immediately following a lesson are ideal for using the journal. This transitional time allows flexibility for the "fast finishers" and for the students who need another minute or two to complete the task.

The journal may be used solely in one subject area or as a focused follow-up at randomly selected spots during the lessons presented throughout the day. It can be structured formally with designated sections for information or it can be informally structured through student preference and use.

LEAD-INS FOR JOURNALS

Journal "lead-ins" can "lead" students to higher-level thinking processes and provide the needed versatility to develop alternative patterns for thinking. The lead-in dictates to some degree the mode of thought. For example, lead-ins can encourage responses that are analytical, synthetic, or evaluative. They also can be used to promote problem solving and decision making, or to foster a particular intelligence. The chart on the opposite page suggests some possibilities to illustrate the focus flexibility of lead-ins.

As students grapple with new material and struggle with fleeting, disconnected thoughts, the journal impacts in yet another way. The students begin to become aware of the thought process itself. Again, the sensitive teacher captures the moment by prodding the youngsters to think about their thinking in deliberate and intentional metacognitive discussions. Students start to see that they do have patterns for thinking as they find the words to articulate their thought processes, labels that identify strategies like reasoning by analogy, classification, logical thought, and intuitive leaps. They begin to choose *how* they want to process new ideas. They

Lead-Ins That Promote Development of the Multiple Intelligences

Verbal/Linguistic
A quote that fits is
I discovered
I want to ask about
Another way of saying this is

Musical/Rhythmic
It sounds as if
If I were a song, I would
A dance that reminds me of

Logical/Mathematical
Compared to
The best part
A logical sequence is
By contrast

Visual/Spatial
Imagine
My picture of this idea
I see
I wonder
My point of view is

Bodily/Kinesthetic
I feel
I sense
If I were a ____ muscle, I would

Naturalist
I need
I feel I belong when
To survive, I
(I, he, she, it) lives

Intrapersonal
I do my best when
My goal this week is
I prefer ____ because
My major concern with____ is

Interpersonal
What we did well was
What we want to accomplish is
I contributed by

begin to build a repertoire of thinking patterns as they express their ideas in writing. They "begin inking their thinking."

The journal also becomes an indicator for instructional assessment as teachers note the inner language of the thinking mind. The students are deliberately and consciously given the most precious commodity of modern man—*time!* They are given time to think, to wrestle with new ideas, to absorb strange bits of information, and to attempt to fit the pieces into the tapestry of personal experiences.

The journal, then, is a pathway to higher thought. It is a place to store, track, and review their most important ideas. It is a chance to develop their ability to put thoughts to words without interference, pressure, or influence from any voices but the voices in their heads.

Journals are not diaries. A diary, which will appeal strongly to the intrapersonal student, is very private. Students may want to keep a diary for their own personal use. Encourage them to use the diary if they want, but its entries are not for your eyes. Journal entries, however, are part of your approach to encouraging development of this intelligence. Advise students that you will collect the journals, read them, and provide commentary. You may even want to set up the journal for double entry. On the back side of each page, the student will make entries; you will make your comments on the opposite front side.

For ease in working with journals, invite students to follow these guidelines:
- Write only one entry per page. Take your time and try to use the whole page.
- Multiple-page entries are O.K.
- Use pencil. Erase as much as you like.
- Sign and date each entry.

Self-Assessment Organizers

Students can use the PMI (de Bono, 1992) to self-evaluate their goals. After thinking about a possible goal for the week, the student can use the PMI chart to evaluate each one: What are the Pluses of each idea? What are the Minuses? What are the Interesting questions about each idea?

The student can also use the PMI as a journal reflection guide: "What were the Pluses of my school week? What were the Minuses? What were the Interesting points?" The teacher may assign each student to complete a PMI when handing in a major assignment or evaluating a portfolio.

PMI

P (+)	I completed all of my homework assignments this week.
M (-)	I did not start my research paper yet and it is due very soon.
I (?)	I discovered an interesting source to include in my research paper.

Another reflective organizer is de Bono's OPV (Other Point of View). After the student sets a goal, she can evaluate it with an OPV. For this chart, she selects two to five names of persons whose point of view will be different from her own, but whose point of view she wants to consider. She may respond as she thinks those persons would to her goal, or she can interview each and make the entry.

SAMPLE OPV

My goal: _____ *is to make the varsity basketball team* _____ .

My point of view: _____ *it is the most important thing to me* _____ .

Other points of view:

Mom _____ *Great, but make sure your grades don't suffer* _____ .

Dad _____ *Practice very hard; Maybe you can get a scholarship* _____ .

Rev. Jones _____ *Wonderful, but make sure you find time for other things* _____ .

Mary, my older sister _____ *Good luck! It's really tough!* _____ .

Suzanne, my best friend _____ *That's nice, but I hope you still have time for fun* _____ .

Structured Activities

STRENGTH BOMBARDMENT

At the beginning of the school year, tell the class that for each birthday (don't forget the summer birthdays) each child will receive a special gift from the class. On each birthday, end the day with a strength bombardment. With the birthday child sitting in the middle of the room, have the other children write down one positive thing they see in the birthday child. Use small index cards. Give each child a piece of masking tape. All the children go up and attach the cards to the birthday child's arms and shoulders. As each attaches the word, they speak it softly to the birthday child. After all cards are attached, the class applauds or sings to the birthday child. The birthday child takes the cards home to save.

ME COLLAGE

Students create collages with magazine pictures. The collage will show their positive characteristics. Post the collages. (For a variation, have cooperative groups brainstorm a list of the positive characteristics of each member and then build a "We Collage.")

GALLERY WALK

Ask students to bring in series of photographs of themselves. They should start with a baby picture. On poster board, have each student make a timeline with the pictures. If a picture is missing from some important event, have the student sketch it in. The timelines should remain anonymous. When all are ready, post the timelines with a blank piece of paper under each one. Let students gallery walk and guess to whom the timeline belongs by writing the individual's name below it.

HERITAGE BOOK

Ask each student to work with his or her family to make a small book that celebrates the family heritage. They can include photos, artifacts, or magazine pictures. Invite the parents to a display day as students share their heritage with the class.

CULTURE POSTER

This is a good follow-up to the heritage book. After all the students have shared heritages, the next task is to make a poster for all the different cultures in the classroom. The poster can show the culture's uniqueness, its contributions to the arts and/or modern society, its outstanding personages, its customs, etc.

CULTURE DAY

Each culture represented in the classroom will have a special day. Students from each culture will work as a team. They may recruit family and friends to help plan a day for the class to celebrate. The group must decide what the celebration will be and then prepare it so that all students in the class are involved. At the end of the celebration, hold a circle discussion with all the students to determine what they learned about the culture.

ANIMAL ANALOGIES

For journal entries, use the forced relationship technique. Invite each student to think of an animal. List the names on the board. Discuss what positive characteristics they associate with several of the animals.

Have each student pick a name from the list and complete this sentence in the journal: "I am most like_____because I _____ _____." (You may vary this by picking famous people, physical objects, etc.)

GRAPHIC ORGANIZERS

The web, thought tree, KWL (Donna Ogle), sequence chart, and concept map are graphic organizers students can use for reflection.

- *The web* "My strengths." Use the web to generate personal positive points.
- *The thought tree* At the top, put a desired attribute. Put the student's name at the bottom. Construct the tree.
- *KWL* What do I Know about (subject)? What do I Want to know? What do I want to Learn about this subject?
- *Sequence chart* Sequence biographical high points.
- *Concept map* Make an autobiographical concept map.

Lesson Example 1: Me T-Shirt

TARGETED INTELLIGENCE: Intrapersonal

SUPPORTING INTELLIGENCES: Visual/Spatial, Verbal/Linguistic, Naturalist

THINKING SKILL: Inventing

SOCIAL SKILL: Giving and getting positive feedback

CONTENT FOCUS: Self-awareness

MATERIALS: Large piece of newsprint, markers or crayons

TASK FOCUS: Each student will design a T-shirt reflecting his or her likes, favorite book characters, goals, or strengths.

PRODUCT: T-shirt

PROBLEM: How to accept positive feedback

ACTIVITY:

1. Have each student cut or tear the shape of a large T-shirt out of newsprint.
2. Give the following directions:
   a. Put your name in the center of the T-shirt in graffiti style.
   b. On one sleeve, draw two things you like to do in your spare time. (If they wish, students may label them.)
   c. On the other sleeve, draw ways that you learn the best.
   d. In one of the bottom corners, draw what or who you want to be ten years from now.
   e. In the bottom of the other corner, draw and write about a goal you set for yourself next year.
   f. Under your name, write an adjective that describes the way you want others to describe you.
   g. Include a symbol of your favorite character from a book.
   h. Design the rest of your T-shirt with your favorite sketches, doodles, and colors. NOTE: Exercise may end here.
   i. Take a long rectangular piece of newsprint and tape it above the T-shirt for the head and neck. Don't cut it out.
   j. During the next three minutes, go around the room and ask others to give you a word that describes you. Write them around your head. Only positive words!
   k. When a friend gives you a word, you give him or her a word in return.
   l. Display the T-shirts.

REFLECTIONS: Make a journal entry about how you felt when friends gave you those positive words.

PRIMARY SCHOOL EXAMPLE: You may do the activity as described or as a student-of-the-day activity. When the student is the star for a day, the total class gives information to the star and he or she decorates the shirt. The questions that are asked by the teacher are answered and illustrated by the star.

MIDDLE SCHOOL EXAMPLE: Do the activity as described. Establish the rule that students must give the positive word quickly, sincerely, and with a smile.

HIGH SCHOOL EXAMPLE: Use a 5 x 7 index card instead of a T-shirt. Put names in the middle and a question response in each corner. Have a silent milling so students can read each other's cards before doing a journal entry.

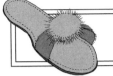

Lesson Example 2: If the Shoe Fits

TARGETED INTELLIGENCE: Intrapersonal

SUPPORTING INTELLIGENCES: Visual/Spatial, Verbal/Linguistic, Naturalist

THINKING SKILLS: Interpretation, Analysis of Data

SOCIAL SKILL: Self-awareness

CONTENT FOCUS: The multiple intelligences

MATERIALS: Worksheet, pen or marker, overhead projector

TASK FOCUS: This is a concrete way to help learners assess their intelligences and discover how they are unique and intelligent in different ways.

PRODUCT: Completed survey

PROBLEM: How to identify strong intelligences

ACTIVITY:

1. Each participant has a worksheet.
2. Tell the definition and a story of each of the intelligences.
3. As you discuss the intelligence and draw your own "shoes" on the overhead, invite students to draw the shoes that fit.
4. At the end, all eight intelligences will be drawn and represented on the graphic.
5. Discuss with the class how every brain is unique. The shoe is a mental image of each intelligence. Everyone has all eight of Gardner's intelligences. The shoes change in size by the growth of learning. Each shoe represents an interpretation of our learning capacity.
6. Invite students to double check their shoe selections with the quizzes provided. After the quiz, label the intelligence that fits.

REFLECTIONS: In the journal, write your response to one or more of these lead-ins:

The "shoe" that I like best is _____ because_____.

The "shoe" I would most like to fit better is _____ because_____.

PRIMARY SCHOOL EXAMPLE: Ask students these simple questions to help them identify their strongest intelligences. They can respond by raising their hands.

1. Do you love to dance? .... (Musical/Rhythmic)
2. Do you like to write? .... (Verbal/Linguistic)
3. Do you love to play sports? .... (Bodily/Kinesthetic)
4. Do you like to work in a group? .... (Interpersonal)
5. Do you love to work with computers and calculators?....................................(Logical/Mathematical)

6. Do you enjoy nature walks? .... (Naturalist)

7. Do you keep a diary or write in a journal? .... (Intrapersonal)

8. Do you know the words to a lot of songs? .... (Musical/Rhythmic)

9. Do you like to imagine things and play pretend games? .... (Visual/Spatial)

10. Do you like to draw and color? ....(Visual/Spatial)

11. Do you like puzzles, problems, and brainteasers? .... (Logical/Mathematical)

12. Do you like to work by yourself? .... (Intrapersonal)

13. Do you like to read? .... (Verbal/Linguistic)

MIDDLE SCHOOL AND HIGH SCHOOL EXAMPLE: Ask the students to answer "yes" to the following questions that describe them best. (The questions are modified slightly for older students.)

1. Do you like to dance? .... (Bodily/Kinesthetic and Musical/Rhythmic)

2. Do you enjoy writing? .... (Verbal/Linguistic)

3. Do you excel at sports? .... (Bodily/Kinesthetic)

4. Do you prefer to work in a group? .... (Interpersonal)

5. Do you love to work with computers and calculators? .... (Logical/Mathematical)

6. Do you enjoy nature walks? .... (Naturalist)

7. Do you keep a diary or personal journal? .... (Intrapersonal)

8. Do you know the words to a lot of songs? .... (Musical/Rhythmic)

9. Do you like to solve logic problems and puzzles? .... (Logical/Mathematical)

10. Do you enjoy drawing or photography? .... (Visual/Spatial)

11. Do you like to study while listening to music? .... (Musical/Rhythmic)

12. Do you prefer to work on your own? .... (Intrapersonal)

13. Do you enjoy reading for pleasure? .... (Verbal/Linguistic)

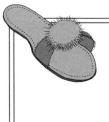

Lesson Example 3:
Portrait of ...as a Young...

TARGETED INTELLIGENCE: Intrapersonal

SUPPORTING INTELLIGENCE: Verbal/Linguistic, Naturalist

THINKING SKILL: Inventing

SOCIAL SKILL: Reflection

CONTENT FOCUS: Autobiography

MATERIALS: Paper. (For the primary and middle grades, use cardstock for binding the books.)

TASK FOCUS: After studying autobiographies, each student will write an autobiography using the portrait metaphor (from James Joyce's *A Portrait of the Artist as a Young Man*).

PRODUCT: Autobiographical sketch

PROBLEM: How to write an autobiography

ACTIVITY:

1. After reading an autobiography and discussing how autobiographies are written, assign each student to write an autobiography of one incident in his or her life.

2. Coach students through the process with a prewriting activity such as a web or concept map, the writing phase, and the final editing.

3. Display the completed works or have a "read-a-thon." After each reads someone else's autobiography, students can add positive comments on a comment sheet.

REFLECTIONS: Before the student turns in the final work, request written responses to these questions:

1. What did you do well in this assignment?

2. If you did the same assignment again, what would you do differently?

3. What would you like the teacher to comment on?

PRIMARY SCHOOL EXAMPLE: Have students do the personal timeline activity first. After that, they can draw pictures and invent words to describe each major event from the timeline. Name and bind each book.

MIDDLE SCHOOL EXAMPLE: Brainstorm with the class the types of events that can be included in an autobiography. Invite the students to plan the event descriptions carefully. Follow concept maps with a sequence chart before they begin writing.

HIGH SCHOOL EXAMPLE: Study Joyce's book, *A Portrait of the Artist as a Young Man*. Contrast that book with another autobiography. Encourage each student to select the "voice" they want to use in writing their autobiographical event. After the events are done, form cooperative groups to edit the works and to use a Venn diagram to contrast their works to Joyce's book.

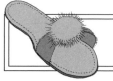

Lesson Example 4: My Strengths

TARGETED INTELLIGENCE: Intrapersonal

SUPPORTING INTELLIGENCE: Interpersonal, Naturalist

THINKING SKILL: Attributing

SOCIAL SKILL: Cooperation

CONTENT FOCUS: Strengths

MATERIALS: Newsprint, markers, tape

TASK FOCUS: Students will generate lists of their personal strengths.

PRODUCT: Strength web

PROBLEM: How to identify personal strengths

ACTIVITY:

1. Ask students to make a private list of their qualities or characteristics that are considered good points or strengths. Give a few examples of your own as a model.

2. Discuss with students why different players on a football team play different positions. Highlight how physical characteristics such as size or speed help identify a particular player's strengths or special characteristics that make the player good or strong at a position. Ask the students to think of examples of athletes with special strengths that make them good at special positions on the team.

3. Have each student web his or her list of strengths. Begin with the positive characteristics that the student generated in the beginning of this activity.

4. Instruct the students to take their webs to at least ten other people in the room. Each person selected by the student will add one new characteristic that is a noticeable strength. When a student writes a strength on another's web, the "peer" should sign his or her initials. You can participate too.

5. Instruct the students to take the webs to other teachers, parents, friends, employers, etc., and have more characteristics added. If someone cannot come up with a new strength for the list, he or she may sign a strength already on the web.

REFLECTIONS: Post the completed webs with each student's name. Ask the class to discuss:

1. What was easy about getting the strengths from others?

2. What was difficult about the task?

3. What did you learn about your own confidence to take risks?

PRIMARY SCHOOL EXAMPLE: Ask each student to pick a "best characteristic" and tell why it was picked.

MIDDLE SCHOOL EXAMPLE: Have students do a second round of the webmaking. What are the differences?

HIGH SCHOOL EXAMPLE: Select a character from a book or a historic incident. Have pairs generate webs on the character and then make a Venn diagram comparing themselves to the character.

Make Your Own

LESSON NAME: _____

TARGETED INTELLIGENCE: Intrapersonal _____

SUPPORTING INTELLIGENCES: _____

THINKING SKILLS: _____

SOCIAL SKILLS: _____

_____

CONTENT FOCUS: _____

MATERIALS: _____

_____

TASK FOCUS: _____

_____

PRODUCT: _____

PROBLEM: _____

ACTIVITY:

_____

_____

_____

_____

_____

_____

_____

REFLECTIONS:

1. _____

_____

2. _____

_____

3. _____

_____

Make Your Own

LESSON NAME: _____

TARGETED INTELLIGENCE: _Intrapersonal_____

SUPPORTING INTELLIGENCES: _____

THINKING SKILLS: _____

SOCIAL SKILLS: _____

_____

CONTENT FOCUS: _____

MATERIALS: _____

_____

TASK FOCUS: _____

_____

PRODUCT: _____

PROBLEM: _____

ACTIVITY:

_____

_____

_____

_____

_____

_____

_____

_____

REFLECTIONS:

1. _____

_____

2. _____

_____

3. _____

_____

Working in This Intelligence, I Am . . .

When I use this intelligence, I am . . .

|——|

very uncomfortable   totally at ease

When I ask students to use this intelligence, I am . . .

|——|

very uncomfortable   totally at ease

In what ways does this shoe fit me personally?

What can I do to polish this shoe for my professional use?

What am I going to do to provide for students in this intelligence?

What to continue	New things to do

IRI/SkyLight Training and Publishing, Inc.

Journal Page

Reflections on My Pathway to Intrapersonal Intelligence

_____
_____
_____
_____
_____
_____
_____
_____
_____
_____
_____
_____
_____
_____
_____
_____
_____
_____
_____
_____
_____
_____
_____
_____
_____
_____
_____

Interpersonal Intelligence

The football cleats were chosen to represent the teaming of the interpersonal intelligence. Each member must do his or her part to make the team plays. Movements must be synchronized with the movement of every other player on the team. Working for and with others is one of the goals.

What Is It?

The interpersonal intelligence is the ability to get along with, interact with, work with, and motivate others toward a common goal. It involves the capacity to understand and interpret others' moods, temperaments, motivations, and intentions.

If the Shoe Fits... It Looks Like

Dave has a highly developed interpersonal intelligence, loving his fellow students and appreciating their diversities. He likes to study people in other cultures as well as their history and art. This social person is dependent for success on others and is a team player.

Wearing the Shoe in Life – Career Choices

• Counselor	• Religious Leader	• Political Leader
• Doctor	• Teacher	• Nurse
• Pyschiatrist	• Salesperson	• Social Worker

"E"asing On Down the Road of the Interpersonal Journey

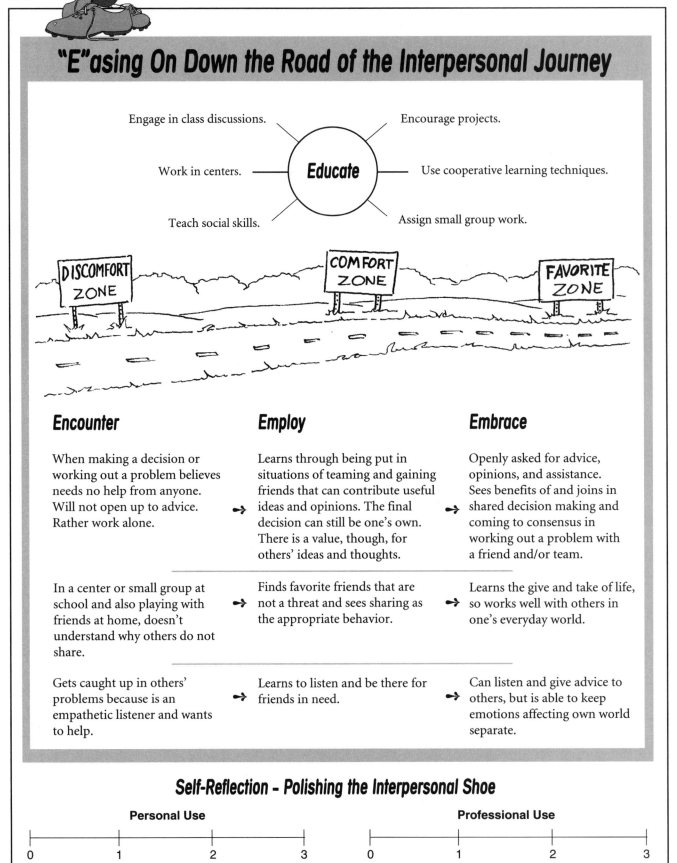

Engage in class discussions.   Encourage projects.

Work in centers. ——— **Educate** ——— Use cooperative learning techniques.

Teach social skills.   Assign small group work.

DISCOMFORT ZONE   COMFORT ZONE   FAVORITE ZONE

Encounter

When making a decision or working out a problem believes needs no help from anyone. Will not open up to advice. Rather work alone.

In a center or small group at school and also playing with friends at home, doesn't understand why others do not share.

Gets caught up in others' problems because is an empathetic listener and wants to help.

Employ

Learns through being put in situations of teaming and gaining friends that can contribute useful ideas and opinions. The final decision can still be one's own. There is a value, though, for others' ideas and thoughts.

Finds favorite friends that are not a threat and sees sharing as the appropriate behavior.

Learns to listen and be there for friends in need.

Embrace

Openly asked for advice, opinions, and assistance. Sees benefits of and joins in shared decision making and coming to consensus in working out a problem with a friend and/or team.

Learns the give and take of life, so works well with others in one's everyday world.

Can listen and give advice to others, but is able to keep emotions affecting own world separate.

Self-Reflection – Polishing the Interpersonal Shoe

Personal Use

0 — 1 — 2 — 3
Discomfort Zone   Comfort Zone

Professional Use

0 — 1 — 2 — 3
Discomfort Zone   Comfort Zone

IRI/SkyLight Training and Publishing, Inc.

What do a basketball player, a corporate executive, a lieutenant commander, and Ph.D. candidate in physics have in common? First, each has highly developed, gifted intelligences: bodily/kinesthetic and logical/mathematical. Second, each works with individuals whose talent, knowledge, skill, or experience in the same field are less developed. Third, each is dependent for success on the other people with whom he or she works. Fourth, each has a highly developed, perhaps gifted interpersonal intelligence. Through the talent, skill, and experience with these intelligences, these individuals are able to motivate teamwork that makes the sum of all their energies more successful than any one person, including themselves, could accomplish alone. Without his teammates' special talents, the basketball player cannot function. Without her workforce ready to follow, the executive has no increase in production. Without each private and sergeant carrying out his role, the commander cannot win the battle. Without her younger graduate student colleagues, the Ph.D. candidate has no thesis and no degree. In their highly complex worlds, each demonstrates that no one person on the team is sufficient because each and every one is necessary, including at least one person with a highly developed interpersonal intelligence.

Football cleats were chosen to fit the interpersonal intelligence. This intelligence involves the ability to get along with, interact with, work with, and motivate others toward a common goal; it evokes an image of a championship football team. On the team, each player is responsible for each movement he makes on each play. Every movement must be synchronized with the movement of every other player on the team. When the touchdown is scored, one player captures the roar of the crowd and celebrates with a victory dance. But that player knows that the glory was not his alone.

What Is Interpersonal Intelligence?

This intelligence is the capacity to understand and interact with other people with a win-win result. It involves verbal and nonverbal communication skills, collaborative skills, conflict management, consensus-building skills, and the abilities to trust, respect, lead, and motivate others to the achievement of a common beneficial goal. Empathy for the feelings, fears, anticipations, and beliefs of others, the willingness to listen without judgment, and the desire to help others raise their level of performance to the highest level are all critical traits of this intelligence.

What Is the Developmental Path for This Intelligence?

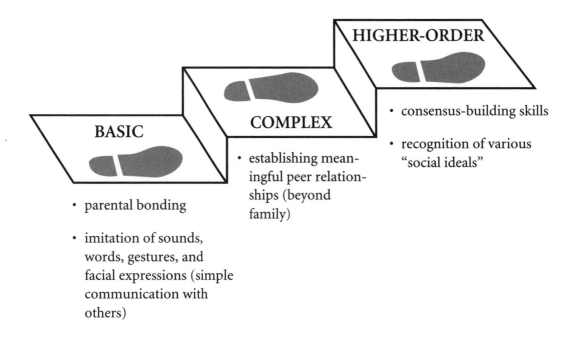

BASIC
- parental bonding
- imitation of sounds, words, gestures, and facial expressions (simple communication with others)

COMPLEX
- establishing meaningful peer relationships (beyond family)

HIGHER-ORDER
- consensus-building skills
- recognition of various "social ideals"

How Is This Intelligence Developed in Other Cultures?

British Columbia, Canada, values the interpersonal intelligence very highly. In Canadian schools, cooperative learning is more than a teaching tool; it is an essential value. Already one of the most multicultural societies in North America, Canadians believe that cooperation is a way of life. They see American competition as unproductive. Getting along, working together, solving problems together, and living in harmony are deeply rooted traditions that owe as much to the ancient Inuits as to the eastern philosophies of the more recently arrived immigrants from Asia.

In Norway, interpersonal interaction is also a highly valued tradition. Stories are told that the tradition had its roots in the long, cold, and dark winters on the mountain farms. Each evening, the landowners would share the simple meal of cheese and milk with the farmers. This would start the long hours of storytelling, discussion of philosophical and religious issues, and teaching of traditions. From parent to child, neighbor to neighbor, the families talked about problems, found solutions, and supported each other through the long, lean months of the winter solstice.

IRI/SkyLight Training and Publishing, Inc.

How Can This Intelligence Be Used for Problem Solving?

"He can talk his way out of a paper bag" is a familiar refrain. Although not always meant in a complimentary way, the refrain does pinpoint the value of this intelligence in a verbal society.

☐ Lynn's math grade was a D-. She knew that her parents would have a fit. Although she knew she had missed several homework assignments, she was sure she could talk her professor into letting her do an extra-credit task.

☐ Beth had a hard time getting a word in edgewise. Her boss was a hyperactive talker. Beth decided the best strategy was to be a good listener and end the one-sided conversation with, "So, what you want me to do is. . . ."

☐ Kate's best friend was gossiping. This made it difficult for Kate. She didn't want to hurt any of her friends' feelings. She decided to sit Casey down and tell her to stop the gossiping.

☐ Bruce knew the meeting was going to be tough. There were several of the office's biggest resisters on the team. He knew if he confronted them, they would just walk out. He also knew he couldn't just ignore them. He decided that he would use the quality circle techniques he had learned in the company's leadership training program.

Who Is the Student With This Intelligence?

Dave has a highly developed interpersonal intelligence, loving his fellow students and appreciating their diversities. He likes to study people in other cultures as well as their history and art.

As students, individuals with this intelligence prefer to work in situations where they can be social, have the chance to talk things over, plan with others, sense their motivation, and encourage togetherness for mutual benefit. The person with this intelligence would rather collaborate to accomplish a task, hates to study or work alone, has a good sense of others' feelings, and possesses well-developed collaborative and communicative skills. On weekends, this person loves a party. The more guests the better. If there is no party, then this person grabs the telephone and may talk on two lines at once.

The Comfort Zone: What Helps This Student Learn?

When this student sees the classroom desks organized into small, clustered workstations with cooperative guidelines posted, he settles in quickly. The more instruction is organized for peer tutoring, cooperative study groups, base groups, group investigations, group games and activities, and informal pair sharing, the more this student achieves. When the teacher guides all-class discussions, this student perks up in the chair ever ready to participate.

IRI/SkyLight Training and Publishing, Inc.

The Discomfort Zone: What Hinders This Student?

This student hates working alone. Individualized study packets, study carrels, self-paced learning, and silent sustained reading are anathema. The student has great difficulty with private reflection time, journal writing, workbooks, and study-alone time. The more time she has to spend in these strategies, the less she achieves.

How Do You Catch This Student's Attention in the Classroom?

The person with this intelligence responds to a "we" atmosphere. First, couch questions to the class in the invitational "we": "How do we feel about this?"; "What did we learn today?"; "What should we do next?"; "How does this make us feel?"

Second, structure the opening of lessons with pair- and cooperative trio-based activities. For instance, use think-pair-share as the anticipatory set: "Think what we know about. . . ."

Third, use cooperative learning structures that foster group interdependence for the core tasks in a lesson. For instance, jigsaw vocabulary or basic math worksheets, use round-robin responses with web organizers, or adapt Kagan's four-heads-together strategy to a lesson on prediction.

Fourth, use cooperative teams for project-based learning. Structure the projects so that each group member is forced to do a fair share. Require signatures from each person on the part of the project he or she completed.

Fifth, structure metacognitive processing so that individual contributions to the group and group successes are highlighted. Use the wraparound for oral, round-robin reporting to the whole class.

How Do You Meet the Challenge of the Special Student?

The special needs child will leave school to live and work in the world beyond the school walls. This child will need to develop cooperative social skills. There is no better place to start than in school where labels challenge the special child to work extra hard to "fit in." The need for acceptance does not disappear for these students; if anything, the labels and the social biases make their need all the more difficult.

- Insist that special needs students participate in cooperative groups in the regular classroom as well as in resource rooms.
- Teach and practice cooperative social skills in the resource room. Make transfer outside of the resource room a priority.
- Provide opportunities to process feelings and ideas with fellow students.

- Give this student a role in cooperative groups that he or she can do with success. Coach and check specific instructions.
- In regular classroom, give an all-class job he or she can do with success.
- Double check task instructions for group work. Have the student repeat the instructions.
- Use two or three as the group size, never four or five.
- Use challenging tasks for the groups. Stay away from cooperative group tasks that use workbooks or other boring tasks.
- Give lots of hurrahs and other celebrations for this student's work in groups.
- With students who experience behavior difficulties, use many team-building, conflict resolution, and bonding activities and process the value of working with others.

What Activities Promote Learning With This Intelligence?

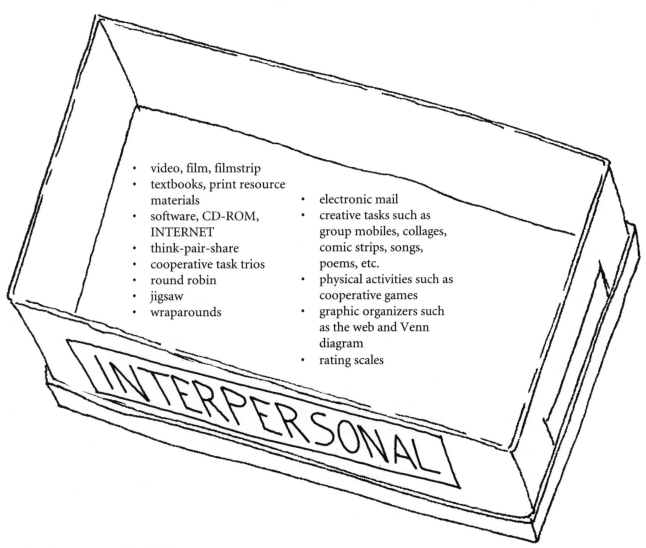

- video, film, filmstrip
- textbooks, print resource materials
- software, CD-ROM, INTERNET
- think-pair-share
- cooperative task trios
- round robin
- jigsaw
- wraparounds
- electronic mail
- creative tasks such as group mobiles, collages, comic strips, songs, poems, etc.
- physical activities such as cooperative games
- graphic organizers such as the web and Venn diagram
- rating scales

How Do You Create an Environment for This Intelligence?

The learning environment for this intelligence is created by integrating management tactics, social skill instruction, and collaborative problem solving into the daily curriculum.

MANAGEMENT TACTICS

At the start of the year, the teacher teaches the students how to form cooperative groups. A cooperative group consists of two to four students of different ability, motivation, intelligence type, socio-economic status, or ethnic/racial origin with a common learning goal. To form these groups, the teacher selects the members of each group, how long the group stays together (usually ten to thirty minutes at the start of the year; longer later in the year), and for what purpose (a single cooperative lesson or an entire unit). Next, she introduces the students to the basic tools they will need to work together: a common goal that all will work together to achieve, roles and responsibilities for each group member, guidelines for behavior in the cooperative groups, a signal for stopping group work and maintaining quiet voices, the use of a simple set of materials, the rationale for cooperative work, a review/assessment of cooperative contributions, and a furniture arrangement conducive to cooperative work. During the first cooperative activities, the teacher takes extra time to introduce each management tactic and guide practice in the tactic's use.

COOPERATIVE GUIDELINES

Post these for all to see. The guidelines detail the expected behavior. Observe the use of the guidelines in the cooperative groups. Below is a list of sample cooperative guidelines for primary, middle, and high school levels.

PRIMARY SCHOOL EXAMPLE:	MIDDLE SCHOOL EXAMPLE:	HIGH SCHOOL EXAMPLE:
• Use low voices.	• Use low voices.	• Control your voice.
• Listen to your neighbor.	• It's O.K. to think.	• Think for yourself.
• Stay with the group.	• Don't interrupt others.	• Respect others' opinions.
• Look at the speaker.	• Help your neighbor.	• Carry your weight.
• Don't hurt the feelings of others.	• Know and do your job.	• Help each other stay on task.
	• Listen to all ideas.	• Explore different points of view.
	• Use encouraging words.	• Include all members.

SOCIAL SKILL INSTRUCTION

After the teacher observes students using the basics of cooperation, it is time to integrate cooperative social skill instruction into each lesson. The social skills she selects will set the norms for interpersonal interactions in the classroom. The level of her students' interpersonal skills will determine which social skill to teach. Essential skills include attentive listening, teamwork, giving encouragement, and praising accomplishments. More advanced cooperative social skills include clarifying, solving conflicts, and creating consensus.

Social skill instruction is most beneficial when the teacher provides explicit instruction. This works well in a direct-instruction model of teaching. In the model, the lesson will include an anticipatory set or hook that connects the students to their prior knowledge and provides a concrete example of the skill, the identification of the specific behaviors used with this social skill, guided practice, imbedded practice, and celebrations of success. The first elements of this lesson require ten to thirty minutes of time; guided group practice with corrective feedback takes the same amount of time, depending on the class's interpersonal skill level. From the time guided practice is done, the targeted social skill is imbedded in the daily cooperative tasks for extended practice. As the teacher notices the students using the social skill with increased regularity and ease, she helps the students recognize and celebrate the development of their interpersonal intelligence. At this point, she will introduce the next, more advanced cooperative social skill.

COLLABORATIVE PROBLEM SOLVING

At times, the cooperative environment can go into a winter freeze. Conflicts between students and among groups of students may arise.

The teacher can most assist the students, not by solving the problems for them, but by teaching them a conflict resolution strategy. The first step in this approach, most strongly advocated by William Glasser, is to set a goal that the students will learn to control their behaviors with a win-win solution to the problem. Just as the teacher taught the basic social skills, she can teach a win-win problem-solving model to the students and guide the practice. It is most beneficial to teach the model to the entire class and practice its use with decisions that affect the entire class (e.g., noise reduction during group activity, violation of the guidelines, etc.). Once she has noted that the students understand the model's use, she can facilitate additional applications when conflicts arise in the cooperative groups or between individuals.

The Responsibility Model

a. Identify the problem.
b. Clarify the issues in the problem.
c. Agree on standards for solutions of quality.
d. Generate possible solutions.
e. Evaluate possible solutions.
f. Select win-win solution with responsibilities and timeline.
g. Implement and evaluate the results.

At times, individual students may elect not to cooperate with the group or with the teacher. In those cases, she may wonder what to do with the kid who misbehaves. The solution is guided by several basic principles: (1) Every student has a right to work alone; it is a privilege to work with others. (2) No student has a right to disrupt the learning of another. (3) All solutions to misbehavior problems must meet the win-win standard.

INSTRUCTIONAL VARIETY

Madeline Hunter points to variety as the most important key to motivation. Variety comes not only in what the students learn, but in how they learn. In the classroom that promotes the development of interpersonal intelligence, the teacher has an almost endless list of usable instructional strategies. Combining these strategies in different ways with the different content allows the teacher to bring variety to the development of the interpersonal intelligence. As students become more skilled in the use of the strategies with the content they are expected to master, they also become more responsible for their own learning, more able to speed the process of learning, and more ready to develop the other supporting intelligences that nest so well with the cooperative model.

CENTERS

There are many ways to take advantage of the Center approach with this intelligence. First, provide print and media information on cooperative learning and teamwork for research tasks. Second, provide art supplies so that students can make projects that show cooperation in action (e.g., a collage on teamwork in the armed forces, sports, or the hospital). Third, provide computer programs that require two to three students to cooperate (e.g., Team Challenge by EBEC and Compton's Multi-Media). Fourth, make a career center to examine career opportunities in which cooperation and interpersonal skills are important (e.g., social work, medicine, therapy, politics, religion, education, etc.). Fifth, and most important, structure all activities in this center for cooperative work.

REVIEWING COOPERATION AND POSITIVE INTERACTION

On a regular basis, put students into groups of three or put the entire class in a circle to review how they are contributing to the cooperative environment of their small groups and the entire classroom. Accentuate positive accomplishments, celebrate successes, and examine ways to improve. These discussions will enable students to keep a focus on their responsibility to make everyone, including themselves, feel included and successful in the classroom.

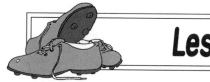

Lesson Example 1: Make a Team

TARGETED INTELLIGENCE: Interpersonal

SUPPORTING INTELLIGENCES: Visual/Spatial, Intrapersonal, Musical/Rhythmic

THINKING SKILLS: Generating Ideas, Selecting from Alternatives

SOCIAL SKILLS: Teamwork, Cooperative Problem Solving

CONTENT FOCUS: Teamwork

MATERIALS: Poster board, art supplies, T-shirts

TASK FOCUS: One way to bond teams is to have them create logos, symbols, and sayings that identify the team. (Note how many people buy hats, T-shirts, banners, etc., to identify with their favorite sports teams.)

PRODUCT: Group symbol

PROBLEM: How to develop teamwork skills

ACTIVITY:

1. This can be a series of cooperative group activities. It works best if the students stay in the same group for these activities and have a chance to know each other better. For other cooperative tasks in the classroom, assign these students to different groups but let them rejoin each other for these team tasks.

2. Select teams of three. Don't put friends together. Make every team as heterogeneous as you can. Assign roles and responsibilities and review cooperative guidelines.

3. Have groups work on the tasks below. Select a different task each time the group meets. (Note: If gangs are a problem in your community, you must set the parameter of no gang symbols and be sure that your groups are heterogeneous.) All products must reflect the contributions and the personalities of all members.

   • Make a group name from positive characteristics of the members in the group.

   • Make a group motto and flag that represent the commonalities in the group.

   • Make a T-shirt or cap with the group name and symbol.

   • Make group goals for working together better and depict them on a chart.

   • Make an ad for renting your group. Highlight the best and most common traits of the group.

   • Make a play or video about your group.

   • Write a song or poem about the greatness of your group.

   • Make a strength chart for each member of the group.

   • Make a mobile or collage showing the positive characteristics of each member and the whole group.

   • Make a cartoon strip of your group solving a problem together.

- Write an essay describing what each member contributes to the group.
- Make a team cheer.
- Make a graph to show how the group's cooperation has improved after each meeting.
- Make a team shoe.

REFLECTIONS:

1. What did you do to work as a team?
2. Where and how could you use the teamwork skills you are developing in your daily lives

PRIMARY SCHOOL EXAMPLE: Select one team-building activity to do each week. Select stories to read that illustrate teamwork. Discuss how teamwork helps students' favorite sports heroes.

MIDDLE SCHOOL EXAMPLE: Use these activities as part of the advisor/advisee program. Display the products around the homeroom. Each quarter have a team day so that teams can wear their T-shirts, eat lunch together, or perform for the class. Discuss the importance of teamwork in school, in sports, and in the work world. Have each team select a work site to visit on career day.

HIGH SCHOOL EXAMPLE: Start each week with team goal setting. End the week with an evaluation of the goals. On the day after a unit test, celebrate with a team-building activity.

Lesson Example 2: Know Your Job

TARGETED INTELLIGENCE: Interpersonal

SUPPORTING INTELLIGENCES: Intrapersonal, Visual/Spatial

THINKING SKILL: Clarifying

SOCIAL SKILLS: Roles and Responsibilities, Encouraging

CONTENT FOCUS: The Roles of a Cooperative Group

MATERIALS: Index cards, cartoon strip

TASK FOCUS: Groups of three will use cards and the round robin to coach each other in learning the basic group roles.

PRODUCT: Job role card

PROBLEM: How to learn cooperative roles and responsibilities

ACTIVITY:

1. Give each student an index card with a role title and responsibilities written on it and a piece of a comic strip. (There are three pieces to each strip.) They must find the two persons that have the other parts of their comic strip.

2. Once the students are seated, each will read his or her card to the new group.
   Encourager: You are the cheerleader. No put-downs allowed.
   Guide: You make sure that everyone understands the task and stays on task.
   Checker: You make sure everyone agrees and can explain his or her job. Watch the clock.

3. Ask for examples of put-downs and encouragement (verbal and nonverbal).

4. Have each person in a group draw a picture on the back of the index card. The picture should represent the job.

5. With only the picture showing, each will explain his or her job. The checker will check for accuracy on the back of the card. If the explanation is not complete, the other group members may coach.

6. If there is time, the checker can do a round robin final check.

REFLECTIONS:

1. What is the responsibility of each job?
2. How do you think doing these jobs will help with cooperation?

PRIMARY SCHOOL EXAMPLE: Review all the jobs with the class, especially if there are nonreaders. If you have enough readers to assign one per group, that person can be the guide and read each job to the group. Review the roles before every group task and reinforce students when you see them doing the jobs.

MIDDLE SCHOOL EXAMPLE: Repeat the task twice as outlined. Each time, rotate the roles so that all members learn all roles. Before each cooperative lesson, have the groups assign and review each role. Introduce the cooperative guidelines on a bulletin board or handout. Clarify terms and have the groups review the guidelines before each cooperative task.

HIGH SCHOOL EXAMPLE: Make a handout with the roles, responsibilities, and guidelines. Once a week review the use of the roles and guidelines and ask the groups to assess how well they are performing both.

Lesson Example 3: The Dinosaur Problem

TARGETED INTELLIGENCE: Interpersonal

SUPPORTING INTELLIGENCES: Verbal/Linguistic, Visual/Spatial, Naturalist

THINKING SKILL: Problem Solving

SOCIAL SKILLS: Contributing to a Team, Clarifying, Listening

CONTENT FOCUS: Science

MATERIALS: Transparency of the problem-solving model, newsprint, markers, journals

TASK FOCUS: Students will use a problem-solving model to escape from a dinosaur that has trapped them in a cave.

PRODUCT: A solution

PROBLEM: Creating steps to solve a problem

ACTIVITY:

1. Set up your cooperative groups of three. Assign and explain the roles of reader, recorder, and task leader. Review the cooperative guidelines.

2. On the overhead, show the transparency of the problem-solving model:

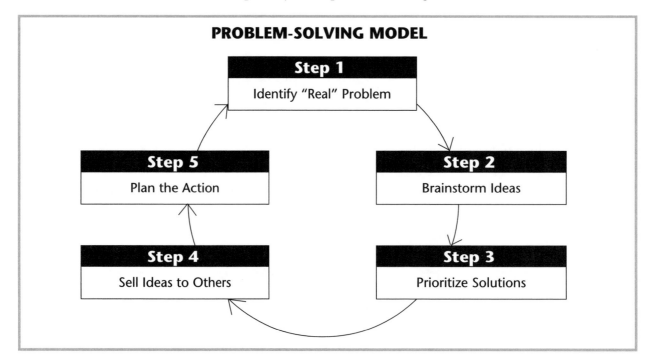

3. Give each reader a copy of the problem paragraph:

   "Maria, Samuel, and Vicky had gone hiking in the mountains north of the city. When a heavy thunderstorm came, they found a cave for shelter. As they were sitting in the cave, the storm passed. They looked out. To their surprise, a giant tyrannosaurus rex was seated twenty feet away. It was getting dark. Maria reminded the group that they were expected home before sundown."

4. Guide the groups through the problem-solving steps, one step at a time. Each group will record answers on newsprint. After each step ask for one or two groups to share. Call on different groups to share each step.

   Step 1: Identify the real problem. Each group writes an answer on the newsprint. Check for the correct response: the dinosaur sitting outside. "Being late" and "being scared" are not the problem. "Being late" will be a problem only if they can get past the dinosaur.

   Step 2: Brainstorm ideas. Every group should have at least five ways to escape the dinosaur.

   Step 3: Prioritize the solutions. Mark the best solution #1.

   Step 4: Sell the idea to others. What are the good reasons for this solution?

   Step 5: Plan the action. Use a sequence chart on the bottom of the newsprint. Have at least six steps in the plan.

5. All group members sign and help post the newsprint. Have a silent gallery walk. No talking as the students look at the different charts.

6. (optional) Give more newsprint and markers to the groups. Have each group make a storyboard of its solution.

REFLECTIONS:

1. What did your group do well as co-workers?
2. If you did the same task over, what would you do to improve your teamwork?
3. How else might you use this problem-solving model? Give an example that fits all the steps.

PRIMARY SCHOOL EXAMPLE: Simplify the story. Read it aloud to the entire class and have four students act out the events in the cave. Use think-pair-share at each point in the model. What is the problem? How can they get away unharmed? Why would you do that? What would you do first to escape?

MIDDLE SCHOOL EXAMPLE: Use the activity to introduce the problem-solving model. After they complete the activity, ask each group to select a real issue that they think is a problem at school. Working with their group, have students follow the same model and find solutions to their "school" problem.

HIGH SCHOOL EXAMPLE: Use the activity to introduce the model. Keep the same groups and have them apply the model for a discussion of a short story (e.g., "The Pit and the Pendulum" by Edgar Allan Poe), a historic event (e.g., Lincoln and the slave issue), a current event, or critical social issue. Assess the groups' improvement with the problem-solving model by having them reflect in their journals.

Lesson Example 4: Symbol Search

TARGETED INTELLIGENCE: Interpersonal

SUPPORTING INTELLIGENCES: Visual/Spatial, Verbal/Linguistic

THINKING SKILLS: Making Analogies, Finding Attributes

SOCIAL SKILLS: Clarifying and Encouraging

CONTENT FOCUS: Language Arts, Literature

MATERIALS: Newsprint, markers, story copies for each student

TASK FOCUS: This activity can follow the reading of any piece of literature with characters.

PRODUCT: Symbols of group members and story characters

PROBLEM: How to create specific symbols

ACTIVITY:

1. Form mixed-ability groups of three and assign the roles of recorder, encourager, and clarifier. The job of the clarifier is to make sure all the group members can find the sections of the story used in the symbol search.

2. Do a round-robin review of the roles in each group. Spot check for understanding.

3. Explain the meaning of a symbol: an object that represents an idea or belief. Give several examples: a heart is a symbol for love; a skull and crossbones is a symbol for piracy or poison. Ask students for some examples they know.

4. Divide the story into parts (a novel by chapter). Each person in the group will select one main character to follow through the story. On the newsprint, the recorder will draw three webs of equal size. At each stopping point, each person in the group will have the recorder write down important behaviors of the selected character. (Give an example.) At the end of the story, the group will look at the information and decide on an appropriate symbol from the book for each character.

5. Remind the encourager to lead the encouragement in the group and suppress put-downs.

6. On the basis of the interactions on this task, have the group make a symbol for each group member. Add the symbols in the corner of the newsprint.

7. Ask for all members of several volunteer groups to share with the class and explain the symbol choices.

REFLECTIONS:

1. How well did each member carry out his or her job?

2. What were some of the ways members encouraged each other?

3. How did encouragement help the group succeed?

PRIMARY SCHOOL EXAMPLE: Select a story familiar to the students such as "The Three Little Pigs." In each group have a reader who will read the story to the others in the group. When the story is done, have groups select a symbol for each of the major characters.

Invite each group to show and explain the symbols to the class. Remember to give emphasis to the social skill of encouragement.

MIDDLE SCHOOL EXAMPLE: Use the model with a short story such as Jack London's *To Build a Fire* or a short novel such as *Johnny Tremain* by Esther Forbes. Have each group concentrate on the main character only.

HIGH SCHOOL EXAMPLE: The strategy will work with a wide variety of plays, short stories, and novels. You may want to have each group select a different piece of literature and make a super symbol for the selection.

Make Your Own

LESSON NAME: _____

TARGETED INTELLIGENCE: Interpersonal _____

SUPPORTING INTELLIGENCES: _____

THINKING SKILLS: _____

SOCIAL SKILLS: _____
_____

CONTENT FOCUS: _____

MATERIALS: _____
_____

TASK FOCUS: _____
_____

PRODUCT: _____

PROBLEM: _____

ACTIVITY:
_____
_____
_____
_____
_____
_____
_____
_____

REFLECTIONS:

1. _____
_____

2. _____
_____

3. _____
_____

Make Your Own

LESSON NAME: _____

TARGETED INTELLIGENCE: _Interpersonal_____

SUPPORTING INTELLIGENCES: _____

THINKING SKILLS: _____

SOCIAL SKILLS: _____

_____

CONTENT FOCUS: _____

MATERIALS: _____

_____

TASK FOCUS: _____

_____

PRODUCT: _____

PROBLEM: _____

ACTIVITY:

_____

_____

_____

_____

_____

_____

_____

_____

REFLECTIONS:

1. _____

_____

2. _____

_____

3. _____

_____

Working in This Intelligence, I Am . . .

When I use this intelligence, I am . . .

very uncomfortable   totally at ease

When I ask students to use this intelligence, I am . . .

very uncomfortable   totally at ease

In what ways does this shoe fit me personally?

What can I do to polish this shoe for my professional use?

What am I going to do to provide for students in this intelligence?

What to continue	New things to do

Journal Page

Reflections on My Pathway to Interpersonal Intelligence

_____
_____
_____
_____
_____
_____
_____
_____
_____
_____
_____
_____
_____
_____
_____
_____
_____
_____
_____
_____
_____
_____
_____
_____
_____
_____
_____
_____
_____

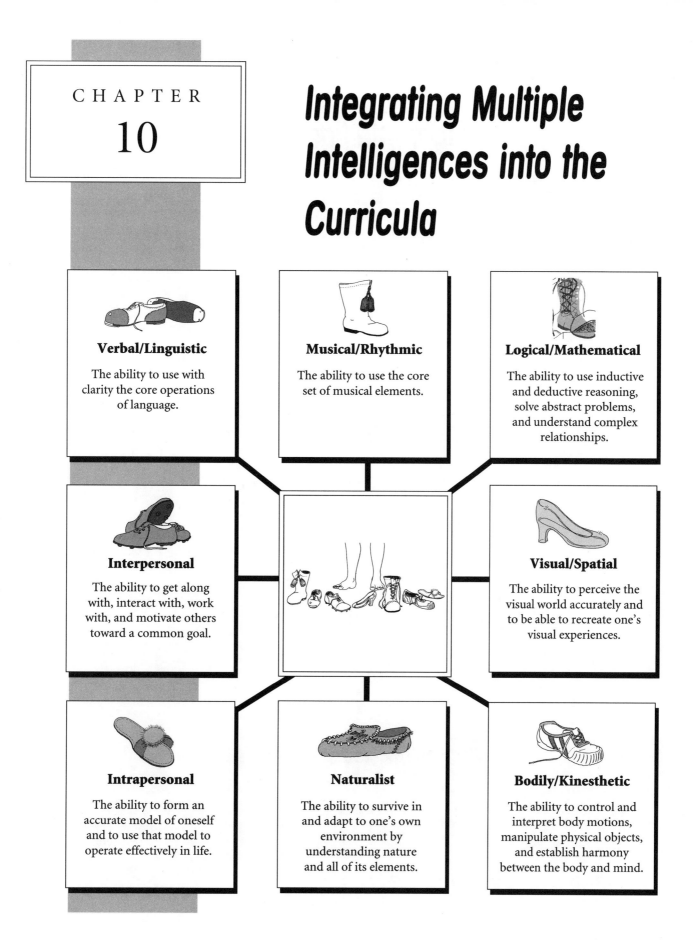

CHAPTER 10

Integrating Multiple Intelligences into the Curricula

Verbal/Linguistic

The ability to use with clarity the core operations of language.

Musical/Rhythmic

The ability to use the core set of musical elements.

Logical/Mathematical

The ability to use inductive and deductive reasoning, solve abstract problems, and understand complex relationships.

Interpersonal

The ability to get along with, interact with, work with, and motivate others toward a common goal.

Visual/Spatial

The ability to perceive the visual world accurately and to be able to recreate one's visual experiences.

Intrapersonal

The ability to form an accurate model of oneself and to use that model to operate effectively in life.

Naturalist

The ability to survive in and adapt to one's own environment by understanding nature and all of its elements.

Bodily/Kinesthetic

The ability to control and interpret body motions, manipulate physical objects, and establish harmony between the body and mind.

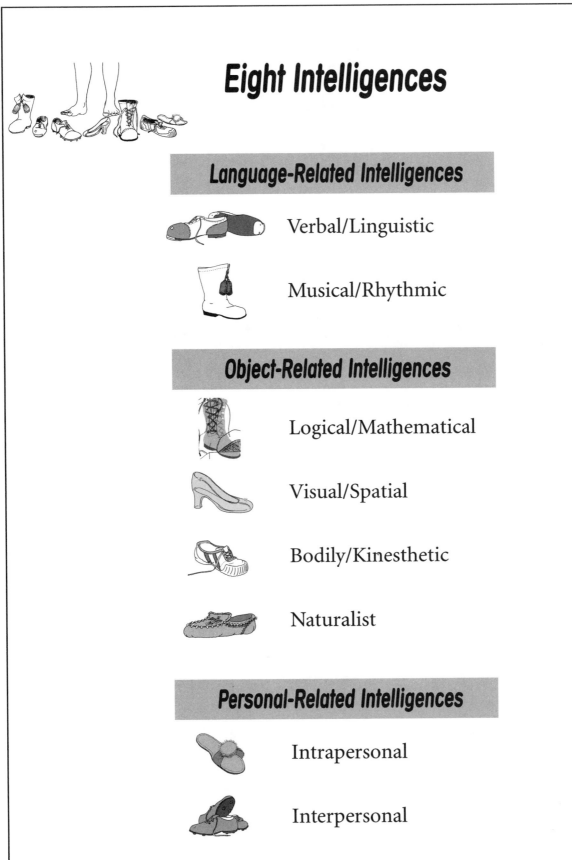

Eight Intelligences

Language-Related Intelligences

Verbal/Linguistic

Musical/Rhythmic

Object-Related Intelligences

Logical/Mathematical

Visual/Spatial

Bodily/Kinesthetic

Naturalist

Personal-Related Intelligences

Intrapersonal

Interpersonal

IRI/SkyLight Training and Publishing, Inc.

In today's classrooms, there is a resurgence of emphasis on the integrated curriculum. Because of the high-tech information overload and inflexible time schedules, school curricula are overburdened with more content to cover and little change in the time allotted to teach. Some compare the school curricula to a sausage that everyone and anyone can stuff with anything they desire (including state bird day, state flower day, and the life cycle of the cockroach). This leaves teachers to wait for the overstuffed curriculum to explode or to find meaningful ways to abandon the trivial.

In addition to an overloaded curriculum, there is also much fragmentation in the learning process as students bounce from one subject to another and from one classroom to another. Based on the study of Caine and Caine (1990), a focus on more holistic learning seems more brain compatible. Their finding that the brain processes information simultaneously, that it learns from the cognitive and affective realms, and that it is unique, suggests that an integrated approach is beneficial to the natural process of learning.

There are many ways to integrate the curricula. One of the most valuable is Howard Gardner's theory of multiple intelligences. As Gardner has noted, learners favor certain ways of knowing and problem solving. Often the individual's culture predisposes which way of knowing the individual will favor. For instance, in the United States, favor, communicated by standardized testing priorities and textbook content, is given to the development of the verbal/linguistic and the logical/mathematical intelligences. As one way to overcome this intelligence development bias, integrated curriculum models can assist teachers in giving greater balance to the development of the other six intelligences about whose existence Gardner has theorized.

The key to success with an integrated curriculum is the quality of the planning that precedes classroom instruction. In one sense, the integrated approach is no more than a different way to deliver instruction. In another, it is the window of opportunity to rethink what is most important for students to learn, a way to abandon the trivial and out of date, and to restructure what students learn so that they can focus on meaning and concept rather than on facts alone.

A quality lesson in an integrated curriculum focuses on what Fogarty, Perkins, and Barell (1992) call "fertile" themes and meaningful units of study. Fertile themes use significant issues, concepts, and idea relationships as the connectors of content in and across disciplines. In this approach, textbooks become resources from which students select information relevant to the theme in focus, rather than a document to be "covered."

In the outcomes-based learning approach, fertile themes spark thoughtful outcomes as well as thoughtful pathways to significant insights into the heart of the various disciplines. For interdisciplinary outcomes, the learner looks to understand the connections between ideas in a course of study (e.g., the hero in literature, the role of competition in the development of our nation, the importance of responsibility in friendship) to develop specific thinking skills or social skills or to expand a particular intelligence from the eight that Gardner has posited. As pathways to outcomes in a discipline, interdisciplinary curricula help guide the learner to significant connections among the disciplines (e.g., using writing [verbal/linguistic], art [visual/spatial] and music [musical/rhythmic] to facilitate a language arts study of a novel).

Whether using multiple intelligences to connect disciplines by thoughtful outcomes or well-chosen instructional strategies, teachers can plan integration of the curriculum in a variety of ways. Fogarty's (1991) nested, webbed, shared, threaded, and integrated models are especially adaptable to integration via the multiple intelligences.

Nesting a Lesson With the Multiple Intelligences

The Nested Model is the foundation of every lesson in the multiple intelligences classroom. When using this model the teacher analyzes what is being taught and realizes the important targets being addressed. Therefore, one is able to see what the learners will be learning in many areas at one time.

The model can be used in two ways. Both are beneficial for selecting quality activities to use in instruction.

Model A: Nesting With a Targeted Intelligence

During the planning time, the teacher targets a content goal and the core activity. Then, decisions are made about appropriate life skills and umbrella concepts that are inherent in the selected activity. For example, thinking skills and social skills are easily nested into any content lesson. In addition to the content goal and the skill development, and with an eye on the multiple intelligences approach to learning, one of the intelligences is also nested into the total lesson focus.

For example, the lesson depicted in Model A delineates a number of skills that are simultaneously nested into the Mac-A-Lena activity.

1. Content Goal and Core Activity: Health/Science Unit, Parts of the Body, and Mac-A-Lena Activity
2. Thinking Skills: Sequencing, Following Directions
3. Social Skill: Accepting Self and Others
4. Target Intelligence: Musical/Rhythmic

While the academic goal is to learn the parts of the body, the core activity, Mac-A-Lena, provides the platform for the thinking skills of sequencing and following directions and the social skill of accepting self and others. The musical/rhythmic intelligence is also a target in this nested model.

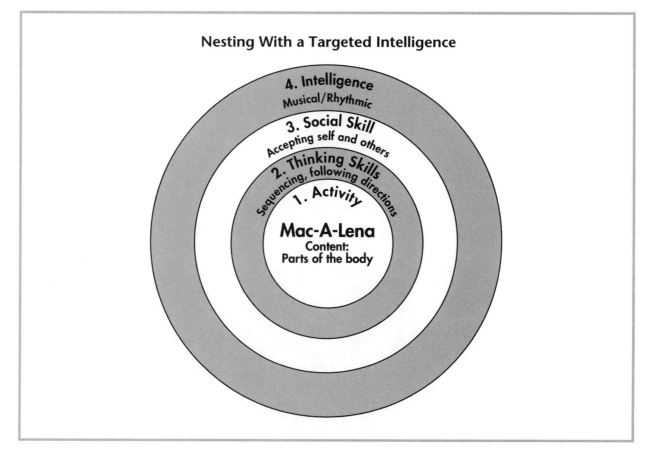

Model B: Nesting With a Targeted Intelligence, Plus Other Intelligences

For a more complex unit, the teacher may develop this even further. As illustrated in Model B, the content goal and core activity, as well as other life skills and one of the multiple intelligences, are nested together, just as in Model A. In this more complex example, however, several supporting intelligences are also highlighted.

1. Content Goal & Core Activity: Health/Science Unit, Parts of the Body, and Mac-A-Lena Activity
2. Thinking Skills: Sequencing, Following Directions
3. Social Skill: Acceping Self and Others
4. Target Intelligence: Musical/Rhythmic
5. Supporting Intelligences: Visual/Spatial, Verbal/Linguistic, Interpersonal, Intrapersonal

Again, using the parts of the body as an academic focus, not only is there opportunity to teach thinking skills and social skills, and the musical/rhythmic intelligence, but also to use other supporting intelligences.

By analyzing the integration of the multiple intelligences in the classroom unit, the teacher epitomizes the natural integration of intelligences that occurs in the human mind as it learns and grows and develops.

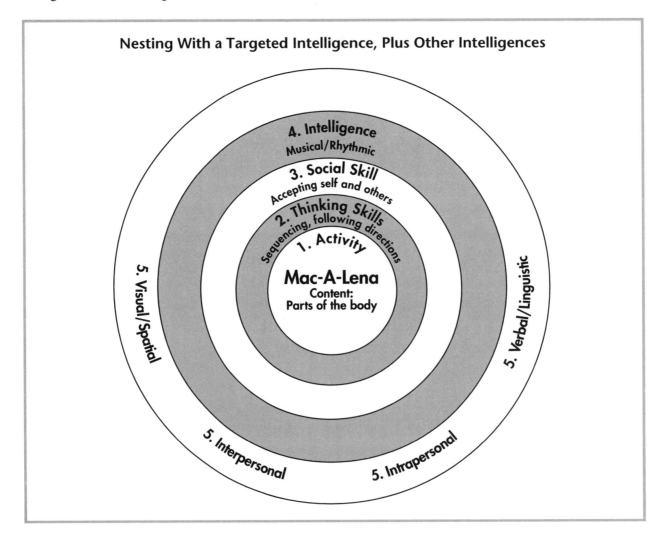

Nesting With a Targeted Intelligence, Plus Other Intelligences

Webbing a Lesson With the Multiple Intelligences

Webbing is the most popular model of integration (Fogarty, 1991). Most commonly, teachers use a single, fertile theme such as responsibility or cooperation; a common topic such as the individual and society or the community; or a category such as the Renaissance or fiction to connect the students' learning. One way to use the web model with the multiple intelligences is to use a single piece of literature as the core. Activities and projects that develop each intelligence can spin from the story.

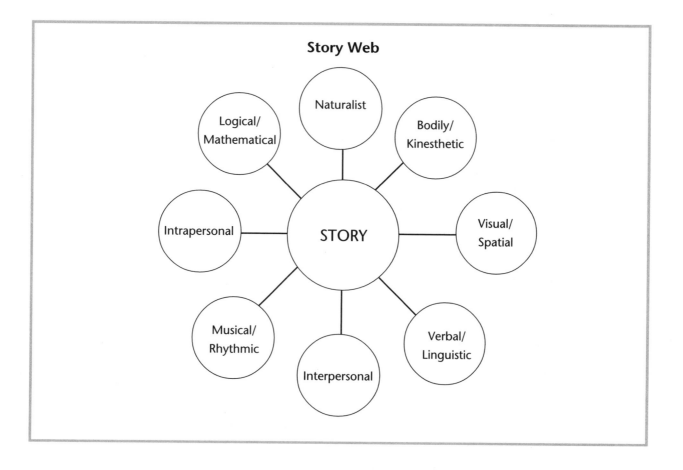

Primary School Web Sample

Caps for Sale by Esphyr Slobodkina

A peddler travels each day through the town and then out into the country saying, "Caps! Caps for sale! Fifty cents a cap!" One day while resting under a tree, a group of monkeys takes his caps. The adventure continues with the monkeyshines of retrieving the caps.

STORY EXTENSIONS USING THE MULTIPLE INTELLIGENCES

Verbal/Linguistic
1. Read the story to the whole class.
2. Have students tell and/or read the story again to a partner.
3. Ask students to respond to the story, draw, and write about it.
4. Read other related literature.
   a. *Curious George* by H.A. Rey
   b. *Five Little Monkeys Jumping on the Bed* by Eileen Christelow
5. Write the story line from each page and invite children to illustrate.
6. Walk a story. Cut footprints from plastic carpet runner and have students step from footprint to footprint as they read each page.
7. Make cap-shaped books.
   a. Write a magical cap story.
   b. Write monkeyshine cartoons.
   c. Write important parts of the story in a sequence and illustrate.

Musical/Rhythmic
1. Write a catchy jingle or rap to sell caps.
2. During a shared reading of the story, have students do "monkeyshines" as they mimic the peddler in the story.
3. Sing a song about the story. Make up some new verses and place on your language experience charts.
   a. Caps (tune: "Frère Jacques")
   Teacher: Caps for sale.
   Students: Caps for sale.
   Teacher: Fifty cents a cap.
   Students: Fifty cents a cap.
   Teacher: Orange, green, and purple caps.
   Students: Orange, green, and purple caps.
   Teacher: Please buy a cap.
   Students: Please buy a cap.
   (Next verse: class repeats each line)
   b. Caps for Sale
   Fifty cents a cap.
   Red, blue, and yellow caps.
   Please buy a cap.
   (Again, class repeats each line.)

Primary School Web Sample (continued)

   c. Caps for Sale
      Fifty cents a cap.
      Pink, black, and brown caps.
      Please buy a cap.
4. Put the words to the song on a chart to read as the students sing.
5. Use paper caps of different colors and distribute to the students. Have students march in a cap parade, sing the song, and wave their caps when their color is sung.

Logical/Mathematical

1. Sorting
   a. Have a collection of caps. Let the class brainstorm many ways to sort caps. In groups, have children classify caps into the brainstormed categories. Discuss how they sorted, why, which set has more, less, same, etc.
   b. Put caps in a learning center. Have children sort the caps and tell another student what they did.
2. Measuring and Graphing
   a. Assign a travel problem of the week for homework. Ask students at the beginning of the lesson to find out how many miles it is from their home to a downtown landmark. Plot homes and downtown distances on a city/county map.
   b. Graph the distances.
3. Money Word Problems
   a. Make up problems involving cap-purchasing stories at fifty cents per cap. Let students purchase caps for $.50 each.
   b. Vary prices if children are ready.
   c. Use pennies, nickels, and quarters for purchasing.
4. Recipe: Chocolate-dipped frozen bananas
   a. Peel banana.
   b. Push popsicle stick in and freeze overnight in a pan covered with foil.
   c. For every three whole bananas, melt one cup of chocolate chips and one tablespoon of shortening in a double boiler or microwave.
   d. Dip bananas in melted chocolate.
   e. Eat bananas and note the quality, taste, and desire for more.

Visual/Spatial

1. Tell students, "Dream of sitting under a big tree out in the country on a beautiful day… (Pause)… Think about how things look… (Pause)… smell… feel… (Pause)… Now draw the picture of this dream."
2. Have students close their eyes and think of the story, *Caps for Sale.* Ask them to capture their favorite part by drawing and writing about it.
3. Ask students to design a new style cap and logo.

IRI/SkyLight Training and Publishing, Inc.

Primary School Web Sample (continued)

Bodily/Kinesthetic

1. Bake money-shaped cookies.
2. Role play the story. You will be the narrator, one student will be the peddler, and all the other students the monkeys. Remind the monkeys to steal the caps quietly so they do not wake up the peddler. Also, rehearse monkeyshines before their role play begins. Show the scene on an overhead transparency or chalkboard to create the setting.
3. Have a cap day. Everyone wears a cap on a special day. Have a cap parade.
4. Have a cap relay for P.E. class. Balance caps on heads. Add one cap each round. See which team can complete the relay with the most caps balanced at the end.

Naturalist

1. Compare life in the country with life in the city.
   a. Make a Venn diagram. Label one side city and the other side country.
   b. Brainstorm ways that surviving in the city and the country are alike and different.
   c. Plot the information of the Venn diagram.
2. Pet Monkey Care
   a. Pretend you have a pet monkey.
   b. Make a list of responsibilities you would have in taking care of a monkey as a pet.
   c. Analyze your data. Write all the reasons to get a pet monkey and all the reasons not to get a pet monkey.

Intrapersonal

1. Have students write down all they know about monkeys. They may need to research monkeys to find out more.
2. Designate a day for students to wear a favorite cap and tell someone about their cap and why it is special.
3. Ask students to tell or write about something that they have lost or has been taken from them in the past.
4. Encourage students to write in their journal about how they would feel and what they would do if they were a monkey for a day.

Interpersonal

1. In cooperative learning groups, design a cap for the school, class, or team including logo, name, colors, etc.
2. Write a modern-day version of a cap dealer losing his caps and getting them returned. Have students work with a partner.
3. In literary study groups discuss the plot, setting, character, problem, and solution of the *Caps for Sale* story.
4. Ask students to bring a favorite sports cap and share in pairs about the team and its players.
5. Problem: While the peddler was asleep the monkeys stole his caps.
   Solution: Decide in groups how students would advise him to get his caps back. Have each group make a skit showing its solution.

Middle School Web Sample

Tales of a Fourth Grade Nothing by Judy Blume
Peter finds his demanding two-year-old brother Fudge an ever-increasing problem.

STORY EXTENSIONS USING THE MULTIPLE INTELLIGENCES

Verbal/Linguistic

1. Tell students to do a compare/contrast chart with another Blume book.
2. In groups, have students write and act playlets of a favorite scene.

Musical/Rhythmic

1. Ask students to write a rap song or poem that tells about Fudge's adventures and then perform it for the class.
2. Select a popular song you think would be a Fudge favorite. Play it for the class and explain your choice.

Logical/Mathematical

1. Have students make a matrix with the major characters in the story.
2. Tell students to use the story on a rope exercise.
3. Request that students make a map showing in proportion the distances between their home and school, a hospital, the police department, and two other important spots in the town.

Visual/Spatial

1. Make a short video or magazine print ad about the book.
2. Fudge tried to fly in the story. Have students imagine they are birds. Ask them where they would fly. Encourage them to draw the image in a four-picture sequence using no words.

Bodily/Kinesthetic

1. Plan a Fudge Fun Day. Do a sequence of physical activities that Fudge would like.
2. Allow students to invent a "bird exercise" to imitate different ways different birds fly (with feet on the ground!).

Naturalist

1. Write *The Hardest Day I Survived at School* stories
2. Write a survival rap.
3. Have a Clean-Up Our School Environment campaign.

Intrapersonal

1. Invite students to write and compile their school day memories in a journal.
2. Encourage students to construct an "All About Me" mobile.
3. Instruct students to do a Venn comparison of themselves with Fudge.

Interpersonal

1. Have cooperative learning groups write the after chapter.
2. Have students convince a friend they need a brother just like Fudge.
3. Tell students to do an "expert jigsaw." Read another book and coach each other in the setting, plot, and characters.

High School Web Sample

Death of a Salesman by Arthur Miller
The story of an aging traveling salesman, Willy Loman, and his estranged relationship with his sons. Extension activities in the high school may necessitate team planning with other course instructors.

Verbal/Linguistic
1. Place students in cooperative groups of seven. Divide the roles in each group for a group reading.
2. Use pairs to select the character to web.
3. Use trios to construct a concept map that shows the relationships in the Loman family.

Musical/Rhythmic
1. Invite a group of students to select one scene from the play and turn it into a musical with at least one song.
2. Invite students to write a ballad about Willy Loman.

Logical/Mathematical
1. Have students identify the logical fallacies in Willy's thinking. Use logic to correct these.
2. Ask students to plan an itinerary for Willy from his home to six cities in the Midwest. Calculate mileage for each trip and costs for fuel, food, and lodging.
3. Invite students to construct a question matrix about Willy and his sons. Use age, dreams, weaknesses, and results as the top headings.

Visual/Spatial
1. Use groups of three to pick a visual medium to communicate the critical attributes of a character.
2. Use groups of three to design a magazine ad for the play.
3. Use groups of three to make a mobile about the play's conflicts.

Bodily/Kinesthetic
1. Imagine that Biff cannot play football. Invent a game with rules that could be substituted in the play.
2. Plan a Willy Loman Walk-a-thon. Why would you have it? How far? Rules? Carry it out with the class and evaluate the results.

Naturalist
1. List Willy's habits to survive when he is traveling on the road and when he is at home.

Intrapersonal
1. Invite students to write a critique of Willy Loman's decisions.
2. Have students keep a journal about their dreams and aspirations after high school.
3. Invite students to complete a Venn comparison of themselves with Biff.

Interpersonal
1. Structure a think-pair-share about key quotations from the play.
2. Use a vocabulary jigsaw for the key drama terms you want students to recall.
3. Use a matrix for cooperative groups to create a play about one of the minor characters from *Death of a Salesman*.

Threading a Lesson With the Multiple Intelligences

Another way to integrate multiple intelligences is to use Fogarty's threaded model. In this model a particular "intelligence" threads its way through a series of lessons in different subject areas.

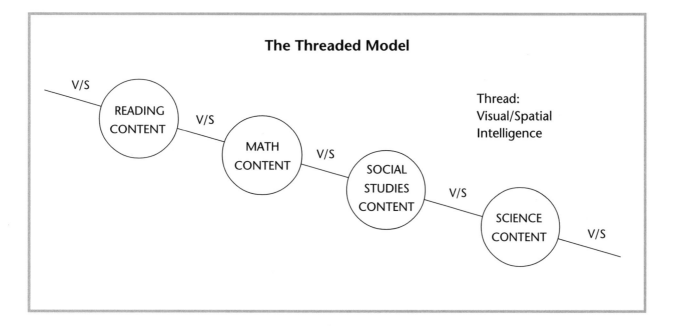

The Threaded Model

Thread:
Visual/Spatial
Intelligence

Primary School Threaded Sample

Reading
Read the story *Pigs* by Robert Munsch. Invite students to draw a picture of his or her favorite pig in the story. Post the sketches.

Math
Work with partners. After you teach a pattern, invite students to use two-color crayons to sketch the pattern.

Science
Do a scavenger hunt to find samples of tree bark. Have students pair and use a Venn diagram to compare bark from two trees.

Social Studies
Draw a map of the school. Label each room.

Sharing a Lesson With the Multiple Intelligences

A fourth model is called the shared model. In the shared model, topics and units from two related disciplines can be integrated in a variety of ways, including a sharing of intelligences.

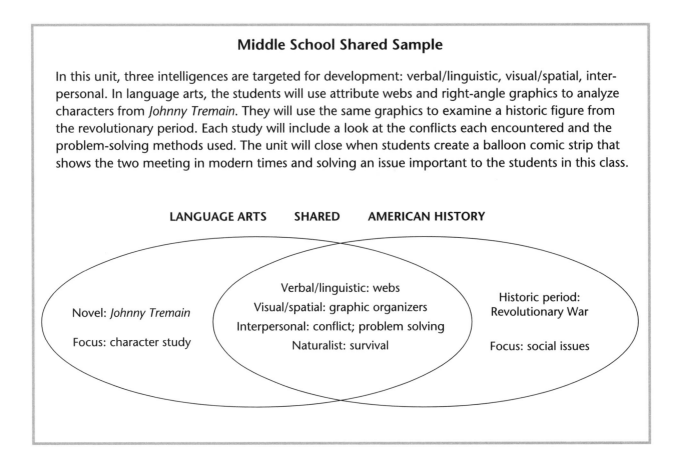

Middle School Shared Sample

In this unit, three intelligences are targeted for development: verbal/linguistic, visual/spatial, interpersonal. In language arts, the students will use attribute webs and right-angle graphics to analyze characters from *Johnny Tremain*. They will use the same graphics to examine a historic figure from the revolutionary period. Each study will include a look at the conflicts each encountered and the problem-solving methods used. The unit will close when students create a balloon comic strip that shows the two meeting in modern times and solving an issue important to the students in this class.

LANGUAGE ARTS   SHARED   AMERICAN HISTORY

Novel: *Johnny Tremain*

Focus: character study

Verbal/linguistic: webs
Visual/spatial: graphic organizers
Interpersonal: conflict; problem solving
Naturalist: survival

Historic period:
Revolutionary War

Focus: social issues

Integrating a Lesson With the Multiple Intelligences

The most sophisticated model is called "integrated." As a cross-disciplinary model, it enables teams of teachers to blend four or more disciplines. In the case of multiple intelligences, the model facilitates integrating four or more intelligences, often in a single project.

High School Integrated Sample

For this unit, the secondary content is the four intelligences: logical/mathematical, visual/spatial, musical/rhythmic, and interpersonal. Lessons can include the examination of the critical attributes of each intelligence through exemplary performers and the examination of those attributes that produce individual excellence across the intelligences. Cooperative groups may study each "producer" and construct concept maps within the assigned intelligence. Using an expert jigsaw, the disciplines can cross so that students can identify the common characteristics of the central notion of individualism. To ensure individual accountability, this study will end with students preparing an essay relating any two, randomly assigned "performers" to the core theme.

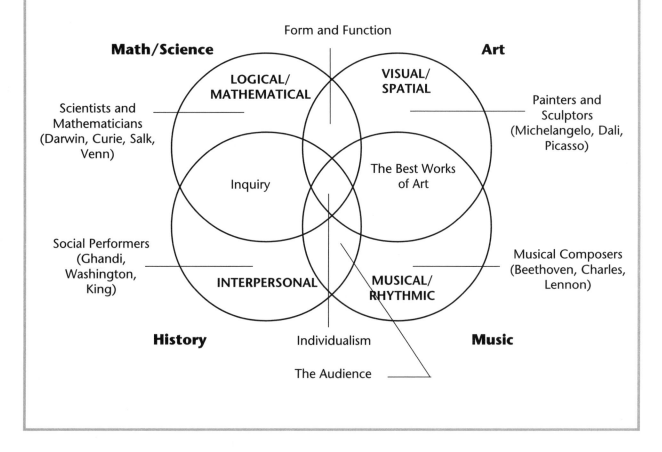

Beyond these models and samples, there are many other possibilities for integrating the multiple intelligences across the curriculum. (For a fuller development of the integrated approaches, see Robin Fogarty's *The Mindful School: How to Integrate the Curricula*, IRI/Skylight Publishing, Inc., 1991.)

Make Your Own

LESSON NAME: _____

TARGETED INTELLIGENCE: _Integrated_____

SUPPORTING INTELLIGENCES: _____

THINKING SKILLS: _____

SOCIAL SKILLS: _____

_____

CONTENT FOCUS: _____

MATERIALS: _____

_____

TASK FOCUS: _____

_____

PRODUCT: _____

PROBLEM: _____

ACTIVITY:

_____

_____

_____

_____

_____

_____

_____

_____

REFLECTIONS:

1. _____

_____

2. _____

_____

3. _____

_____

Make Your Own

LESSON NAME: _____

TARGETED INTELLIGENCE: _Integrated_ _____

SUPPORTING INTELLIGENCES: _____

THINKING SKILLS: _____

SOCIAL SKILLS: _____

_____

CONTENT FOCUS: _____

MATERIALS: _____

_____

TASK FOCUS: _____

_____

PRODUCT: _____

PROBLEM: _____

ACTIVITY:

_____

_____

_____

_____

_____

_____

_____

_____

REFLECTIONS:

1. _____

_____

2. _____

_____

3. _____

_____

Working in This Intelligence, I Am . . .

When I use this intelligence, I am . . .

|————————————————————————————————————|

very uncomfortable   totally at ease

When I ask students to use this intelligence, I am . . .

|————————————————————————————————————|

very uncomfortable   totally at ease

In what ways does this shoe fit me personally?

What can I do to polish this shoe for my professional use?

What am I going to do to provide for students in this intelligence?

What to continue	New things to do

Journal Page

Reflections on My Pathway to Integrated Intelligences

CHAPTER
11

The Grading Dilemma

Howard Gardner was one of the first of the current school reformers who revisited the issue of grades. In 1990, he wrote: "An important part of any plan to encourage a variety of abilities and to provide multiple paths between those abilities and the standard curriculum, is the broadening of assessment conceptions. Even educators who appreciate their students' different needs and strengths often give grades that credit only a narrow range of skills, mainly those that exploit language and logic" (White, Blythe, & Gardner in Costa, Bellanca, & Fogarty, eds., 1992b, p. 132).

Approximately once every twenty years, the grading issue resurfaces. Each time reformers bemoan the inadequacy of grades, list their negative consequences, and suggest numerous alternatives. Each time, there is a brief stir, some superficial switching from letters to numbers on report cards and a few brave schools that challenge the status quo. For the most part, there is no essential change, and "wad-ja-get" echoes through the school halls as loudly as ever.

In the current reform movement, there is a difference. The antigrading issue of the late '60s was connected to other cries for reform more as an afterthought, disconnected from such reforms as the open classroom and values clarification. Today's cries for a more authentic assessment of student performance are directly connected to calls for reform in curriculum and instruction. Reformers such as Gardner not only see the inadequacy of grades in the current system, but also for the whole new look of education that he is advocating in his theory of multiple intelligences.

The current competitive grading system is designed to separate skilled memorizers of factual information from the less skilled and uninterested. So limiting to learning is this approach that *Business Week* lambasted Harvard University's Graduate School of Business for using grades to discourage cooperation among its students. "The school trails in the number of group exercises and projects assigned to students to develop teamwork and leadership. One recent graduate says she participated in only three group projects over two years. 'Students at Harvard don't work well together,' complains a 1992 alumnus. 'The grade system makes people animals'" (*Business Week*, July 19, 1993).

Gardner wants schools and classrooms to provide curriculum that will develop students' multiple intelligences. He knows that the narrow tests that schools use to measure performance cannot do the job for several reasons. First, the grading curve induces competition that is contrary to the developmental approach. Although this is most obvious for the interpersonal intelligence, it is true in the others as well. Second, the single-answer, fact-oriented test that is most commonly used as the basis of grades in American schools may be one necessary component for assessing what students know, but it is insufficient for measuring the complex thinking processes inherent in the development of the intelligences. As many reform critics have noted, "assessment drives instruction." As long as the single-answer test of factual knowledge is the dominant, or in many schools the sole source of information, there is little chance that Gardner's theories will receive wholesale implementation in the classroom.

In the place of recall tests, Gardner joins many business leaders, learning theorists, and practicing educators in wanting to see multiple forms of assessment used to assist the intelligent performances of students.

What Are Some of These Multiple Forms of Assessment?

In addition to the overdone local, state, and soon-to-be added national standardized tests, there are other activities that can provide the variety of "snapshots" needed for a student's complete photo album of learning (Ferrara & McTighe, in Costa, Bellanca, & Fogarty, eds., 1992b, p. 337–348). For example, teacher-made tests with different types of questions including thoughtful essays; products of student tasks such as essays, poems, stories, storyboards, paintings, journals, drawings, sculptures, mathematical designs, science experiments, dioramas, videos, and architectural models; performances in math problem solving, storytelling, dance, music, physical conditioning, and cooperative learning; demonstrable skills and understanding of principles in all disciplines as well as in creative and critical thinking.

As soon as parents and educators see the list of possibilities, many give a welcome smile with an "It is about time" nod. Others, however, have to shake their heads. They know the questions. One: "When am I going to find time to grade all this stuff?" Two: "Who is going to show me what is important and train me how to use these assessment tools?" Three: "What will happen when most of the parents still want grades?" And then there will be those educators who simply say: "Déjà vu. This too will pass."

Let's focus on one issue at a time. If the reform of assessment is to succeed, assessment (the gathering of information about a child's school performance), evaluation (the judging of the quality of the child's performance), and grading (the reporting of a child's performance usually associated with a number or letter scale on a quarterly report card) will need separate treatments.

Collection and Selection

There are a multitude of ways to collect information about a student's performance. For a classroom teacher using Gardner's theory, multiple ways of assessment are a must, not only for parents and teachers to get a picture of the whole child, but also for the child to have a multiple perspective view of his or her multidirectional growth and development. Thus, over a marking period, the camera can capture "snapshots" of how the student works with other students, the student conducting a botany experiment, a language arts report, a math project where the student applies problem-solving skills, the student's knowledge in social studies, and a snapshot of the student's journal reflections.

As the student and teacher collect the snapshots in an album, commonly referred to as a portfolio, Gardner suggests that teachers be careful to avoid only including polished, finished products. He recommends the use of "processfolios" as employed in Arts PROPEL. "A processfolio," he says, "is a record of learning that captures a student's process of creation. The activity of focus may be in any domain: music, drama, science, English, history, or the like." He notes that the PROPEL processfolios sample a very different set of skills than ordinarily examined in a school. Included in these are "craft, pursuit (revision and development over time), expressiveness, inventiveness" and other reflections of the creative process (White, Blythe, & Gardner in Costa, Bellanca, & Fogarty, eds., 1992b, p. 132).

Whichever means you select to provide assessment data from the multiple intelligences classroom, you will want an efficient approach to evaluate the gathered data. One or two packed photo albums won't overload a teacher; thirty-five will. The efficiency starts with the teacher's identification of the significant outcomes that will provide students with exit standards of performance for the year. Although it is beneficial when these standards are aligned with state and district curriculum outcomes, it is more important that they serve as a guiding beacon for the individual development of students' multiple intelligences in that classroom that year.

For instance, New York State has the Compact for Learning. Among the Compact's goals for students are the following:

Compact for Learning Goals

- Students will acquire knowledge, understanding, and appreciation of the artistic, cultural, and intellectual accomplishments of civilizations and develop the skills to express personal artistic talents.

- Students will develop the interpersonal, organizational, and personal skills needed to work as a group member.

- Students will learn to think logically and creatively and apply reasoning skills to issues and problems.

A school or teacher interested in using the theory of multiple intelligences can readily formulate a set of schoolwide or classroom and lesson outcomes that fit the Compact's goals for students. For instance, a school could easily adopt, word for word, the above statements. A teacher, needing to be more specific, could adapt these goal statements to her classroom. A first grade teacher using the first statement might rephrase the wider goal like this: "First grade students in the Martin L. King Primary School will acquire knowledge, understanding, and appreciation of the artistic, cultural, and intellectual accomplishments of the nations represented in the classroom." A middle school teacher might rephrase the goal, "Students in Stevenson Middle School will acquire knowledge, understanding, and appreciation of the artistic, cultural, and intellectual contributions of ancient Egypt to western civilization." A high school world history teacher might phrase it like this: "Students in the World Civilizations course will acquire knowledge, understanding, and appreciation of the artistic, cultural, and intellectual contributions of five civilizations to western civilization."

Aligning Outcomes

Selecting aligned outcomes is the first step in this adaptation process (every class in a school does not have to take *all* the state goals). One major benefit of selective outcomes is the opportunity for you to fine-tune and focus your course content so that your curriculum is one that "uncovers" ideas rather than "covers" all the facts. It helps to remember that the infinitive "to cover" can mean "to hide from view." As more and more information is packed into textbooks, covering the curriculum results in more and more superficial attention to what is most important for all students to learn. In the textbook (read curriculum) coverage game, there is little room for multiple intelligences.

Setting Criteria

The second step is to identify the criteria of success and the products, processes, and performances that you will assess. After reviewing the items collected, you will use these criteria for the evaluation. Here is a selection of teacher-made statements that align with the outcome statements given above.

FIRST GRADE

"Each student will make a culture capsule about the culture of his or her family heritage. The capsule will include at least three items brought from home that represent some aspect of the artistic, cultural, or intellectual accomplishments of that heritage. The student will share these items with the class."

FIFTH GRADE

"Each student will soap sculpt a miniature copy of one monument of ancient Egypt and describe its contribution to today's society. The description will include at least three contributions of significance and a reason for each selection."

"Each student will contribute to a group collage or mobile that reflects one of the following aspects of the culture of ancient Egypt: music, art, architecture, dress, home life, religion, or government. The collage will represent at least five examples of the aspect selected. Any student in the group will be prepared to give a reason why each of the objects was selected."

HIGH SCHOOL, WORLD HISTORY

"Each student will write a persuasive essay arguing why a specific contribution of ancient Egyptian culture should be included in the 'World Civilization Hall of Fame.' The essay must follow the rules of writing prescribed by the English department and provide at least three documented reasons for the selection."

"Each student will contribute to a group Venn diagram that compares and contrasts ancient Egypt with our modern society. Each element of the diagram must include at least seven items."

To assist the students to know what is most important, it is beneficial to review the products and the criteria with the students at the start of the unit and when you make the assignments. When all students in the class know the criteria, you can eliminate the guessing game and provide a model for helping the students attend to the most important concepts rather than getting mired in facts.

The use of the criteria will benefit you too. First, preset criteria make it easier to focus on what written feedback is important. Second, when the class is targeting a specific intelligence, it makes it easier for you to reinforce that intelligence. Third, preset criteria make it easier to announce a grading scale, if grades are required, and to put grades in their proper perspective for students.

The Grading Game

If grades are required, you can minimize the negative effects of the grading game by providing a simple scale. Using the criteria for success, you can determine the benchmarks for each letter grade. For instance, the first grade teacher might tell her students that three objects merit a C, four a B, and five an A. The fifth grade teacher might benchmark the soap sculpture explanations using a similar quantitative measure. However, for the second criteria, she might describe benchmarks that have a qualitative standard based on the logic of the arguments used. In addition to sharing the benchmarks with the students, she can review examples from previous classes.

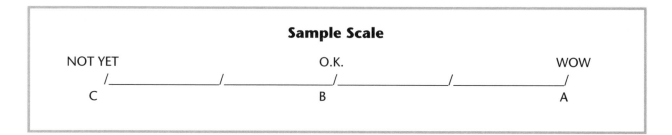

After the teacher uses the criteria to evaluate the product, she can assign a grade on the scale. It is best to limit grade giving to (a) final products or performances, (b) unit exams, and (c) observation charts. Daily quizzes, interim tasks, single journal entries, and other "contributing pieces" and checks for understanding may merit a + or - mark, but don't merit intense bean counting. Because teachers are not accountants, it is *not* helpful if they have to spend long hours entering a grade for every classroom activity.

When deciding how to give a final grade, you can help the students and save time by preplanning how a portfolio checklist will lead to a final course grade. Each student can keep the checklist in her or his portfolio, mark down the grade earned, and file the product or the product evaluation sheet. At the end of a grading period, the student can total the grades earned and do the division work to determine the final grade.

There are at least two alternatives for organizing the portfolio. You can provide a blank outline and indicate which materials go into the portfolio as the assignments are made. Or, you can provide the list with each item filled in when the students receive it. The following examples include the outcomes described above with other products from the grading period. (If grades are not required, eliminate that aspect of the sheet.)

IRI/SkyLight Training and Publishing, Inc.

Examples of Evaluation Sheets

FIRST GRADE EXAMPLE

Name _Sam Ramirez_ Grade _1_ Period 1 ②3 4
Teacher's Name _Ms. Mance_ School _Country View_

	Not Yet	O.K.	WOW	Comments
Journal		✓		
Culture capsule		✓		Good presentation of family background—interesting!
Partner work	✓			Interpersonal skills need to improve, especially for cooperation.
Silent reading chart		✓		
Math pattern chart			✓	Excellent grasp of patterns, very creative visual/spatial.
Reading sketches		✓		
Shoe tying			✓	
Desk organizer			✓	
Home folder			✓	Very well organized; good reflection of your work.
Terrarium log		✓		

FIFTH GRADE EXAMPLE

Name _Jamie Hennessy_ Grade _5_ Period ①2 3 4
Teacher's Name _Mrs. Witas_ School _Buffalo Grove_

	1	2	3	Comments
Egypt sculpture		✓		
Sculpture description			✓	High verbal, linguistic skills—description is detailed and logical.
Collage and contribution		✓		
Journal	✓			
Egypt test			✓	Demonstrates knowledge and understanding of material.
Story grid			✓	
Book report			✓	
Grammar unit test		✓		
Math model		✓		
Math analysis sheet		✓		Shows improvement in logical/mathematical skills.
Science project	✓			
Science unit test	✓			
Base group checklist			✓	
Video self-assessment			✓	Intrapersoanl skills are highly developed

SCALE: A=38–42 B=32–37 C=26–31

MIDDLE SCHOOL EXAMPLE

Name _Alyssa Moskwa_ Grade _7_ Period 1 2 ③ 4
Teacher's Name _Mrs. Simmons_ Section _3_

	Not Yet	O.K.	WOW	Comments
INTRAPERSONAL	✓			
Journal	✓			
Portfolio self-assessment		✓		
INTERPERSONAL			✓	Great job working with others!
Observation of cooperation			✓	
Peer assessments			✓	
Role of self-rating		✓		
LOGICAL/MATHEMATICAL	✓			Needs work—perhaps extra practice & review!
Math pattern project	✓			
Science lab report	✓			
VISUAL/SPATIAL		✓		
Concept map		✓		
Group cartoon		✓		
VERBAL/LINGUISTIC			✓	Excellent—your analysis shows in-depth thinking.
Attribute web			✓	
Character analysis			✓	
MUSICAL/RHYTHMIC		✓		Very good—creative and interesting rap!
Social studies rap		✓		
BODILY/KINESTHETIC		✓		
Walk-a-thon		✓		
NATURALIST	✓			
Animal diorama		✓		

SECONDARY SCHOOL EXAMPLE

Name _Michael Rocha_ Grade _12_ Period 1 ②3 4
Teacher's Name _Mrs. Banks_ Subject _World History_

	1	2	3	Comments
Intelligence goal sheet		✓		
Essay			✓	Verbal/linguistic skills are excellent—great job!
Journal			✓	Journal is well written—shows a great degree of creativity.
Group diagram		✓		
Self-assessment summary	✓			Need to develop more intrapersonal skills to better evaluate work.
Unit test		✓		Good work on unit test!
Group assessment		✓		
Cooperative learning checklist		✓		
Survival kit			✓	

SCALE: A=22–24 B=19–21 C=16–18

Based on ideas found in *The Mindful School: How to Assess Thoughtful Outcomes* (1993) by Kay Burke. IRI/Skylight Publishing, Palatine, IL.

IRI/SkyLight Training and Publishing, Inc.

The examples demonstrate how a teacher interested in building the theory of multiple intelligences into classroom curriculum and instruction can take advantage of a state mandate and, at the same time, restructure so that assessment, evaluation, and grading (if required) are aligned. Some other states have similar tight mandates that differ in what outcomes are required. Others have no such controls over curriculum and instruction. Whatever is the case, it is important to remember that the process suggested in the examples is a simple way of assessing and uses the theory of multiple intelligences even when grades are required. This diagram outlines that process.

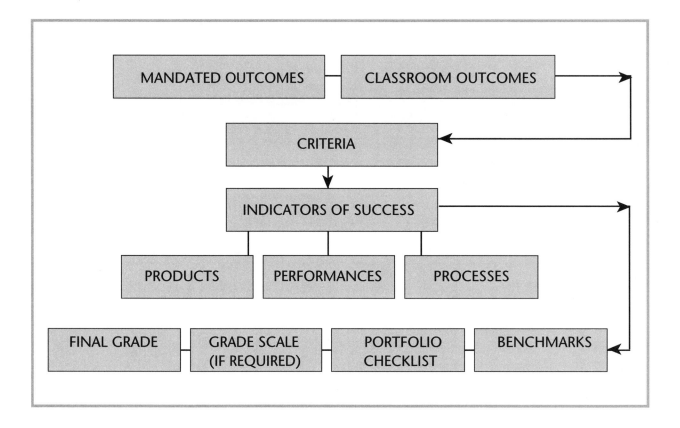

Processfolio Checklist

If the same teacher wants to adapt the **processfolio** that Gardner favors, the portfolio reporting sheet might look like this. Contrast the listed "process skills" as well as the use of scales and the amount of space for comment with the **product** example on the previous page.

Processfolio Checklist

Name _Craig Panwell_   Teacher's Name _Mrs. Simmons_   Grade _6 c_

EXPRESSIVENESS

not yet   on the way   wow

/_____/_____/

Comments _Your contributions are valuable—let's hear them more often!_

_____

_____

ABILITY TO WORK ALONE

not yet   on the way   wow

/_____/_____/

Comments _Wonderful improvement during independent work._

_____

_____

ABILITY TO WORK COOPERATIVELY

not yet   on the way   wow

/_____/_____/

Comments _Social skills are excellent, works well with all students in every role: leader, materials manager,_
and checker.

_____

PERSISTENCE

not yet   on the way   wow

/_____/_____/

Comments _Sticks with a task until complete no matter how difficult—great job!_

_____

_____

(Continued)

Processfolio Checklist (continued)

INVENTIVENESS

not yet   (on the way)   wow

/_____/_____/

Comments   *Need to rely less on group, develop your own ideas—they are good ones!* _____

_____

_____

SELF-ASSESSMENT

not yet   (on the way)   wow

/_____/_____/

Comments _____

_____

_____

FOLLOW THROUGH

not yet   on the way   (wow)

/_____/_____/

Comments _____

_____

_____

SUMMARY COMMENT

not yet   (on the way)   wow

/_____/_____/

Comments   *Keep up the good work—each semester I see an improvement in all areas of your work!* _____

_____

_____

Portfolio Checklist

When a teacher has the opportunity to define her classroom outcomes in terms of the multiple intelligences without the requirement for grades, she will have a greater chance to spotlight the intelligences. If focusing on product review, her portfolio checklist might look like the following.

IRI/SkyLight Training and Publishing, Inc.

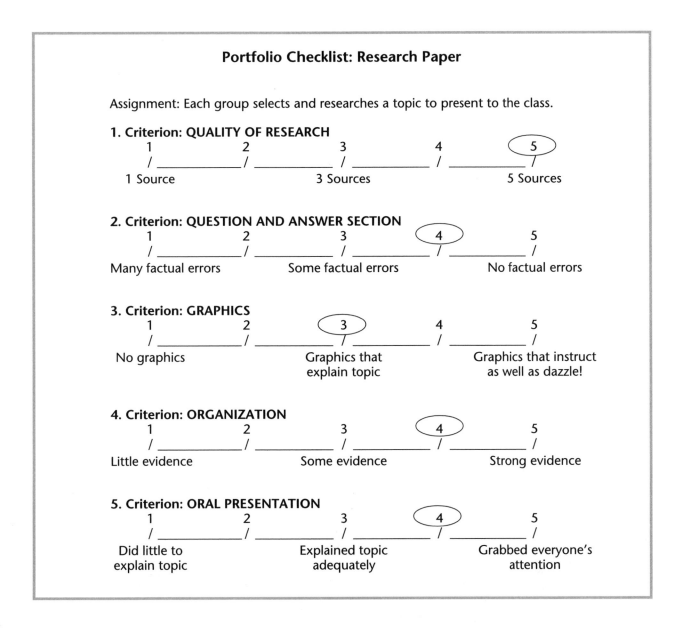

Portfolio Checklist: Research Paper

Assignment: Each group selects and researches a topic to present to the class.

1. Criterion: QUALITY OF RESEARCH

1   2   3   4   ⑤

1 Source   3 Sources   5 Sources

2. Criterion: QUESTION AND ANSWER SECTION

1   2   3   ④   5

Many factual errors   Some factual errors   No factual errors

3. Criterion: GRAPHICS

1   2   ③   4   5

No graphics   Graphics that explain topic   Graphics that instruct as well as dazzle!

4. Criterion: ORGANIZATION

1   2   3   ④   5

Little evidence   Some evidence   Strong evidence

5. Criterion: ORAL PRESENTATION

1   2   3   ④   5

Did little to explain topic   Explained topic adequately   Grabbed everyone's attention

Although these examples of product and process portfolio differ greatly in their focus, it is important to remember that there is no fixed recipe. A teacher can mix product and process evaluation. The key questions are (1) how does assessment fit with the instructional priorities of the classroom? and (2) how can a teacher use more authentic assessment without being overwhelmed with major classroom changes? The above examples of more authentic assessment show that there is little need to change the classroom culture. As Gardner points out, the other adjustments that widen the possibilities for what is assessed in the classroom and help students see a "bigger picture" are the best. Because these adjustments help the teacher put assessment, evaluation, and grades into a more learner-centered perspective, the adjustments also provide a simpler, more student-responsible path to effective evaluation, and if necessary, grade reports. This KISS approach (Keep It Simple and Structured) is a sound solution to a senseless dilemma.

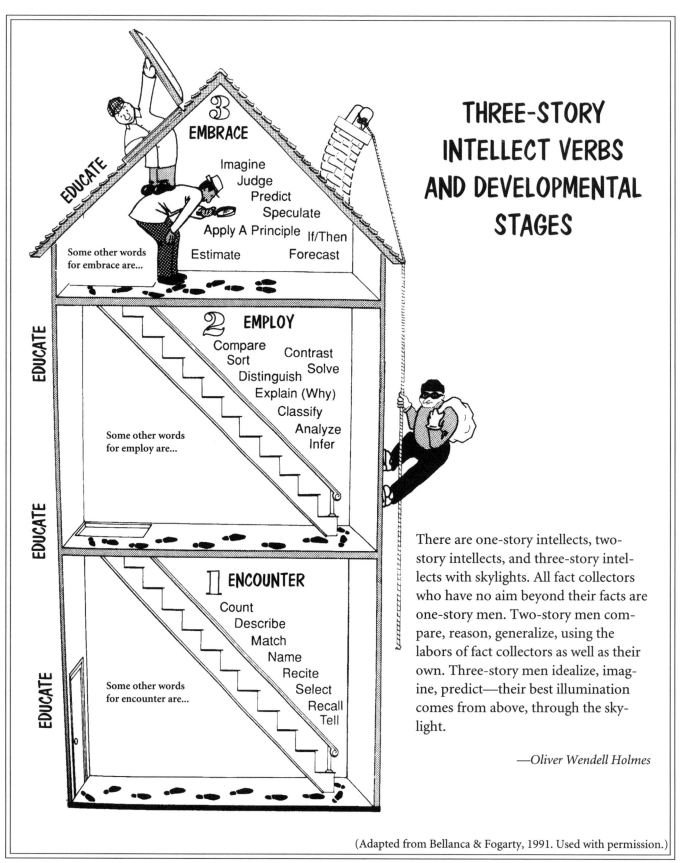

THREE-STORY INTELLECT VERBS AND DEVELOPMENTAL STAGES

EDUCATE

3 EMBRACE

Imagine
Judge
Predict
Speculate
Apply A Principle   If/Then
Estimate   Forecast

Some other words for embrace are...

2 EMPLOY

Compare   Contrast
Sort   Solve
Distinguish
Explain (Why)
Classify
Analyze
Infer

Some other words for employ are...

1 ENCOUNTER

Count
Describe
Match
Name
Recite
Select
Recall
Tell

Some other words for encounter are...

There are one-story intellects, two-story intellects, and three-story intellects with skylights. All fact collectors who have no aim beyond their facts are one-story men. Two-story men compare, reason, generalize, using the labors of fact collectors as well as their own. Three-story men idealize, imagine, predict—their best illumination comes from above, through the skylight.

—*Oliver Wendell Holmes*

(Adapted from Bellanca & Fogarty, 1991. Used with permission.)

IRI/SkyLight Training and Publishing, Inc.

Bibliography

ABC News. (1993). *Common miracles: The new american revolution in learning* [Video]. New York.

Armstrong, T. (1993). *Seven kinds of smart: Identifying and developing your many intelligences.* New York: Penguin Books.

Baugh, A. (1978). *A history of the English language.* Englewood Cliffs, NJ: Prentice Hall.

Bellanca, J., & Fogarty, R. (1991). *Blueprints for thinking in the cooperative classroom* (2nd ed.). Palatine, IL: IRI/Skylight Publishing, Inc.

Berman, S. (1993). *Catch them thinking in science: A handbook of classroom strategies.* Palatine, IL: IRI/Skylight Publishing, Inc.

Blythe, T., & Gardner, H. (1990, April). A school for all intelligences. *Educational Leadership, 47*(7), 33–37.

Boulding, E. (1966). *The image.* Ann Arbor: University of Michigan Press.

Brewer, C., & Campbell, D. G. (1991). *Rhythms of learning: Creative tools for developing lifelong skills.* Tucson: Zephyr Press.

Burke, K. (1992). *What to do with the kid who...: Developing cooperation, self-discipline, and responsibility in the classroom.* Palatine, IL: IRI/Skylight Publishing, Inc.

Buzan, T. (1977). *Use both sides of your brain.* Richardson, TX: Magnamusic-Baton.

Caine, R., & Caine, G. (1990, October). Understanding a brain-based approach to learning and teaching. *Educational Leadership*, pp. 66–70.

Caine, R. N., & Caine, G. (1991). *Making connections: Teaching and the human brain.* Alexandria, VA: Association for Supervision and Curriculum Development.

Campbell, J. (1989). *The improbable machine: What the new upheavals in artificial intelligence research reveal about how the mind really works.* New York: Simon & Schuster.

Campbell, L. (1992). *Teaching and learning through multiple intelligences.* Seattle: New Horizons for Learning.

Carr, E., & Ogle, D. (1987, April). K-W-L Plus: A strategy for comprehension and summarization. *Journal of Reading, 30*(7), 626–31.

Ceci, J. (1990). *On intelligence—more or less: A bio-ecological treatise in intellectual development.* Englewood Cliffs, NJ: Prentice Hall.

Costa, A. L. (1991). *The school as a home for the mind.* Palatine, IL: IRI/Skylight Publishing, Inc.

Costa, A. (1988). Fostering intelligent behavior. *On the beam* (Vol. VII). Seattle: New Horizons for Learning.

Costa, A. (Ed.). (1985). *Developing minds.* Alexandria, VA: Association for Supervision and Curriculum Development.

Costa, A., Bellanca, J., & Fogarty, R. (1992a). *If minds matter: A foreword to the future (Vol. 1).* Palatine, IL: IRI/Skylight Publishing, Inc.

Costa, A., Bellanca, J., & Fogarty, R. (1992b). *If minds matter: A foreword to the future (Vol. 2).* Palatine, IL: IRI/Skylight Publishing, Inc.

Csikszentmihalyi, M. (1990). *Flow: The psychology of optimal experience.* New York: Harper & Row.

de Bono, E. (1992). *Serious creativity: Using the power for lateral thinking to create new ideas.* New York: HarperCollins Publishers, Inc.

de Bono, E. (1985). *Six thinking hats.* Boston: Little, Brown.

Dickinson, D. (1987). *New developments in cognitive research.* Seattle: New Horizons for Learning.

Ferguson, M. (1980). *The Aquarian conspiracy.* Los Angeles: J. P. Tarcher.

Fogarty, R. (1991). *The mindful school: How to integrate the curricula.* Palatine, IL: IRI/Skylight Publishing, Inc.

Fogarty, R., & Bellanca, J. (1989). *Patterns for thinking: Patterns for transfer.* Palatine, IL: IRI/Skylight Publishing, Inc.

Fogarty, R., & Bellanca, J. (1986). *Catch them thinking: A handbook of classroom strategies.* Palatine, IL: IRI/Skylight Publishing, Inc.

Fogarty, R., Perkins, D., & Barell, J. (1992). *The mindful school: How to teach for transfer.* Palatine, IL: IRI/Skylight Publishing, Inc.

Fowler, C. (1990, September). Recognizing the role of artistic intelligences. *Music Educators Journal, 77*(1), 24–27.

Gardner, H. (1995, November). Reflections on multiple intelligences: Myths and messages. *Phi Delta Kappan.*

Gardner, H. (1993). *Multiple intelligences: The theory in practice.* New York: Basic Books.

Gardner, H. (1987a). Developing the spectrum of human intelligences: Teaching in the eighties, a need to change. *Harvard Educational Review, 57, 187–193.*

Gardner, H. (1987b). The theory of multiple intelligences. *Annals of Dyslexia, 37,* 19–35.

Gardner, H. (1983). *Frames of mind.* New York: Basic Books.

Gardner, H., & Hatch, T. (1990). *Multiple intelligences go to school: Educational implications of the theory of multiple intelligences* (Report No. 4). New York: Center for Technology in Education.

Gardner, H., & Hatch, T. (1989, November). Multiple intelligences go to school: Educational implications of the theory of multiple intelligences. *Educational Researcher, 18*(8), 14–9.

Glasser, W. (1990). *The quality school.* New York: Harper, Perennial.

Glasser, W. (1986). *Control theory in the classroom.* New York: Harper & Row.

Gawain, S. (1978). *Creative visualization.* New York: Bantam Books.

Harman, W. (1988). *The global mind change.* Indianapolis: Knowledge Systems.

Harman, W., & Reingold, H. (1985). *Higher creativity.* Los Angeles: J. P. Tarcher.

Hatch, T. C., & Gardner, H. (1986, February). From testing intelligence to assessing competencies: A pluralistic view of intellect. *Roeper Review, 8* (3), 147–150.

Johnson, D., & Johnson, R. (1987). *Learning together and alone: Cooperative, competitive, and individualistic learning.* Englewood Cliffs, NJ: Prentice Hall.

Jones, B. F., Palincsar, A., Ogle, D. S., & Carr, E. G. (1987). *Strategic teaching and learning: Cognitive instruction in the content areas.* Alexandria, VA: Association for Supervision and Curriculum Development.

Kagan, S. (1992). *Cooperative learning.* San Juan Capistrano, CA: Resources for Teachers, Inc.

Lazear, D. (1991a). *Seven ways of knowing: Teaching for multiple intelligences.* Palatine, IL: IRI/Skylight Publishing, Inc.

Lazear, D. (1991b). *Seven ways of teaching: The artistry of teaching with multiple intelligences.* Palatine, IL: IRI/ Skylight Publishing, Inc.

Lowe, D. (1983). *The sphinx and the rainbow.* Boulder & London: Shambhala Publications.

Machado, L. (1980). *The right to be intelligent.* New York: Pergamon Press.

Marcus, S. A., & Bellanca, J. (1988). *Early stars.* Palatine, IL: IRI/Skylight Publishing, Inc.

Mason, K. (1991). *Going beyond words: The art and practice of visual thinking.* Tucson: Zephyr Press.

Miller, L. (1990, March). The roles of language and learning in the development of literacy. *Topics in language disorders, 10*(2), 1–24.

Ogle, D. (1986, February). K-W-L: A teaching model that develops active reading of expository text. *The Reading Teacher, 37*(6), 564–570.

Orlick, T. (1978). *The cooperative sports and games book: Challenge without competition.* New York: Pantheon Books.

Palincsar, A. S., & Winn, J. (Eds.). (1990). Assessment models focused on new conceptions of achievement and reasoning. Symposium at the International Conference of the American Educational Research Association. [San Francisco, CA, March 27–31, 1989]. *International Journal of Educational Research, 10*(5), 409–483.

Russell, P. (1983). *The global brain.* Los Angeles: J. P. Tarcher.

Samuels, M., & Samuels, N. (1975). *Seeing with the mind's eye.* New York: Random House.

Scearce, C. (1992). *100 ways to build teams.* Palatine, IL: IRI/Skylight Publishing, Inc.

Shone, R. (1984). *Creative visualization.* Wellingborough & New York: Thorson's.

Sperry, R. W. (1983). *Science and moral priority: Merging mind, brain, and human values.* New York: Columbia University Press.

Sternberg, R. J. (1990). *Metaphors of mind: Conceptions of the nature of intelligence.* New York: Viking.

Sternberg, R. J. (1986). *Intelligence applied: Understanding and increasing your intellectual skills.* Boston: Harcourt Brace Jovanovich.

Sternberg, R. J. (1984). *Beyond IQ: A triarchic theory of human intelligence.* New York: Cambridge University Press.

Vaughn, F. (1986). *The inward arc.* Boulder: The New Science Library, Shambhala Press.

Walsh, R., & Vaughn, F. (Eds.). *Beyond ego.* Los Angeles: J. P. Tarcher.

Walters, J., & Gardner, H. (1990). *Domain projects as assessment vehicles in a computer-rich environment* (Report No. 4). New York: Centers for Technology in Education.

Williams, R. B. (1993). *More than 50 ways to build team consensus.* Palatine, IL: IRI/Skylight Publishing, Inc.

IRI/SkyLight Training and Publishing, Inc.

Index

PROFESSIONAL DEVELOPMENT

We Prepare Your Teachers Today
for the Classrooms of Tomorrow

Learn from Our Books and from Our Authors!

Ignite Learning in Your School or District.

SkyLight's team of classroom-experienced consultants can help you foster systemic change for increased student achievement.

Professional development is a process not an event. SkyLight's experienced practitioners drive the creation of our on-site professional development programs, graduate courses, research-based publications, interactive video courses, teacher-friendly training materials, and online resources—call SkyLight Professional Development today.

SkyLight specializes in three professional development areas.

Specialty # 1

Best Practices

We **model** the best practices that result in improved student performance and guided applications.

Specialty # 2

Making the Innovations Last

We help set up **support** systems that make innovations part of everyday practice in the long-term systemic improvement of your school or district.

Specialty # 3

How to Assess the Results

We prepare your school leaders to encourage and **assess** teacher growth, **measure** student achievement, and **evaluate** program success.

Contact the SkyLight team and begin a process toward long-term results.

2626 S. Clearbrook Dr., Arlington Heights, IL 60005
800-348-4474 • 847-290-6600 • FAX 847-290-6609
info@skylightedu.com • www.skylightedu.com

There are

one-story intellects,

two-story intellects, and three-story

intellects with skylights. All fact collectors, who

have no aim beyond their facts, are one-story men. Two-story men

compare, reason, generalize, using the labors of the fact collectors as

well as their own. Three-story men idealize, imagine,

predict—their best illumination comes from

above, through the skylight.

—Oliver Wendell

Holmes